FROM STAR WARS
TO SUPERMAN

FROM
STAR WARS
TO
SUPERMAN

CHRIST FIGURES IN SCIENCE FICTION AND SUPERHERO FILMS

JAMES L. PAPANDREA

SOPHIA INSTITUTE PRESS
Manchester, New Hampshire

Sophia Institute Press
Box 5284, Manchester, NH 03108
1-800-888-9344

www.SophiaInstitute.com

Sophia Institute Press® is a registered trademark of Sophia Institute.

Library of Congress Cataloging-in-Publication Data
Names: Papandrea, James L., 1963- author.
Title: From Star Wars to Superman : Christ figures in science fiction and
   superhero films / James L. Papandrea.
Description: Manchester, New Hampshire : Sophia Institute Press, 2017. |
   Includes bibliographical references.
Identifiers: LCCN 2017038652 | ISBN 9781622823888 (pbk. : alk. paper)
Subjects: LCSH: Jesus Christ—In motion pictures. | Science fiction
   films—History and criticism. | Superhero films—History and criticism.
Classification: LCC PN1995.9.J4 P37 2017 | DDC 791.43/651—dc23 LC
record available at https://lccn.loc.gov/2017038652

First printing

To all Christian sci-fi fans, who understand that faith and science are not incompatible, that the ability to be rational and creative is a gift from God, and that a balanced and truthful anthropology is one that affirms the great potential of humanity while still admitting that we need a Savior

CONTENTS

SECTION III: TIME TRAVEL AS INCARNATION

SECTION IV: JESUS CHRIST, SUPERHERO

ACKNOWLEDGMENTS

Any fan of science fiction knows that you don't love sci-fi all by yourself. As a sci-fi fan, you are part of a community of people who love science fiction and who love to talk about it. It's a little like the Church, which is why it can be so tempting for non-Christians (or nonpracticing Christians) to make the science-fiction community a substitute for Church, and science fiction itself a substitute for religion. But even Christian sci-fi fans all know what it's like to love the conversation, and the speculation, and the debates. So I have to thank those in my own sci-fi circle — starting with my sons, Rick and John Papandrea. Then there are my *Doctor Who* companions: Paul Jarzembowski, Ron Lovatt, and Stephanie Bliese; and my superhero league: Matt Forbeck, Mark Teasdale, and Brooke Lester. I also want to thank my research assistants, Jordan Sprunger and Larry Green. And I especially want to thank Ronald D. Moore for being such a good sport and granting me the interview, and his assistant Nick Hornung for facilitating it. Special thanks to my daughter-in-law, Shiann Papandrea, for transcribing the interview.

FROM STAR WARS
TO SUPERMAN

SCRIPT AND SCRIPTURE

This is not another "Gospel according to [fill in the blank]" book. If we're honest with ourselves, we should be able to fill in the blank with anything, because a believer should be able to find evidence of God and divine activity just about anywhere — especially in stories. This book is more specific than that. It's about *Jesus Christ* (the subject of the greatest story) and how He keeps popping up in one particular kind of story: science fiction.

So this is a book specifically about Christology — that is, what we believe about Jesus Christ, who we think He is, what kind of a Savior He is, and how that salvation works. In this book, you will find all the Christology a Trekkie, Whovian, or Matrix Dweller needs to know.

But this is not a book for theologians; it's a book for insightful, imaginative people who love stories about heroes having adventures that take them out of the ordinary world into alternative worlds. The interesting thing is that these alternative worlds have at least one thing in common with the real world. People need to be rescued. Somebody needs to save the day, or even the world. In other words, people need a savior. And that's what a hero is.

Christology is taught in the Bible, and in the Church Fathers, and in the *Catechism*—but not only there. Christology is also taught in popular fiction—in books, on television, and on the big screen. And that especially includes the genre of science fiction. The question is not whether these media teach Christology; the question is whether they teach *good* Christology. Another way of saying that is with a question: How well does the hero, or Christ figure, of any given story represent the *real* Christ? Is this character a faithful analogy of who Christ really is and how salvation really works—or is it some kind of alternative version that pales in comparison with the Jesus Christ who is God made flesh?

These questions, and, in fact, the seeds for this book, were planted in my mind back in my days as an adjunct professor at Elmhurst College. There I designed a Religion in Film class at a time when the idea of a class on religion and film was relatively new. I was excited to discover the ways in which films in general, and science fiction in particular, led to great discussions about the important things in life: philosophy, religion, ethics, life, and death, and what it means to be human.

Some might argue that science fiction, by definition, cannot deal with the metaphysical because it seeks to *explain* the imaginations of its extraordinary worlds. That's what makes it *science* fiction. And metaphysics, or theology in its broader sense, asks us to embrace mystery.[1] But in spite of protestations to the contrary, sci-fi does trade in mythology, and it does capitalize on the mystery inherent in ancient and esoteric religious symbols. To be sure, much sci-fi, when it does depict religion, often does

---

[1] Gabriel McKee, *The Gospel according to Science Fiction: From the Twilight Zone to the Final Frontier* (Louisville, KY: Westminster John Knox Press, 2007), xi–xii.

it from the perspective of uninformed outsiders (or prodigals), critiquing a caricature of something with which it has little or no experience. But whether science fiction is written by believers or unbelievers, from a sympathetic or critical perspective, it does try to appropriate the symbols of religion as talismans to add an air of mysticism (or mystery) to the stories.

Sometimes the stories themselves are meant to convey the writers' beliefs — often including the belief that the only thing worthy of our faith is science and human progress. A common theme in sci-fi is "religion is the opiate of the people," which is the implied moral of any sci-fi story that includes the assumption that given enough time, humanity will evolve beyond the need for religion — that somehow religion is not rational, and eventually people will become so rational that they will no longer need faith. The notions that "the Church is hiding something from you" and that "all the war and hate in the world can be blamed on religion" are also common themes.[2] We will note some common themes in our analysis below. The point, for some sci-fi writers, is the assumption that humanity is its own highest authority and religion only holds us back.[3] But wasn't this the original sin of Adam and Eve?

At this point it will be helpful to define a few terms. "Orthodoxy" is the term we use to describe the good (or correct) Christology. In other words, *orthodox* Christology describes Jesus Christ in ways that are consistent with the witness of the apostles in the New Testament, with the teachings handed down from

---

[2] See Mike Aquilina and James Papandrea, *Seven Revolutions: How Christianity Changed the World, and Can Change It Again* (New York: Random House/Image, 2015).

[3] McKee, *The Gospel according to Science Fiction*, 7–8.

them to the early Church Fathers, with the early and medieval Christian scholars, and with the Church's lived experience. By contrast, "heresy" is a word that means a deviation, going off on a tangent. It's the word we use to describe christologies that fall short of the truth in one way or another.[4]

With regard to science fiction, it's becoming fashionable to use the phrase "speculative fiction" as an umbrella term to include both science fiction and fantasy in a single genre.[5] I've found this to be less than helpful when it comes to talking about sci-fi as distinct from fantasy. In science fiction, things are explained: even if the explanation is implausible, some explanation is offered. In fantasy, there is often no attempt to explain what the audience is supposed to simply accept as magical. The problem is that it's becoming increasingly common to find elements of both science fiction and fantasy within the same story, making it hard to categorize. Even *Doctor Who* has, in the more recent seasons, crossed the line into fantasy on occasion. And for someone who is more of a fan of sci-fi, and less of fantasy, that can be disappointing. Time-travel stories that offer no explanation for how the time travel works can also be frustrating for a sci-fi fan. We want to see time travel, but we are not satisfied if we're not told how the time machine works or why the time travel takes place.

Nevertheless, the real appeal of science fiction for many people is that it doesn't simply speculate about what the future will

---

4 For more detail on this, see James L. Papandrea, *The Earliest Christologies* (Downers Grove, IL: Intervarsity Press/IVP Academic, 2016).

5 James F. McGrath, *Theology and Science Fiction* (Eugene, OR: Cascade Books, 2016), 5.

be like. It goes beyond merely imagining new technologies: it includes the *implications* of those technologies, and the *consequences* of the differences between the alternate world and our own.[6] In other words, science fiction is never just about science. It's about philosophy. It's about what it means to be human, what it means to be a responsible human agent (that is, moral or ethical), and what it means to be a finite subject (a self-aware mortal who is aware of his mortality).

There have been many other books on the connection between science fiction and religion. Some of them take a kind of academic, nonsectarian approach and analyze science-fiction stories for elements that may be influenced by any religion, or by religion in general. That is not the approach of this book. Here I will analyze science-fiction stories from a decidedly Christian perspective, looking for the stories' specifically Christian elements—whether or not the stories were written by Christians or the parallels are intentional. I've chosen stories that are, in my mind, "classic" science fiction—meaning that they have gained a wide audience and have become a part of popular culture. When it comes to the superheroes, I also will not dwell too much on the many reboots and alternate universes in the comic books, preferring instead to focus on the films, since those are the versions to which most people are exposed. Please note that the inclusion of a film or show in this book is not an endorsement of that film or show for all audiences. While I do love the stories I've included in this book, some may not be appropriate for younger audiences, and many include rough language and scenes of sinful behavior. I write this book as a lover of sci-fi, but also as a critic of it. Science and faith are not enemies, but

---

6   McKee, *The Gospel according to Science Fiction*, xiii.

7

when science fiction elevates science to a level of arrogance that assumes that faith is outdated or ignorant, it must be challenged.

In each chapter, we will examine the alternate reality that's created for the story in question, and we will seek to uncover the assumptions behind that reality—if possible, even the beliefs that the writers hold and presumably want to communicate to us. Then we'll look at the hero, or savior character, and ask what kind of "Christ figure" the story presents us with, and what that says about humanity and salvation. We will do all of this using theological categories, by looking at the story's inherent *anthropology, Christology,* and *soteriology.*

Anthropology, simply put, is the study of humanity. We will look at what each story tells us about what it means to be human. We can say at the beginning that from a Christian perspective, being a human means being made in the image of God. But what does that mean? As I have written elsewhere, the aspects of the image of God in us are our spirituality (we are spiritual beings), our rationality and active self-awareness (we have free will), our creativity, and our potential for self-sacrificing love and compassion.[7]

The problem is that people find themselves in a predicament—and that predicament will take different forms depending on the story—but the point is that by our failure to live up to our potential, we have caused the very situation from which we need to be saved. So part of asking what it means to be human

---

[7] James L. Papandrea, *Spiritual Blueprint: How We Live, Work, Love, Play, and Pray* (Liguori, MO: Liguori Publications, 2010), viii–xi, 37. See also McKee, *The Gospel according to Science Fiction,* 40.

is also asking what went wrong: what has caused our need for salvation, and what will it take to make things right?

All good stories (of any genre) are also about relationships. Humans cannot exist in isolation, and so part of the solution to the human condition is that we all need other people: to help us, to love us, to teach us. In fact, if we are to live in a way that does justice to the image of God within us, we will need to find opportunities to show love to others.[8] And if being truly human requires interacting with other humans, we cannot be truly human without our bodies. In other words, being human is not being a soul only, or worse, being a soul trapped in a body. Being human means being embodied—a soul/mind/spirit with a body—all of this together is the *substance*, or the essence, of humanity.[9] This is human nature, and incidentally this is why we could never live forever in a computer, because our God-created body is part of what makes us human, and our minds and bodies cannot be permanently separated—not simply because an uploaded mind is without a soul, but because it has no chance of resurrection, and there is no eternal life without resurrection (a seed has to die to grow [John 12:24; 1 Cor. 15:36]). Memories, divorced from a human *subject*, are just data, but a human subject requires a body to be human; the whole thing is required for humanity.[10]

---

[8] McKee, *The Gospel according to Science Fiction*, 52.

[9] See Gregory of Nyssa, *On the Making of Man* 29.1.

[10] The question of whether an android can be considered human is a common theme in sci-fi, and it could be the topic of a whole book in itself, but we will leave it outside the scope of this book. See, for example, McKee, *The Gospel according to Science Fiction*, 58. Some would argue that if the *imago Dei* evolved into humanity, then why not into machines? This brings up the question of

Humans have free will to make choices about how they will interact with other human beings in the world and to make decisions about their own future. Sci-fi often deals with questions of free will and fate, and this is an important question for all of us to wrestle with because we all want to believe that our lives have purpose.[11]

But what is more conducive to the feeling that our lives have purpose: the idea that with free will we control our destiny, or the idea that we are part of something greater than ourselves and we have a destiny? How you answer that question may depend on whether you are generally optimistic or pessimistic about humanity. If you have an optimistic anthropology (if you think people are generally good and will usually do the right thing), then you might want more free will so you can be the master of your own destiny. But if you have a pessimistic anthropology (if you think people are generally selfish and usually sinful), then it might be attractive to think in terms of a kind of predestination that prevents us from screwing up God's plan for us.

Or maybe the truth is somewhere in the realm of "both-and." Can free will and destiny coexist? We hope they can, because (being what we are) we want to have free will but also want God's providence to protect us. We want to make our own decisions, but we also want to believe that there is a greater purpose and we are part of it. Any sci-fi writer has to decide (consciously or unconsciously) whether to take an optimistic approach or a pessimistic approach to human nature. That will drive the story in certain directions. More importantly, how the writer views

---

evolution as well. I will proceed, however, on the assumption that the *imago Dei* is created ex nihilo and is unique to people.

[11] McKee, *The Gospel according to Science Fiction*, 64.

humanity will determine what it is that humanity needs, which will in turn determine what kind of savior the hero has to be.

Christology is our attempt to answer Jesus' question: Who do you say that I am? (Matt. 16:13–20; Mark 8:27–30). And this question is relevant because Christians believe that Christ is *the* mediator between the Creator and His creation: the reconciler of God with humanity. In other words, if part of the question of anthropology (what it means to be human) is to ask what went so wrong that humanity finds itself in need of salvation, then part of the question of Christology is to ask what it will take to fix the problem. What kind of savior is needed to rescue humanity from its predicament? As the book of Revelation puts it, "Who is worthy to open the scroll?" (5:2).[12]

Another term we should define is *incarnation*. The Incarnation refers to the humanity of Jesus Christ—that "the Word became flesh," as the Gospel of John tells us (1:14). In His earthly life and ministry, Jesus was not simply a good example, showing us how to live up to our potential as humans; He was the embodiment of the divine. Then He gave His life for our sake, to make it possible for us to overcome our alienation from God and be reconciled to our Creator. This means that as we analyze science-fiction stories to see how the sci-fi heroes measure up to the real Christ, we will be taking note of some important recurring themes, such as the savior's descent from another realm (or lack thereof), self-sacrifice, and resurrection.

Some science-fiction writers try to explain away the mystery inherent in Judeo-Christian religion. For example, when gods

---

[12] See also James L. Papandrea, *The Wedding of the Lamb: A Historical Approach to the Book of Revelation* (Eugene, OR: Pickwick Publications, 2011).

turn out to be aliens, and everything once thought to be mystery turns out to be explainable as futuristic or alien technology, then we are back to the assumption that religion is needed only by primitive cultures.[13] Again, the assumption (or the message) is that any culture cannot truly progress as long as it holds on to religious faith. The interesting thing is that even science-fiction stories that are antagonistic to faith often turn out to be stories of faith in one way or another. In this book, I'm interested in sci-fi that is an allegory for the Christ event—even when the writer is trying to explain it away or replace it—and even if (or especially if) the analogy is unintentional or antagonistic.

As we look at the savior characters in some of the most fa-mous and popular sci-fi stories of all time, we're going to analyze these characters to see how the stories answer the question as if they had been asked, "Who do *you* say that he is?" Sometimes this means we will look at what the story says about the nature of God and divinity. To what extent is the savior character di-vine, more than human? To what extent is the savior character a mere human? We can then compare the different portraits of a savior to the historical Christian understanding of who Jesus Christ is. We can also see how "there is nothing new under the sun," and how many alternative pictures of a savior have been tried in the past—that is, descriptions of Christ that were de-termined to be incorrect in the early centuries of the history of the Church, or what were labeled heresies. In the end, we can use the criteria of history, and historic orthodoxy, to determine how well our fictional Christ figures stand up to the real thing. And in the interest of being scientific, we'll give them each an orthodoxy score. The score will be based on the description of

---

[13] McGrath, *Theology and Science Fiction*, 26–27.

Christ in the Nicene Creed, Christianity's common definition of orthodoxy. We'll give a possible 5 points for each element, including the divinity of Christ, His humanity, His uniqueness among humanity, His Incarnation, and His sacrificial death and Resurrection.

Soteriology is what we believe about salvation. If the question of anthropology is what we think about what it means to be human (and what went wrong in the human condition), and the question of Christology is what we think about what kind of savior is needed to fix the problem, then the question of soteriology is the question of how the savior saves: the nuts and bolts of salvation itself. "Science fiction is always concerned with salvation."[14] Science fiction always includes an element of people trying to overcome whatever predicament they find themselves in. Although I would say that some science fiction attempts to replace religion with other kinds of salvation, every human culture that has ever existed has recognized the existence of divinity and the need for divine help.[15]

In some stories, the salvation may be the solution to a very down-to-earth problem. The hope of salvation may be simply a desire for personal improvement, rising above an immediate predicament. In other stories, the hope of salvation is the promise of love. In others, the threat may be a fate worse than death, demanding the kind of spiritual salvation for which it becomes

---

[14] McKee, *The Gospel according to Science Fiction*, 128.

[15] For more on science fiction as a replacement for religion, see McKee, *The Gospel according to Science Fiction*, 129–130. Also, it must be noted that the religion of scientology began as science fiction, and even when it's unintentional, fans can turn a fictional belief system into a real-life religion, as in the case of Jediism.

a metaphor. However salvation is defined, the thought of it offers hope for a better future. On the other hand, some stories do not offer hope, but rather a nihilistic pessimism that leads to cynicism, hedonism, and eventually, despair.

Jesus is not just a good teacher who lived two thousand years ago. He is at the center of our very existence and indispensable to the salvation of humanity. Of course, I can't prove that in any scientific way. The truth of the Christian convictions about Christ, however, is demonstrated by the very existence of the Church: the fact that Christianity converted the Roman Empire, influenced Western culture for good, stood the test of time, and now exists everywhere in the world. But also, the truth of the story of Christ is demonstrated by the way the human psyche seems to be hardwired for stories of heroism, selfless sacrifice, and resurrection—and the way these savior themes keep popping up in myth, popular culture, and fiction. My own conviction is that the greatest story ever told is encoded in the human spirit, and elements of that story repeat themselves throughout popular media and storytelling. Even for nonbelievers, the Christ event is such a powerful story that they can't help trying to exploit it. There is no question that themes inspired by the life, death, and Resurrection of Christ keep popping up in fiction. The question is whether the authors are aware of it, whether they do it intentionally, and whether they do justice to the real Christ.

When we compare *Script and Scripture*, we will be looking at heroes as Christ figures, how they are incarnated into the world that needs them, and how they save that world. In cases in which there are multiple films, sequels, or reboots of a certain character, we will be more concerned with their origin stories than with the details of every chapter. We will explore questions such as these: How do they become heroes if they don't start out that way? In what ways are they willing to sacrifice themselves? Do they die, and, if so, do they stay dead? How do they overcome death?

As I said above, we are focusing on classic (popular) stories —and I would claim that they are popular *because* they are Christ stories, which means they are stories that resonate with the way people are hardwired to respond to Christ. My purpose for this book is twofold: to make the case that the story of Christ is hardwired into our psyche, and to use science fiction stories as a way to teach about the real Christ. I encourage the reader to read the chapters in order, since I will develop some themes over the course of multiple chapters. I also encourage the reader to watch these films and shows again, after having read my analyses of them. My hope is that doing this will open up new ways to think about the important questions these stories raise. Good fiction, by asking questions and answering them in a certain way, invites us to think about how we would answer the same questions.

SECTION I

ALIENS INCARNATE

CHAPTER 1

STAR TREK

Perhaps the words are more important than the man.

—(CLONE) KAHLESS

Like all good sci-fi, "*Star Trek* is not about science or technology, except as aspects of its real focus: humanity and human nature."[16] And *Star Trek* certainly has a particular point of view about humanity, in spite of the fact that the universe of *Star Trek* is almost as vast as the actual universe. I have always thought that there was something a bit paradoxical about the fact that in the *Star Trek* universe, the human race on Earth has long outgrown the need for religion, and yet on worlds both in and outside of the Federation of Planets, the religions of all the alien peoples are an analogy for the religions (and religious relations)

[16] Kevin C. Neece, *The Gospel according to Star Trek: The Original Crew* (Eugene, OR: Cascade Books, 2016), 42.

of present-day Earth cultures. To put it another way, the show presents an earthly utopia that is basically atheist, while making a virtue of tolerance toward the religions of other planets.

Paradox or not, the fact that the universe is a macrocosm of present-day Earth is part of the genius of *Star Trek*, but for Christian viewers, it has always been something of a frustration: the idea that humanity will evolve to a point at which everyone on earth is an atheist obviously flies in the face of Christian theology. As the character Chris Agnello wondered in the novel *Time Signature*, by Carlo Kennedy,

> In all those science fiction movies where you get to see what it might be like in the distant future ... most of the time people are portrayed as having "evolved" beyond the need for God—as if belief in God was some kind of superstition that humanity would outgrow. And anyway, Christians are supposed to believe that someday Jesus will come back. All those futuristic scenarios pretty much assume that's not happening, at least not for hundreds of years. Is science fiction anti-Christian?[17]

Many believers have asked the same question.

However, although the Earth in *Star Trek* is apparently too enlightened for religion, there are a variety of religious beliefs represented on the *Enterprise*.[18] These are usually found in the

---

[17] Carlo Kennedy, *Time Signature* (Chicago: 220 Publications, 2014), 47–48.

[18] Neece, *The Gospel according to Star Trek*, 40, 47. On the other hand, there are hints of religious faith among earthlings in the original series, and the *Enterprise* is equipped with a chapel. See the interview in the next chapter for comments on this.

various nonhuman species included in the crew, not least of which is Mr. Spock, whose Vulcan culture has significant religious commitments. And where religious belief is found among the aliens, our human heroes exhibit respect and tolerance, especially during the time of the original series, coming as it did in the latter part of the civil rights movement.

Most books that deal with religion in *Star Trek* take on two primary stories: the "Bread and Circuses" episode of the original series, and the story arc of *Deep Space Nine*, in which Captain Sisko turns out to be the messiah for the people of the planet Bajor.[19] I will touch on these briefly, but only as background for the primary focus of this chapter, which will be a particular episode of *The Next Generation*, which I believe exemplifies the general approach of *Star Trek* to anthropology, Christology, and soteriology.

The episode "Bread and Circuses," which originally aired on March 15, 1968, finds the crew of the *Enterprise* on a planet very much like Earth, with the exception that its Roman Empire never fell.[20] So although they have television and cars, Christianity is still outlawed and persecuted. Part of the point of the episode is something of a social commentary on Roman—and American—culture as one that exploits people for entertainment.[21] There's also a clever play on words used throughout the episode so that until the very end, the viewer thinks that the

---

[19] On this story line, see McKee, *The Gospel according to Science Fiction*, 63–64, 75–76, 137–139.

[20] On this episode, see Neece, 53–56.

[21] For a recent treatment of this and related themes, see Aquilina, Mike, and Papandrea, James L. *Seven Revolutions: How Christianity Changed the World and Can Change It Again* (New York: Random House/Image Books, 2015).

persecuted religion is sun worship. In the show's epilogue, we find out that all along it has been about worship of the Son of God. The episode ends with a hint that Christianity will triumph over this planet's Roman Empire just as it did on Earth. Some have dismissed this epilogue, however, as having been required by network censors. As we will find out in my interview with *Star Trek: The Next Generation* and *Deep Space Nine* writer Ronald D. Moore, there is no evidence that this is the case, yet it seems to be assumed by many people that *Star Trek's* creator, Gene Roddenberry, could never have written such an ending. This conviction is based on the widely held assumption that Gene Roddenberry was an atheist.

Kevin C. Neece, in his book, *The Gospel according to Star Trek: The Original Crew*, has done a great job of setting the record straight on this point.[22] A brief summary will suffice here. Gene Roddenberry went to church while growing up, but his father was a skeptic. He thought Christianity (or any religion) was basically superstition, and for Gene, his father was the perfect example of a man who could be a decent guy without going to church. Ultimately, Gene Roddenberry came to believe that Christianity was useful for promoting morality, but the actual doctrines of the Faith amounted to unenlightened mythology.[23] Yet he seems to have been fascinated with mythology, judging by the sheer number of *Star Trek* episodes that incorporate aspects of ancient myths. In truth, Roddenberry was perhaps more of a humanist than an atheist. He did not condemn all aspects of religion or all religious people, but he was antichurch, because of what he

---

[22] Neece, *The Gospel according to Star Trek*, 3–27.

[23] Ibid., 4–5.

saw as intolerance, and the exploitation of the uneducated by (some) organized religion.[24]

Gene Roddenberry never called himself an atheist, nor did he ever say that he did not believe in God. In fact, there are hints in some *Star Trek* episodes (including "Bread and Circuses") that he believed in some sort of divinity and that he had respect for at least some religious people — if only on principle based on his commitment to tolerance. For him, as long as religion promoted tolerance and peace, it was useful. To the extent that he believed that religion did not promote tolerance and peace, he considered it harmful and oppressive. In fact, a recurring theme of *Star Trek* is the conflict between the Prime Directive (do not interfere with less-advanced cultures) and the desire to liberate primitive cultures from oppressive systems, be they totalitarian regimes or backward belief systems. More often than not, traditional or mythological deities turn out to be aliens — sometimes benign and sometimes malevolent — but never the Judeo-Christian God of monotheism.[25] In the end, while the religious beliefs of individuals are always respected, religion itself is often depicted as exploitive of less evolved peoples.

Based on what Roddenberry said about his own faith, his personal theology seems to have been basically gnostic; that is, he believed that we all have divinity in us, and therefore we are all gods (or potential gods).[26] A line in *Star Trek V: The Final Frontier* seems to speak for Roddenberry. McCoy wonders, "Is God really out there?" and Kirk responds, "Maybe he's

---

[24] Ibid., 6–17, 53.

[25] Ibid., 51.

[26] Ibid., 21.

not out there, Bones. Maybe he's right here … in the human heart."[27] Therefore, if every person is a god, then respect and tolerance (loving your neighbor) is about the only worship that's necessary.

As it turns out, Roddenberry, and by extension *Star Trek*, was not anti-Christian, per se. Roddenberry was fine with the teachings of Jesus as interpreted through the lens of his late-twentieth-century liberalism.[28] This explains why religious themes keep coming up in *Star Trek*. On the other hand, presumably Roddenberry would be happier with the teachings of Jesus if they were detached from Jesus. And this brings us to Kahless.

The *Star Trek: The Next Generation* episode "Rightful Heir" (season 6, episode 23, or 6:23), revolves around a figure named Kahless, who is the Klingon messiah. As the episode opens, Lieutenant Worf is going through a spiritual crisis. He is praying in his quarters. There is a shrine, with a statue of Kahless, the ultimate Klingon warrior. There are candles, and a fire pit in the middle of the room. Worf is sweating and deep in meditation, and he misses his shift on the bridge. When Captain Picard confronts him about his dereliction of duty, Worf explains that he feels empty. He had encountered a group of young Klingons who did not know the traditions of their culture. Worf tells the captain, "I told them about Kahless, how he had united our people long ago, how he gave us strength and honor, and how he promised to return again one day and lead us again." The reference to a promise to return is the clue that this Kahless is the savior figure

---

[27] McKee, *The Gospel according to Science Fiction*, 8–10; Neece, *The Gospel according to Star Trek*, 135.

[28] Neece, *The Gospel according to Star Trek*, 22–24, 26.

of the story, and that he is in some way based on Jesus Christ. In any case, Worf is left questioning his faith, and even questioning whether he ever had any real faith at all.

The captain reasons that Worf may not be able to find what he's looking for on the *Enterprise*. Picard (with great tolerance and just a little condescension) says, "Perhaps you need to immerse yourself in Klingon beliefs in order to discover if they can hold any truth for you." Here the condescension breaks the fourth wall, as the relativism of the show's worldview shines through. The fact that something can be true "for you" without at the same time being true for me betrays a postmodernist approach to truth that assumes it is anything but absolute. Pontius Pilate asked, "What is truth?" (John 18:38). Relativism supplies the implied answer: "Whatever is true according to the perceived experience of the individual."

Picard gives Worf permission to go on retreat to what amounts to a monastery, where devoted followers of Kahless are waiting for him to return. There Worf prays for a vision of Kahless, and is disappointed when he doesn't get one — and frustrated when a younger devotee does have a vision. He is discouraged, but one of the older monks (known as the Guardians) encourages him to stick it out and keep praying. Eventually, Kahless does appear, but not as a vision. He appears in tangible form and proclaims that he has returned. Naturally, some doubt whether this could be the real Kahless, returned after an absence of fifteen hundred years.[29] He does look like the paintings of Kahless, and he knows

---

[29] In the *Star Trek: Deep Space Nine* episode "The Sword of Kahless" (season 4, episode 8), which takes place later, it is said that the life of Kahless was fourteen hundred years prior. Since both *The Next Generation* and *Deep Space Nine* take place in the twenty-fourth century (the year is 2369), that would put the

things only Kahless would know, such as the story of the origin of the Bat'leth (the Klingon battle sword). He proves himself a charismatic leader and begins to rally the Klingons around their pride and honor. He says, "I have returned to restore faith and hope to my people—to lead them back to the way of honor, and the glory that once was theirs, and can be again."

Anthropology

It's ironic, but a fair assessment of human nature, that the very messiah who comes to unite the people ends up creating division. Jesus Himself said, "Do you think that I have come to establish peace on the earth? No, I tell you, but rather division. From now on a household of five will be divided, three against two and two against three" (Luke 12:51–52; cf. Matt. 10:34–36).

Kahless says he has returned to unite the Klingons, but (just as Jesus predicted of Himself) Kahless's very existence causes division among the Klingons over whether to accept and follow him. Even Worf is on the fence. He confides in Kahless, saying, "I want to believe." Kahless responds, "That is a beginning." Later, when Worf is criticized by the Guardians for having doubts, he quotes what seems to be a Klingon proverb, "Questions are the beginning of wisdom." This sounds a lot like the Hebrew proverb, "The fear of the Lord is the beginning of wisdom," except

time of Kahless in the ninth or tenth century by our calendar. According to Christian Domenig, Kahless died in A.D. 822. See the interesting comparison between Kahless and Charlemagne in Christian Domenig, "Klingons: Going Medieval on You," in *Star Trek and History*, ed. Nancy R. Reagin (Hoboken, NJ: John Wiley and Sons, 2013), 295–306.

that the authority of God is replaced by the authority of human reason, in another nod to relativism (see Job 28:28; Ps. 111:10; Prov. 1:7; 9:10; Sir. 1:16).[30]

Kahless claims that he has come because Klingons are fighting among themselves and need someone to unite them. But then, isn't fighting supposed to be the defining factor in Klingon identity? When Worf and Kahless fight with Bat'leths, Kahless breaks off the combat to deliver a speech about how fighting is supposed to be joyful, and he criticizes the Klingons for having lost the joy of battle. This seems to present a mixed message, and I think that here the assumption about religion being naturally pacifist is coming into conflict with what we know about Klingons. Peace has never been the goal of Klingons—until later perhaps, when we see an evolution in Klingon politics in *Star Trek VI: The Undiscovered Country*. But the Klingon savior is not the Jesus of the Sermon on the Mount ("Blessed are the peacemakers" [Matt. 5:9]); the Klingon savior is the ultimate warrior. So Worf, who represents contact and relationship between Klingon and human culture, is conflicted, and skeptical.

Data asks Worf, "In the absence of empirical data, how will you determine whether or not this is the real Kahless?" Worf responds, "It is not an empirical matter—it is a matter of ... faith," to which Data replies, "Faith. Then you do believe Kahless may have supernatural attributes? As an android, I am unable to accept that which cannot be proven through rational means."

Much has been written about whether Data (or any android) can be considered human, in the sense of having personhood.[31]

---

[30] Note that in *Star Trek V: The Final Frontier*, Spock says, "Logic is the beginning of wisdom, not the end."

[31] See McKee, *The Gospel according to Science Fiction*, 44–45.

Most treatments of this issue seem to come down to whether the android in question—or whether any android ever—could express feelings, or emotions.[32] But emotions in and of themselves are not an aspect of the image of God in humanity. Aspects of the image of God—what makes us truly human—are things such as spirituality, rationality and free will, self-awareness and active agency, creativity, and yes, love—not as a feeling, but as the capacity for empathy, compassion, and self-sacrifice.[33] These could arguably be called emotions, but at the heart of the matter (pun intended) they are not feelings; they are decisions. They are matters of the will. And as it turns out, in the ancient world, the heart was not considered to be the place where emotions come from. The ancients thought that emotions came from the guts, and the heart was the seat of the will, the place where decisions come from. So when Jesus said that everyone must forgive his brother "from his heart," He meant that we all have to make the *decision* to forgive, whether or not we feel like it (Matt. 18:35). The ability to forgive requires the ability to *believe* that one should forgive (despite one's baser emotions), so ultimately the question is not whether Data can *feel* love or any other emotion; the question is whether Data can *decide* to act in ways that are compassionate and self-sacrificing. This is a question of free will, of rationality, and of spirituality. In other words, he would need to have the ability to have faith. I would argue that if an android cannot have faith, he can never be considered a person.

Data has just told us that he is "unable to accept that which cannot be proven through rational means." But the following dialogue later in the episode shows us that this is simply not true:

[32] Ibid., 56.

[33] See Papandrea, *Spiritual Blueprint*, viii–xi.

DATA. I once had what could be considered a crisis of the spirit.

WORF. *You?*

DATA. Yes. The Starfleet officers who first activated me on Omicron Theta told me I was an android—nothing more than a sophisticated machine with human form. However, I realized that if I were simply a machine, I could never be anything else. I could never grow beyond my programming. I found this difficult to accept. So I chose to believe that I was a person, that I had the potential to be more than a collection of circuits and subprocessors. It is a belief which I still hold.

WORF. How did you come to your decision?

DATA. I made a leap of faith.

So it turns out that Data is capable of faith after all, and even capable of encouraging another person's faith. The episode "The Measure of a Man" (2:9), is well known for featuring the trial for Data's personhood. In the context of the trial, there are three criteria for sentience: intelligence, self-awareness, and consciousness.[34] Gabriel McKee comments, "Data's desire to be human seems to be an emotion in itself, and thus we as the audience believe what he does not: the quest for humanity means that Data has already achieved his goal."[35] In other words, the desire to be human, and to be more like the humans he lives with, proves that he is self-aware (which implies free will), and that he can understand the differences between himself and the biological humans. In the episode, Data's self-awareness and intelligence are

[34] McKee, *The Gospel according to Science Fiction*, 44–45.

[35] Ibid., 56. McKee is commenting here on the episode "Data's Day" (4:11).

proven, and it is determined that consciousness is not provable. Certainly, something like spirituality would also not be provable in any kind of Turing test. But we are left with the hope that Data can be considered human.

So what does it mean to be human according to Gene Roddenberry and the *Star Trek* universe? First of all, if an android can be human, then humanity does not require a creator other than prior humans, and it does not require anything like what we understand as the image of God. On the other hand, it could be argued that if we are all gods in the gnostic sense, then any sentient being we could create would indeed have our image stamped on it and would be made in the image of its creator(s). So sentience, some level of intelligence, and self-awareness are required for humanity, but not spirituality. In fact, as we have seen, *Star Trek* is based on the assumption that spirituality will diminish as humanity evolves toward its potential. Therefore, the implication is that spirituality is a hindrance to human self-actualization, in spite of the fact that Data had to take a leap of faith to believe that he could grow beyond his programming.

In "Rightful Heir" Worf's skepticism is rewarded, demonstrating that it's better to be skeptical than faithful. We are supposed to learn that doubt and probing questions with regard to religion will be rewarded and are better than blind faith. Organized religion is often portrayed as stifling human potential. Born as it was in the civil rights era, *Star Trek* looks forward to a utopian Earth, where all people are respected as equals, where there is no war or poverty, but also where there is no religion. There is one government for the whole planet, and the planet is part of a peaceful federation of planets. The problems (religious and otherwise) of present-day Earth are projected onto other planets and are arbitrated by a benevolent, highly evolved, enlightened human race, who nevertheless lives by a Prime Directive of noninterference.

This is a very optimistic anthropology, but it also smacks of condescension a bit. There is an assumption that the enlightened ones will educate the less-evolved masses. To be fair, where that education involves equality and tolerance, this is a good thing. Even the Prime Directive itself seems to be a kind of anticolonial apology, as if to say that perhaps the conquistadors should have had the Prime Directive. But here's where it gets tricky, because while we can all agree that it was wrong for the conquistadors to enslave the native people of Central and South America, Christians would not say that it was wrong for them to spread the Gospel.

So this is a kind of optimism that assumes we don't need any god other than ourselves. If God exists, He exists now only because we need Him to, and as soon as we "grow up" enough to realize our potential, God will cease to exist, just as the gods ceased to exist in the episode "Who Mourns for Adonais?" (original series 2:2). At the end of "Bread and Circuses," we are left with the hint that the Roman Empire planet will evolve much the same way as Earth did. On one level, that sounds good to Christians: the Church will convert the empire! But on another level, we remember that in the *Star Trek* world, Earth keeps on progressing until the Church is obsolete—and so is its God. This must make one wonder if the creators of a show where utopia is atheist see themselves as more highly evolved than their viewers who are still believers. The message is that the masses need religion for now, to promote peace, but they also need the enlightened elites to lead them. But this intellectual posture contradicts the very tolerance that the show claims to espouse. When faith is treated as something that humanity needs to outgrow, tolerance becomes little more than a pat on the head.

Christology

In "Rightful Heir" we get an in-depth look at the religion of the Klingons. It features ancient sacred writings complete with traditional stories and songs, a messiah who is the central figure of their glorious past—and who has promised to return—and prayer of some kind, presumably to this messiah, Kahless the Unforgettable. Kahless led the early Klingons to victory in battle, gave them "the laws of honor," and told them about Sto-Vo-Kor, the Klingon heaven, "the life beyond this life where Kahless awaits us." It all sounds very Christian, and on the surface it might seem like Kahless is a thinly veiled analogy for Jesus. But to call Kahless a savior would probably be saying too much. He has never saved the Klingons from anything, certainly not their own violent nature, and he does not point them to any higher power. In the sacred books quoted in the episode, it is written that Kahless once said, "You are Klingons; you need no one but yourselves. I will go now to Sto-Vo-Kor, and I promise one day I will return." Of course, the idea that "you need no one but yourselves," would be inconsistent with the teachings of Jesus, yet it is very consistent with the humanism of Gene Roddenberry and *Star Trek*.

When it is found that Kahless's DNA matches that of a blood sample taken from an ancient dagger, for a short time Worf believes that the man claiming to be Kahless is in fact the ancient warrior returned. But this Kahless doesn't know what authentic War Nog is supposed to taste like, or what Sto-Vo-Kor is like, and he doesn't know the unwritten details of the ancient stories. Captain Picard says, "If he really is an imposter, then you have nothing to worry about," echoing the words of the Pharisee Gamaliel, who advised the Sanhedrin to leave the apostles alone (Acts 5:34–39). Gowron (the leader of the Klingon high council) responds, "Kahless has been dead for a thousand years—but the idea of Kahless is alive. Have you ever fought an idea, Picard?" Eventually Gowron fights Kahless and defeats him (pretty easily, in fact), proving that the man cannot be the greatest warrior ever, and so he cannot be the real Kahless.

Worf loses his faith once again. He says to the Guardians, "You are using the name of Kahless for some twisted game—for that alone you alone should die!"[36] It turns out that the man claiming to be Kahless is a clone, created by the Guardians from the DNA on an ancient relic. Worf calls him, "a copy, a fraud," but the Guardians argue that they have in fact fulfilled the prophecy by bringing Kahless back. They argue over the meaning of truth, and again we are back to Pilate's question, "What is truth?" except this time the Guardians speak for relativism and Worf is taking the moral high ground. Worf says, "You talk to me of truth. They [the Klingons] do not need a false god!" But Koroth (the leader of the Guardians) argues that the clone is "the last chance to restore hope to our people." So even the religious leaders of the Klingons don't actually believe that "the first Kahless" is coming back. The assumption here is that even the "guardians" of the myths don't believe the myths anymore; they just perpetuate them to keep the less educated people hopeful ("the opiate of the masses"). In this case, they take it upon themselves to create his return—making it happen on their terms. To them there is no God who will bring Kahless back; they are their own gods, and they will do what has to be done.

When he's told that some of the Klingons still believe in Clone Kahless, Worf says, "Then they are fools." But later he

---

[36] This may be a criticism of people who use the name of Jesus to endorse things He never intended.

says to Gowron, "It does not matter.... You will still not be able to stand against him." Gowron objects, "What? He's not real; you just said so." Worf responds, "I said he was not Kahless, but in the minds of our people he can be just as powerful as Kahless. Like many of our people they need something to believe in … something larger than themselves — something that will give their lives meaning. They need Kahless." Gowron replies, "But when they find out the truth …" and Worf concludes, "It does not matter. Despite the facts, they will still believe; they will make a leap of faith." So what we are to take from this dialogue is that it is the fool who still believes. Religion exists because we need it to, not because it's true, and faith is something that denies the facts.

In the end, it is decided that the clone will be considered the "rightful heir" of Kahless, reinstating an ancient hereditary monarchy, but one in which the emperor will be little more than a figurehead for the purpose of moral inspiration. However, we come to find out in the *Deep Space Nine* episode "The Sword of Kahless" (4:9) that our cloned messiah will prove to be too weak to stand up to the politicians on the Klingon home planet and will ultimately be a failure as an emperor. At the end of "Rightful Heir," Worf is still full of doubt, saying, "My heart is empty again. I do not know what to believe." He says the same thing again in "The Sword of Kahless," when his hopes of finding the ancient sword to provide him with an "icon" that will give his live purpose are disappointed. The relic becomes only a temptation for people to use to make a grab for power and try to become a new kind of Kahless. Even Worf is not immune to this temptation and almost kills a revered war hero out of selfish ambition.

"Rightful Heir" ends with Clone Kahless accepting the fact that he is not the real Kahless. Speaking of the original Kahless in the third person, he says, "If his words hold wisdom and his philosophy is honorable, what does it matter if he returns? What is important is that we follow his teachings. Perhaps the words are more important than the man." And there it is: we have just been told what we should believe about Jesus Christ. Kahless is the quintessential *adoptionist* savior—the one who achieves hero status, and then shows the way to glory by becoming an example for others to follow (see "Heresy 1: Adoptionism/Arianism"). He is not divine in any sense other than the idea that he has reached a level of achievement that makes him a perfect specimen of realized human (or Klingon) potential. He is not the Son of God in any sense other than being the heir to authority as a lawgiver and teacher of virtues. He does not point his followers to any higher power, though he does hold out for them the promise of an afterlife. Finally, there is no sacrificial death or atonement. It may be that Kahless is an exemplar of honorable death, but only in the sense of inspiring his followers to look forward to their own honorable deaths.

HERESY 1
Adoptionism/Arianism

- This heresy begins with Jewish converts, possibly Pharisees, who followed the so-called Judaizers mentioned in St. Paul's letters (see, for example, Galatians 1).

- It is based on a desire to protect the oneness of God, and the belief that worshipping Jesus would be worshipping two Gods—so adoptionists taught that God is one because Jesus is not God.

- Jesus was a good teacher, a prophet, and an anointed man (Messiah) but still a mere human.

- Jesus was indwelt or inspired by the Holy Spirit, in the same way that the prophets were. Some believed He was "possessed" by an angel, but only temporarily.

- This heresy denies or diminishes the reality of Jesus' divine nature: the Son of God is not eternal but is created.

- Jesus became perfect and earned God's favor, resulting in His being *adopted* as God's Son, but He is not the Son of God by nature.

- In the fourth century, a priest named Arius taught that Jesus' adoption results in His elevation to a status of quasi-divinity, but not a divinity that is equal to the Father's. Arius said He was of a lesser divinity, and therefore not of the same divine nature as the Father.

- So Arianism is a kind of adoptionism that said that Jesus was a mere human who became a god. This is called a Christology of *ascent* because He "rises" to a position of hero status.

- Notice that adoptionism is the opposite of what we read in the New Testament: there Jesus Christ is God (the divine Word) who became a human ("the Word became flesh and dwelt among us" [John 1:14]).

- It denies the reality of Jesus' bodily Resurrection and is understood as a metaphor for eternal life.

- Salvation is by following the law, or by obeying God to the point of achieving perfection — in other words, by human effort. Jesus first saved Himself and, by doing so, showed the rest of us how to save ourselves.

- This heresy assumes an extreme separation between the Father and Son, so that They do not share the same divine nature, and the Son is not essentially any different from the rest of us.

Orthodoxy = God became a human.
Heresy = A human became a god.

In a 1985 interview, Gene Roddenberry explained his thoughts on Jesus. He said, "To me the whole joy and glory of Jesus is the fact that he is one of us. It seems to me that the whole statement of the New Testament is, 'Hey man, you can, too, because I was born like you. I died like you. There's nothing special about me that's not special in you.'"[37] The idea that Jesus is not unique among humanity is a core assumption of adoptionist Christology.

---

[37] Quoted in Neece, *The Gospel according to Star Trek*, 56. Original interview with Terrance Sweeney in *God &* (Philadelphia: John C. Winston, 1985), 19. In the interview, Roddenberry goes on to say of Jesus, "Divine, yes. But so are we. I think that's what he was saying. 'So are you.'" So Roddenberry's own personal Christology was actually gnostic (see "Heresy 2: Docetism/Gnosticism"), while the character of Kahless is an adoptionist Christ figure.

Like the Arian concept of Christ (see "Heresy 1: Adoptionism/
Arianism"), Kahless represents a Christology of ascent, in that
he is no different from every other person, except that he has
achieved something that the others have not: he has risen to hero
status. He is a pioneer and an example to follow, but he is not a
savior, unless salvation is redefined.

Soteriology

In the case of "Rightful Heir," the optimistic anthropology of
humanism leads to an adoptionist or Arian Christology. Since
humanism assumes that humanity's biggest problem is that many
people remain unenlightened, all that is needed to "save" the
human race is progress. In the world of *Star Trek*, humanity is
already on the right path, and it's only a matter of time before it
gets there. So it does not need a savior in the Christian sense. It
needs only leaders, people to show the way to enlightenment.
In the *Deep Space Nine* story line in which Captain Sisko is the
messiah for the Bajorans, there too we have an Arian savior.
In fact, the revelation that Sisko's conception was orchestrated
by the gods (who are actually aliens, of course) based on their
foreknowledge that he would be the chosen one, is actually a
closer approximation to the Arian description of the birth of
Christ than to the orthodox Virgin birth.

Normally, an Arian Christology would lead to a salvation by
works. The adoptionist savior has saved himself and has shown
the rest of us how to save ourselves. It remains for us only to
follow his example. If we want salvation, we have to do what
the savior did and save ourselves. However, Gene Roddenberry's personal theology — which is basically gnostic (see "Heresy
2: Docetism/Gnosticism") — adds an interesting twist to the

equation. For him, and those like him, salvation is actually by knowledge. If people could only "grow" to the point at which they were enlightened enough to know that they are the only gods they need, then the human race would have progressed to utopia. The problem is that the underlying arrogance of gnostic atheism — the condescension toward those who are not "enlightened" and are less "evolved" — means that for the time being at least, most people cannot be trusted to know what's best for them. They need the enlightened minority to show them the way, and like all gnostics, Roddenberry believed himself to be in that enlightened minority.

To be fair, some of this is similar to Christianity. We Christians believe that sin often prevents us from knowing what's best for us, and we also believe that nonbelievers need believers (us) to show them the way. The difference is that the Christian says, *You and I both need Christ*. The gnostic humanist says, *You need us*.

Script and Scripture

Gene Roddenberry's savior figures are Arian because of his fundamental belief that even if God exists, we don't really need Him. We need only ourselves and enough time to grow as a species. As Kevin Neece said, "Roddenberry saw humanity as its own savior ... if it needed saving at all."[38] Interestingly, Roddenberry accepted the idea of intelligent design, though he was never clear on who or what he thought the intelligent "Maker of All Things" was.[39]

[38] Neece, *The Gospel according to Star Trek*, 26.

[39] Ibid., 52.

On the other hand, it may be that the capricious and duplicitous quasi-divine being known as the Q gives us a little more insight into what Roddenberry thought of God. The character of Q is, in fact, consistent with the ancient gnostic belief that the Creator of the material world was either an evil trickster, or incompetent, or both. Gnostics believed that the God of the Old Testament was not trustworthy and was probably the enemy of humanity. If Roddenberry didn't think God was our enemy, he seems to have thought that religion had the potential to be.

Still, Roddenberry accepted the teachings of Jesus (to the extent that he knew them), as long as those teachings could be used to move humanity toward greater tolerance, equality, and peace. True to his humanistic sensibilities, he wanted to promote Jesus' teachings, such as love of neighbor, without promoting the worship of Jesus Himself. Clone Kahless's final statement in "Rightful Heir" makes the point that Roddenberry and his fellow humanists want to make. For them, the words are more important than the man. In fact, the man (Jesus) is not really important at all, at least not for His own sake, and certainly not because He has any unique relationship to God. He is important only for the example He set. But for Christians, the Man is actually *more* important than the message, because the Man is the Son of God, and the Second Person of the Trinity. He is worthy to be worshipped, and by worshipping Him, we are worshipping God. In what is known as the scandal of particularity, Christians believe that while it is true that Jesus Christ is one of us, and fully human, He is also the unique Son of God, and truly divine, and it is only through Him that God chose to reach out to humanity in the Incarnation.

Christians must also reject the idea that humanity will outgrow religion as a fundamentally flawed assumption, if only because it contradicts what our Scriptures tell us. When Jesus instituted the Church, He promised that "the gates of hell will not prevail against it" (see Matt. 16:18). In fact, the Church has outlived every empire that has ever persecuted her. But more than that, even Data understood that the ability to have faith is necessary for a person to be human, because he had to take a leap of faith to believe that he had free will and could grow.

I suppose it all depends on what you put your faith in. Christians put their faith in Christ. Humanists put their faith in humanity. But after the events of the twentieth century, isn't anyone who can't see that humanity is fallen denying the facts? It seems that such an optimistic anthropology is actually a kind of blind faith after all, a blind faith in human progress in spite of the evidence. The truth is that there could be no humanity without spirituality, and to assume that human progress means outgrowing spirituality is to misunderstand completely what it means to be human.

Score

As an Arian Christ figure, Kahless won't be getting any points for being the Son of God, or for divinity. Of course, he gets full points for "humanity" because he is a Klingon just like any other (though I suppose one could argue that he is not fully Klingon because he's a clone). But that's all he gets, because there is no sacrificial death or resurrection—leaving Kahless with the low score of 5.

CHAPTER 2

INTERVIEW WITH RONALD D. MOORE, WRITER OF "RIGHTFUL HEIR"

While working on this book, I sent about fifty e-mail queries to the writers, the directors, and the actors who played the characters in question. I got five responses. Four very polite declines, and one yes. The one person to grant me an interview was Ronald D. Moore, who wrote for *Star Trek: The Next Generation* and *Deep Space Nine*. He was also the showrunner for *Battlestar Galactica* and has worked on a long list of things you would recognize. As far as sci-fi television goes, Ron Moore is at the top of the game, and I'm grateful that he was willing to give up some time for the interview. He is a really nice guy, very intelligent (as you'd expect), down to earth, humble, and gracious. But as you'll see from the interview he's a "fallen-away" Catholic, and

I thought what a shame it is that the Church lost such a sharp mind. Here's the interview.

PAPANDREA. First of all, I want to thank you for taking some time out to answer my questions. And I also want to say at the beginning that all of this is coming from my love for science fiction and my great respect for the people who make great film and television. I'm a huge fan of a lot of what you've done, including, of course, *Star Trek* and *Battlestar Gallactica*.

MOORE. Thanks.

PAPANDREA. *Wikipedia*, which I always take with a grain of salt, says that you describe yourself as a "recovering Catholic" and agnostic. So I just want to start by asking you what that means to you—if you consider yourself a person of faith at all, and if so, what that means.

MOORE. I think it's just, you know, it's been sort of a lifelong evolution in different ways. I was raised Catholic. I sort of always, sort of rebelled against it in my youth just because I didn't like the formality of it, and I didn't like being forced to go to church, catechism, and all of that. So, I sort of grew up waiting to get out of the church, more or less. Then, once I was out, I was like, "Okay, I'm done with all that. I'm an atheist now." But, as you know, as I got older, I got into my twenties and thirties, I just started, seeking, and thinking about bigger ideas and, what's my place in the universe? Is this all that there is? It seems that I was, that we were, playing around with this in *Star Trek* and in science fiction; there was always an existential questioning and a lot of thought about other civilizations, and societies, and cultures, and whether they would have religion or not. It sort of, you know, started to rekindle my interest in the whole subject.

At a certain point, I was becoming interested in Hinduism, in my thirties and into my early forties. I didn't really embrace it as a full-time religion for myself but was sort of intrigued with a nonwestern religion; it was my first encounter with a nonwestern religious system, and I was fascinated with it for a time. I still am to a certain extent, but then I kind of retreated to a place of, "I just don't know." I guess I call myself agnostic by lack of any other definition. I think I'm probably a person of some faith, in that I do have an innate belief that there is something else, that what we perceive in the mortal sphere is not it, and that there is something greater and that there is something beyond our ken, you know, for lack of better term. And I just don't know what that is or that it's knowable to us, who walk around on Earth today. But, I kind of feel that in my bones, that there is something else, that there is a certain other dimensional idea.

PAPANDREA. Okay. One of the reasons I love science fiction too is that it's not really just about science or technology. It tackles the bigger questions. Now, *Star Trek*, of course, is based on this assumption that there is a utopian future in which it seems that humanity has outgrown religion. I think I kind of know where you might go with this based on your answer to the last question. I'd like to get your take on that, and having been so close to the *Star Trek* universe, do you think there's a message there that religion and spirituality are hindrances to human potential and that eventually we will outgrow it as a race? Or do you see ways in which religion and spirituality empower human potential?

MOORE. Well, I think in terms of *Star Trek*, I think it changed certainly over the decades. The original series was not as clearly atheistic and secular as *Next Generation* became. In the early days, in the original series, there was in one episode ... they even establish there is a chapel aboard the *Enterprise*, which is sort

of nondenominational; it has no real decoration. But there is a
chapel. It's where Kirk is going at the beginning of the episode
"Balance of Terror." He's going to perform a wedding there, and
he has a nice opening speech about this place, and it's reflec-
tive of our many traditions and our many beliefs. And there's a
line in another episode where the giant god Apollo appears and
turns out to be an alien. There's a line in there somewhere where
Kirk says, "We have no need of gods anymore. We find the One
quite sufficient." So there was sort of a generalized acceptance
of some sort of monotheistic belief system in the Federation,
even though they really didn't play it very much. But it kind of
was there, around the edges. You move forward in time to *Next
Generation*, Gene [Roddenberry] had a much more definitive
take on it. He flat-out said, "In the twenty-first century, there
is no religion on Earth. All the major religions are gone. It was
all mythology, and it's all done." It was very much an edict from
on high that that is how he saw the future. So, he had kind of
changed as a person over those decades and become much more
of a humanist, and he was celebrated in certain circles as a great
humanist and futurist. He then wanted *Star Trek*, at that point,
to sort of reflect that idea of humanity going forward. Those of
us internal to the show kind of bridled against that because we
just didn't believe that five thousand years or however you care
to count it, of human history with a belief system in place was
just going to get wiped out in a couple of centuries because of
technological progress. We just didn't believe that was what
humanity would become. We, as a staff, all just kind of thought
the religions are still going to be around in some way. They may
not be as prominent. They may not have televised preachers
anymore, and you know, there might be a lot of forced trappings
of organized religion that we know might be long gone, but we

never really believed that idea. However, that was kind of the edict, so we just kind of played it and as a result, any stories that had to do with sort of a questioning for knowledge of a greater existence or a belief in something bigger than the material world all had to kind of get pushed aside and assigned to alien cultures. That was the way that we explored them, particularly in *Deep Space Nine*. There we had the whole thing with the prophets, and the Bajoran religious system was our way then to start to explore religious themes and what religion meant to people's lives and how it could be used and abused and the different cultural traditions, et cetera. It just meant that we could no longer play those stories with the human beings in the Federation, but any alien was still fair game to tell all the same stories.

PAPANDREA. Yeah, I always felt that the alien cultures were kind of used as a metaphor for present-day religions on earth and perhaps even sometimes the conflict between them. Well, since you mentioned the original series, there was an episode called "Bread and Circuses"—do you remember this one?—with the sort of Roman Empire and this persecuted minority, which in the epilogue turns out to be Christians. You're supposed to think throughout the show that they're sun worshippers, and then at the very end of the show there is the punch line, which is that it's the Son of God they worship. And there were rumors that this was sort of mandated by network censors and that it was not part of the original script. Do you know anything about that?

MOORE. I do and actually, there's the definitive history of that episode, and actually every episode of the original series is in a book called *These Are the Voyages* by Marc Cushman. He went through literally every single episode from pitch and story outline to drafts and preproduction and production notes and post; I mean, it's like the definitive notes. And so volume 2 covers season 2, and before we got on the phone, I remembered this question. I went back and I skimmed through the chapter on "Bread and Circuses," which I had read but didn't remember that clearly. I think that's kind of an urban myth. From what I can pick up, it seems like there's no specific mention in Marc's account of when that angle came up, but it does seem like it was always kind of baked in. It was always a satire of network television at the time, and it was also primarily a parallel planet construct about what if Rome had survived until the twentieth century. There are reprints of several of the network notes throughout. There doesn't seem to be any reference to a demand to add that onto the tag, and from the early drafts it looks like it was always just kind of there and didn't seem to get anybody's attention one way or the other.

PAPANDREA. Well, that was my take on watching the episode, that it seemed like the whole episode was building up to that and it would have been strange if that was added later.

MOORE. It looks like it wasn't there in the early drafts but I think it evolved throughout because it's kind of set up and sprinkled in some early places and then it pays off in the tag of the show. It was always a slavery thing; it was always on a TV gladiatorial game, and it's somewhere in the drafts. It kind of added that element, but it definitely wasn't added at the very end.

PAPANDREA. Okay, good. Thanks. What I am focusing on in the chapter of my book is the *Next Generation* episode "Rightful Heir," which I understand you wrote. And in fact, as far as I can tell, you are kind of the expert on Klingon culture, and in this episode we learn a lot about Klingon religion and the character of Kahless, the Klingon savior. Of course, it's pretty clear that he is based on Jesus Christ and the aspects of having been there and having been the Savior, promising to return, and all of that. So

I was just going to ask, what can you tell me about the thought process behind creating the Klingon religion and especially the character of Kahless?

MOORE. I'll try to reconstruct it as best as I can, but it's been a while. Depending on how deep into this particular subject you want to go, I donated all of my story outlines and scripts and notes and memos on every single episode of the entire series to the USC film and television library.[40] So you can go there and ask them for the binder on "Rightful Heir," and it would literally have everything from the pitch through all of the subsequent drafts, if you want to go into that kind of detail. My recollection is that we were talking around the idea of DNA, and I think, if I'm remembering the time of this correctly, I think this episode is around the time that *Jurassic Park* came out. So, I think the subject of resurrecting creatures and then possibly people, based off a DNA sample was something that I think we were talking about in the offices a bit, and in pop culture. Somewhere in that discussion, we started the idea of "What if?" And to my recollection someone said, "What if you could bring Jesus back?" Of course, we aren't doing that on the show. Then it kind of gravitated toward, well we can do it with the Klingons and we established Kahless and, oh let's go down that road. It became kind of fun to start thinking of it that way. The Klingon religion itself had been referenced in different episodes over a series of years, you know. There were little dribs and drabs of it just sort of randomly dropped into different episodes. You got a sense that the Klingons had a belief system and they might have referenced the afterlife here or there in some episodes, and established Kahless as one of

---

[40] USC Cinematic Arts Library, https://libraries.usc.edu/locations/cinematic-arts-library.

the founders of the Klingon society. So, everyone kind of always used the term Kahless, so he was like their Lincoln. He's like one of those chief figures in Klingon history. So writers tended to reference him here and there if you were doing something with the Klingons. And when it came time to do "Rightful Heir," I tried to sort of pull together the threads of things that we had established about them. Also, there was a book. There was a *Star Trek* novelization that I had read growing up that was a Klingon centric novel called *The Final Reflection,* by John Ford. Within that book, it had this reference to the Black Fleet, like some kind of fleet that sailed on in the hereafter. There were different religious aspects to their culture that I remembered when I was a writer on the show. So, I was drawing from a lot of those things as well. But the center of it in this episode was then to establish not only that was Kahless a political and military leader of the Klingon culture but that there was a religious aspect to him. Whether it was a full-blown religion shared by the entire planet or if it had become a cult at that time was one of the things we were sort of kicking around in the writers' room. But the central metaphor was still to get to the idea of: Jesus comes back, and you find out that somebody had cloned Him and re-created Him, and how valid is that? Did that fulfill the idea of returning one day? It just became a fascinating sort of debate to have and to really play around with. We were overtly aping different aspects of Christian mythology while trying to also, you know, at least maintain continuity with certain things we had already established about the Klingon culture.

PAPANDREA. Yeah, well it's a brilliant idea. So, I wanted to press you on this point because earlier you said you were talking about your own faith and coming to the conclusion that if there is something out there, it may be unknowable. In that episode there's a line where Picard is trying to encourage Worf to go off and go on retreat, so to speak. And he says, "Perhaps you need to immerse yourself in Klingon beliefs in order to discover if they hold any truth for you." And when I heard that for the first time, I really latched on to the last two words, "for you," because he seems to be implying that something could be true for Worf without being objectively true, or without being true for others. And so, I wondered if that's in play there too. If there's a kind of implicit assumption here about truth that is sort of going against what traditional religion claims about truth. Was that at all going on?

MOORE. Yeah, yeah, I kind of remember that line because it was meant to sort of, on the one level, it was supposed to protect Picard from endorsing the religion and having an objective religion, and encouraging Worf to go on this kind of quest of his own because he could find something of value and he could find a truth. So, it is kind of what you're talking about. There was a trying to lay out a statement that you can find truth in these traditions and these belief systems, but they may not apply to everyone, and it may not be an objective truth, you know, whatever that means and that there was something of value to be had in this pursuit.

PAPANDREA. With Kahless, though, Kahless is a warrior and Jesus is the Prince of Peace, and so I wondered if there was any sort of conflict going on in the discussions or in your mind about the idea of a warrior Messiah figure? Is that kind of an oxymoron? Or if religion is supposed to be about peace, is Klingon religion even an oxymoron? You know what I mean?

MOORE. Right. I mean, I was thinking about it in terms of what made sense for the Klingons as established. They were, by definition, a warrior culture. Everything about them literally worshipped the martial ideal and the honor system of it and the combat and the definition of a man or woman was in large part how they conducted themselves in some form of battle, and they had to have a battle in order to sort of justify their lives. So, it felt like their Messiah had to be at the core of that in some way. It had to be a martial figure. It had to be a warrior figure. It had to be a figure that would lead them into eternal battle for glory, with something like that in play. There was a line that I originally wrote for the episode "Yesterday's Enterprise" that ultimately got cut from the script, unfortunately, that always bugged me. But there was a line where Worf was sitting in Ten Forward, and the stars were racing by the ship and Guinan was sitting there with him, and she said, "You know, I notice you're the only one who comes in here, and they all stare at the stars, but you don't, and what's up with that?" And Worf's answer was: "To look at the stars is to ask them questions for which there are no answers, and Klingons, we make the stars ask questions of us." And I thought that was connected to this idea of a Klingon belief system that would center on a martial ethos. It was about conquest, it was about glory, but it was righteous conquest and righteous glory, and there was some kind of code that dictated a just battle from an unjust battle, a good cause from a bad cause, and that was sort of the center of their moral universe.

PAPANDREA. That's interesting. Of course, we have that in Christianity too. We have the Crusades mentality. We have the Templars and lots of cultures have this martial monk character. It's just that our Savior didn't really endorse it.

MOORE. Yeah, and in the Crusades and the Christian traditions it's more, "We're going to go defeat our enemies, then plant a kingdom of peace, then all will be well." And with the Klingons it was more the eternal battle. I don't think there is any notion of there ever being an end to that war. In a larger sense, there's always another battle to fight. There's always another land to be conquered, and plant our flag. There's no like, "Oh! Now it's all over. We won against our foes, and everything can be peaceful." They would just hate that.

PAPANDREA. Right, that's interesting. Okay, so at one point Kahless says to the Klingons, "You are Klingons. You need no one but yourselves." And again, that was one of those lines that made my ears perk up, and I was wondering where you were coming from there. Is this a kind of humanistic sermon or is this a cautionary tale in the sense of a critique of a particular kind of self-reliance? What was the thinking there? Do you remember?

MOORE. I was trying to thread a couple of different needles at that point because I had to find a way to get into the episode without destroying the Klingon religion itself and its cultural significance, and at the same time without Kahless saying, "Yeah, you know what, I am a god, and come follow me." He was a clone and a construct so at this point, it felt like he had to sort of acknowledge on some level that he himself did not believe he was the literal reincarnation of the original, whatever it was in a spiritual way, and that the way to convey that to the Klingons was to kind of say, "You don't need me anyway; you don't need the mythological figure to come and lead you to paradise or lead you to the next battle. You're Klingons, and you're already there, and all you need is yourself." And it was in keeping with the Roddenberry-esque kind of rejection of organized religion; and the Klingons, it felt like they could go to that same kind of place.

PAPANDREA. That makes sense. I have a couple of follow-up questions for that. The first one would be, you say you wanted to sort of get out of the episode without destroying the Klingon religion. One of the things that occurred to me as I've seen this episode several times is that when the Guardians make the decision to create Clone Kahless, are they admitting that they have lost their faith and given up hope in the return of the actual Kahless?

Moore. I think they have, but I think they've also rationalized it to themselves in the sense that somehow we are carrying out the master plan. The technology has allowed us now to fulfill the prophecy, and we are now the instruments of destiny. But yeah, I think that probably in their hearts, they're disillusioned and they've come to a place of hopelessness for their belief, and then they've realized, "Oh, there's a way we can make it happen, and we kind of justify it to ourselves like this."

Papandrea. All right. And then the other follow up was, and this is kind of, I think, the whole episode leads to this. This is one of the last lines in the episode. You know where I'm going with this, and actually, this line is the reason I chose this episode to focus on in my chapter. Clone Kahless says, "Perhaps the words are more important than the man." So, what I wanted to ask you about that is, to what extent is this a sort of commentary on Jesus, and are you saying that it would be a good idea to separate the man from his message, in that sense?

Moore. Yeah, that is exactly where I was going with that. I was kind of talking about, does it really matter whether Jesus literally walked on water and whether He was literally the Son of God? Or are the words, and the beliefs, and the message of peace, and brotherhood, and love, and loving thy neighbor, isn't that more important to us on some level? Maybe that's more important than to question whether He was literally all of these things in the traditions. Yeah, that was definitely sort of the place I was going.

Papandrea. Okay, and there's also a line in the episode where Data has this conversation about his own faith and there's the bit where he describes the time where he made a decision to believe that he was more than just a machine, and the way that he did that was by taking a leap of faith, and so I wondered if there was a message behind that, something to the effect that there is something about faith that is essential to humanity. Can a person be a person without faith? And then, if so, does that contradict the idea that humanity is going to sort of grow out of having to have religion?

MOORE. That's an interesting question. I've never thought about it in those terms. I think, to me, there was something about thinking about Data, the machine that does on some level become self-aware and become conscious. That the difference between just a computer and a self-aware being on some level is a leap of faith, that the machine believes in itself and believes that it is a person, ergo it is a person. The power of thinking, as conscious human beings, is almost like an act of faith, in that it does sort of self-actualize ourselves, if I'm using that term correctly. Our belief in ourselves is sort of the first article of faith, you know. I believe that I am here and that this is real and that these are my thoughts is like the first verse of our bible. And then moving on from there, well what is this reality, and so on. Then you ascribe some kind of organization to how you believe the universe works.

PAPANDREA. Okay, so are you saying that it's not that humanity outgrows faith, per se, but that at least in the sort of Roddenberrian Utopia, humanity has replaced faith in a supreme being with faith in humanity, a humanistic faith? Is that kind of where you are going with that?

MOORE. Yeah, I think that's somewhat where I'm going. I mean, I kind of looked at the *Star Trek* universe as saying, even in Roddenberry's construction, that the organized religion that we're familiar with kind of falls away but that there are greater truths. There is an ongoing theme throughout *Star Trek*, like *Star Trek: The Motion Picture*, for instance, where at the end Decker and Ilia essentially go into some kind of heaven-like existence. They transcend our universe. They go to other dimensions, like Spock does. So there are greater realities and things that we cannot know, and *Star Trek* certainly embraced that idea, that there were multiple universes and that there were all sorts of possibilities. The human adventure is just beginning and so on, and by a different definition, that's faith. You have faith in something you can't see, touch, prove exists, and they clearly had faith in that; they just didn't cloak it in the more traditional sense of religious forms.

PAPANDREA. Right, well it does take faith to step out into the unknown, whatever that is.

MOORE. It takes faith to step into a transporter.

PAPANDREA. Yeah, right!

MOORE. If you're going to walk into a machine that's going to take your body apart, turn it into energy, and then it's going to create a copy of you somewhere else, it's an enormous leap of faith that that is still going to be you on the other side.

PAPANDREA. That's right. Well, I mean, you could press that further and say it takes a leap of faith to get on an airplane even today. So, do you think that science fiction has become a substitute for religion for a lot of people?

MOORE. It's certainly a safer way to talk about it. I don't know that it's a substitute. Well, it could be in certain people's lives. Yeah, there's definitely people who treat it like a religion, and it is as meaningful to them in their personal lives as religion is to other people. But I think in a broader sense, it provides a safer context to talk about these things and it's a way that people can discuss these sorts of greater ideas of existence and truth and reality without getting bogged down. Whether that's Judeo-Christian, Muslim belief, or Hinduism, like everything else in science fiction, it cleans it away and you can talk about politics, and society, and race, and culture, and religion in just a safer way and an easier way and really pick it apart and put it back together in different structures and then go, "Hmm, I wonder if it was like this? What if faith was, what if this alien culture had a belief system based on this? And wouldn't that be interesting? And what does that say about faith? And what does that say about culture?" And you can really kind of play around with things in a much safer way.

PAPANDREA. Okay. So, in religion, obviously, if we have a savior figure, that implies that we need to be saved, we need salvation, in some sense from something or for something. What do you think salvation is in the *Star Trek* universe? Do people need some kind of salvation? And if so, what does that look like?

MOORE. In the *Star Trek* universe, exploration is almost the equivalent of salvation. The idea of the final frontier and seeing what's over the next horizon, you know, what's on that star? That's the driving quest of every version of *Star Trek*, and it's almost like that is more important than anything else. Going someplace unknown and doing good once you're there, being a decent person once you're there to embody certain values once you're there, and then to go on to the next one and to discover, to explore, to learn new things about the universe is kind of their version of salvation. Picard would tell you absolutely that learning is everything. It's the greatest endeavor of the human experience and that if you learn, struggle to learn new things until the moment of your death, that would definitely be his version of salvation.

PAPANDREA. Yeah, okay, so you could say that some of the major values of this universe would be increase in knowledge and also tolerance because you have the Prime Directive.

MOORE. Yes. In fact, salvation would be to know everything there is to know. The perfection of the *Star Trek* ideal would be to know everything, to know the universe in its complete form. That's salvation to them, to have perfect knowledge.

PAPANDREA. So, okay, so as you grow in knowledge to knowing everything there is to know, you move toward omniscience and you become more godlike. Interesting.

MOORE. And you see that in the many stories that reflect similar paths, for many characters, usually not ending well. Usually they end up knowing too much; then their human nature turns against them and they become evil. But you can see that that is a driving quest in Rodenberry's humanity.

PAPANDREA. Yeah, interesting, fighting against the tendency toward selfishness in human nature. So, speaking in terms of writing, when you write, how much are you thinking about what lessons the script is teaching about these things, or are you just trying to write a good story, and the lessons kind of come through because they're a reflection of who you are?

MOORE. It's more the latter. You're generally trying to write a good story, you know. There are certain settings and certain characters that are very intelligent people so you have to write them very intelligently, you know. There are societies that are complex, so you seek a greater understanding of how a society functions in order to write a good story about it. So, by trying to tell a story about the Klingon messiah coming back, it made me think more deeply about Christianity than I had, probably, in many years, and wrestle with a lot of the ideas. And so, because that's the story I'm telling, I start to get into, okay what are the themes of religion in this episode, and what does that mean to Worf? You know, it all comes back to the characters in the show—and Picard's position on it. So, I start thinking about the underlying ideas that then come out in the script.

PAPANDREA. Yeah, and to me this is the genius of sci-fi, in that you're also getting the audience to think through these things. In terms of writers in general, do you think, when the religious imagery, especially the Christian imagery, comes up—and I've been going through the most recent Superman and Marvel and DC movies as well and things like that, and there's obviously a lot of Christian imagery there too—how much of that do you think is intentional on the part of the writers versus again just the culture seeping in?

MOORE. I think it depends on the individual writer primarily, but my sense is that it's a similar process to what I described. They're setting out to write a movie about Superman, and you get into it, and you're playing with literally a godlike alien; you start thinking, "Oh, there's some interesting metaphors here to play with, and how will I tackle these metaphors? And hmm, okay, this is an interesting bit of symbolism." My experience with most writers is that they kind of discover it, depending on the project they are working with. I'm sure there are some writers that have a more overt agenda and have a particular message they want to say from the outset, but by and large, in my experience, it usually kind of comes organically out of the material that you're working with.

PAPANDREA. All right. Well, I have to ask about the ending of *Battlestar Galactica*. They get to earth, and then it seems to be thousands of years later or something, and the same characters are there, and it just confused me.

MOORE. Yes, hundreds of thousands of years later, and essentially what we called Head Six, and Head Baltar, which we had established in the last season were both there. And the idea was that they were both representatives of some force, some being that did not like being called god, but that had clearly been a mover and shaker in the series from the beginning. You know, all the way through the show, there was always this sort of religious undertone. The Cylons believe in a single god. The Colonists were polytheists. Baltar's relationship with Six — there were things that happened that could clearly not have happened by accident so they know certain things, certain events had no rational explanation other than some kind of supernatural intervention and that we kind of, as we were wrapping up the show, had to sort of acknowledge that as part of the myth that it was going on. And it was a question of how you did that, and where I wanted to go was to try to not make it as opaque as possible. It's what we talked about earlier. It's my belief that there probably is something else, and we are just not able to understand and know it. It's not within our realm of understanding. So, with the end of the show, rather than really defining what was Starbuck when she came back, and where did she go, and what is this somewhat supernatural force that doesn't like to be called god, well, what is it, and how is it connected with immortality, and all of this has happened before, and all of it will happen again, circle of events, people, and things that seem to be a part of a continuing circle of life. I just didn't want to define any of it, and I just wanted to leave that ambiguous as long as we acknowledge that it was part of it and it was an important part of it, which is why I walk away and let the audience fill it in, in their minds, and they will argue about it for the next fifty years.

PAPANDREA. Well, I mean, it was brilliant, and it's right up there with the end of *The Sopranos*, as endings go. I loved the series. It was great. So, basically, I just have one more question, and this is very general, but I was watching the documentary *Showrunners*, and you said that you got your start by handing a spec script to someone who was able to pass it along to someone else. And I'm assuming that would be a longshot nowadays. Do you have any advice for the young, aspiring writer who wants to be where you are today but right now, he's working a day job and trying to write on the nights and weekends?

MOORE. Yeah, I mean, the answer I usually give is a story that was told to me when I first started at *Star Trek*. I'm sure it's an apocryphal story, but the story goes that the concert violinist Vladimir Heifetz is about to go onstage at Carnegie Hall, and he's in the wings, and a young, like a kid basically, comes up to him, a teenager, and says, "Mr. Heifetz, Mr. Heifetz, I love playing the violin, but I just don't know if I have any talent. Can you just listen to me play for a minute and just tell me if I have it, if I'm ever going to make it?" And Heifetz is like, "All right, kid, let me hear you." I'm sure Heifetz talks like that. So, the kid plays him a minute or two minutes on his violin and finishes, and Heifetz looks at him and goes, "Nope, you don't have it. Give it up." And walks away and goes on stage, and the kid's devastated. And he gives up the violin and walks away. So, time goes by, twenty years later, the kid's now a man, and he's gone into insurance or something, and they're at a cocktail party, and he looks up, and there's Vladimir Heifetz. He goes over and says, "You probably don't remember me. It was a long time ago. I was backstage at Carnegie Hall. I asked you to listen to me play, and you said I didn't have any talent, so I left music, and now I'm married and have kids, and I'm happy. It's all very fine. It all worked out. But the thing I've always wanted to know is how could you tell so quickly that I just didn't have any talent? And how could you do that to me? I was just a kid, and you totally shattered my dreams."

And Heifetz looks at him and says, "I say that to everybody, because it's the kind of business that if you can be discouraged, you will be, and you should find out sooner rather than later." And that is the truest thing about the business I'd ever heard. And to this day, it's still like the most important thing, because it's a business in which, essentially, you've got to believe in your own talent. You have to believe, "I can write. I'm going to make it. I think this is good and I'm going to fight." Because everyone is going to keep telling you no, and everyone's going to reject it and hate it, and they're going to throw it away, and they're going to say it sucks, and you have to have that sort of inner determination and, more importantly, that inner belief that you have that talent and you're going to make it. And I think that the people that succeed are the people that have that fundamental belief.

PAPANDREA. Well, that's great advice. I know you're busy, and you gave me a significant amount of time here, and I appreciate it. It's been a pleasure, and I appreciate meeting you. Thanks a lot.

MOORE. Absolutely, thank you.

CHAPTER 3

STAR WARS

I find your lack of faith ... disturbing.

— DARTH VADER

With the *Star Wars* epic adventure, George Lucas has taken the world on a journey that (so far) has lasted four decades.[41] It began in 1977 with a film that was ahead of its time and yet nostalgic. It was the height of the Cold War, which by definition is something so ambiguous that the ambiguity of it all only heightens the fear. We worried about so many indefinable things, including nuclear holocaust and World War III, but Lucas gave us "A New Hope" by telling us a story about Nazis in space. It's well known that the imagery surrounding the Galactic Empire in *Star Wars* is reminiscent of Nazi Germany. Even the evil empire's stormtroopers

---

[41] For the purposes of this chapter, I will focus on the original three films, episodes IV, V, and VI, using information from the other films as needed.

were named after an English translation of a name for German soldiers. But the reason for basing the Galactic Empire on the Nazis goes deeper than simply making them look like the world's most hated antagonists. In the midst of the Cold War, *Star Wars* reminded the Western world of the last time that it was easy to tell good from evil. For many people, it solidified their suspicion that communism (in whatever form it may take) was no less a threat to freedom than fascism.

And so we have the Galactic Empire, a fascist regime in which a ruling tyrant enslaves an ever-widening sphere of victims through violence and fear. We have the Rebel Alliance, reminiscent of the French resistance, engaging in almost hopeless guerilla warfare against the evil empire for the sake of freedom. And to add a flavor of holy crusade, we have the Jedi Knights, warrior saints reminiscent of the Templars or other medieval militant holy men. They even use swords, of the laser variety. At the beginning of the first film (which was Episode IV in the saga), the Empire has created a weapon of mass destruction, capable of destroying an entire planet, along with everyone on it. This Death Star is a metaphor for the Cold War threat of nuclear annihilation, but it is also a symbol of the absolute power of an invincible government that exists only for the benefit of those in power and considers the vast majority of people expendable.

But this reminds us of another empire, the Roman Empire, and in fact the Nazis patterned their own symbols and images after those of Rome. We can see from their use of the eagle standard of ancient Rome that the Nazis intentionally meant for their icons to give the impression that the Third Reich was the reincarnation of the Roman Empire. And it seems that George Lucas knew his Roman history, because the backstory of the empire — that it had been a republic ruled by a senate until one senator (Palpatine) took control and became the first emperor—parallels the story of Rome. Rome was a republic from the sixth to the first century B.C. In 44 B.C., Julius Caesar was assassinated, sending the Republic into civil war. The result of that civil war was that one man, Octavian—later called Augustus—became the first emperor, and the Roman Republic was transformed into an empire with a single ruler. All of this happened in the few decades leading up to the time when Jesus was born.

The book of Revelation in the New Testament depicts the Roman Empire as the oppressive, seemingly invincible evil empire. Part of the message of Revelation is that behind the violence of the Roman government, driving all the persecution of the early Church, is the "unholy trinity" of the false prophet (sometimes called the "antichrist"), the beast, and the dragon. The beast is the emperor, and the dragon is the devil.[42] The universe of *Star Wars* also has its version of this unholy trinity. There, Darth Vader is the film's antichrist (more on that in a moment), and the emperor is the "beast," true unredeemable evil. But rather than the devil, evil is energized by the dark side of "the Force."

What is the Force? According to Obi-Wan Kenobi, "The Force is what gives a Jedi his power. It's an energy field created by all living things. It surrounds and penetrates us. It binds the galaxy together." We are told that the Force controls your actions, but it also obeys your commands (if you're a Jedi, that is). "May the Force be with you," is a blessing, but the truth is that the Force is not always good. It could be said that the Force is neutral, and that it is the way a person uses it that makes it good or bad, but there is a dark side to the Force that goes beyond simple

---

[42] See Papandrea, *Wedding of the Lamb*. Technically, the word "antichrist" does not actually appear in the book of Revelation.

misuse of it. The dark side tempts people. It seduces people — as it did to Anakin Skywalker. Before we ever know about Anakin, we are told that Darth Vader was seduced by the dark side of the Force. Perhaps this simply means that he was tempted to use the Force for evil — that the temptation of personal power was too much for him to resist. But it seems to mean more than that. It seems to imply that there is a dark side of the Force that exists as an entity, whether anyone misuses it or not. This brings up the question of whether evil is a thing that exists, or whether it is only the rejection of good. I will turn back to that question in the conclusion.

It's clear that the Force is some kind of divinity.[43] But with the inherent dualism of the light and dark sides, it is more like the deity of Zoroastrianism than the Judeo-Christian concept of God.[44] In fact, it was Zoroastrian priests who followed the star to Bethlehem to see the baby Jesus — so, in a way, the Jedi are Magi. They follow (and use) the good, or light, side of the Force, which is never really defined but seems to have something to do with defending the freedom of those who are potential slaves of the empire. Their mortal enemies, the Sith, follow (and use) the dark side of the Force, which is described in terms of anger, fear, and aggression. For anyone who gives in to these, the dark side will dominate their destiny. Nevertheless, both the Jedi and the Sith are believers. The rebels believe in the Force, and so does Darth Vader. It is the military and mercenaries such as Han Solo (at first) who are the unbelievers.

---

[43] McKee, *The Gospel according to Science Fiction*, 17.

[44] McGrath, *Theology and Science Fiction*, 38–39. See also Terry Mattingly, *Pop Goes Religion: Faith in Popular Culture* (Nashville: W Publishing Group/Thomas Nelson, 2005), 142–144.

As everyone knows by now, *Star Wars* is the story of a group of heroes who help the rebels destroy the empire's weapon of mass destruction. But it is also the story of an antihero, Anakin Skywalker, who becomes Darth Vader. He is not just an antihero but an antichrist, in the sense that he has Christ-like features but is a false Christ. We come to find out that he had a "virgin birth," the result of divine sparks known as midichlorians, which are apparently manifestations of the Force in one's bloodstream. Vader also has two natures, symbolized in his two names: the name Anakin Skywalker represents the good and the human in him; while the name Darth Vader (dark father) represents the evil and inhuman—the machine in him. As evil as he is, Darth Vader is a man of faith. But he has put his faith in the power of evil. Anger and aggression have dominated his destiny as he wields the power of the dark side of the Force causing all to fear him. But we had to wait until the end of *Episode VI* (the third film, released in 1983), to find out whether he could be redeemed.

Anthropology

The primary hero of the original three *Star Wars* films is Luke Skywalker. But Luke is not the Christ figure, at least not primarily. Most of the time he functions as the Everyman: the representative of humanity. Luke eventually finds out, much to his dismay, that he is the son of Anakin Skywalker, aka Darth Vader. This means a couple of things: (1) that the Force is strong within him, as it is apparently hereditary (midichlorians again?) and (2) that he has the potential to be turned to the dark side, just as his father was. What this says about humanity is that any of us can use our free will to choose good or evil. We can embrace the light or choose to be selfish, seek personal power, and embrace the dark side. We all have the potential to go either way.

The dark side is very tempting, because it promises power over others. This is, in fact, the real evil behind the Galactic Empire (and during the Cold War, the threat of communism) — that is, the curtailing of people's freedom. To give in to the dark side is to use one's free will to take freedom away from others. This gets a bit confusing, however, in *Episode V: The Empire Strikes Back* (1980). There, Luke is already impatient to complete his training as a Jedi when he finds out that his friends are in trouble. The Jedi master, Yoda, tries to discourage him from cutting his training short to save his friends. But we've been led to believe that unselfishness and the protection of the vulnerable are the hallmarks of the good side of the Force. So clearly, the temptation here is not to give in to the dark side. This whole thing never really worked for me because it seemed to me that Yoda wanted Luke to let his friends die — and then, when he returns to Yoda in *Episode VI: Return of the Jedi* (1983), Yoda tells him his training is complete. So either his training was complete before he saved his friends, and then Yoda was wrong to try to stop him, or he *needed* to save his friends to complete his training, in which case Yoda was wrong to try to stop him. In any case, Luke's impatience is meant to show that there is no guarantee he will not give in to the dark side. And when he loses his hand in the duel with Vader, and that hand has to be replaced by a cybernetic hand, we see what could be the beginning of Luke's loss of his humanity and transformation into a machine — following in the path of his father.

On the other hand, Luke's sister Leia never falters. There is no danger she will turn or be seduced by the dark side of the Force. Even when Darth Vader tries to use a mind probe on her to find out the location of the rebel headquarters, she is able to resist it. Of course, we later find out that Darth Vader is also her father, and that the Force is strong in her — apparently stronger than in Luke. So although the force is supposed to be omnipresent, surrounding and penetrating all living things, there is this recurring assumption that some people have it more than others (that is, they have a higher midichlorian count). Those for whom the force is not so strong are described as "weak-minded," and it's fair game, even for a Jedi, to use the Force to manipulate them. After using the "Jedi mind trick" on some stormtroopers at Mos Eisley, Obi-Wan Kenobi says, "The force can have a strong influence on the weak-minded." Notice that he didn't say "on evil people" but on anyone who is weaker. Although I doubt George Lucas intended this, a gnostic elitist spirituality has crept into the Jedi's religion (see "Heresy 2: Docetism/Gnosticism"). In a context where access to divinity is hereditary, they look down on those to whom less is given.

This elitism effectively divides humanity into two classes. They are the "haves" and the "have-nots," not in the economic sense, but in the spiritual sense. For the haves — that is, for those who are enlightened — there is a more optimistic anthropology. They have access to the Force that others do not have, and assuming they have completed their training and are mature in their faith, they cannot be turned to the dark side. There is also a hint of the gnostic view of humanity, which says that each person has a spark of the divine within himself — meaning that each person *is* divine. Notice the mantra in *Rogue One*: "I am one with the Force, and the Force is with me." To say, "I am one with the Force" goes further than to say that divinity surrounds and penetrates us; it says that we *are* the Force — we are divine.

HERESY 2
Docetism/Gnosticism

- This heresy began with pagans who converted to Christianity but fall back on their old polytheism (see Colossians 2 for Paul's warnings to former pagans).

- It is based on an extreme dualism that says that everything in the material world is evil; only what is spiritual is good.

- Since matter is evil, Christ could not really become human. He only *seemed* to be human (*docetic* means "in appearance only"). Some believed that Jesus was pure spirit, not even tangible. Others believed that He had a tangible body, but that was only a disguise, and He was still not really human.

- Docetism denies the reality of Jesus' human nature.

- However, Jesus is like us in the sense that Gnostics tended to believe that we all have a divine spark within us—so Jesus is divine, and so are we.

- Gnostics believed Jesus came to bring secret knowledge (*gnostic* comes from the Greek word *gnosis*, which means "knowledge").

- Gnosticism denies the reality of Jesus' death and bodily Resurrection: His death was an illusion; the Resurrection was a mystical vision.

- Salvation is by knowledge, by enlightenment.

- Most people can never really be enlightened enough to be spiritual: salvation is for only a select few.

> **Orthodoxy** = The Word became flesh.
> **Heresy** = The Word came disguised as flesh.

For the unenlightened (whether they are evil aggressors or simply ignorant), there is a much more pessimistic anthropology assumed. "Power corrupts," as the saying goes, so anyone who gains power but is not enlightened, as a Jedi is, will most likely give in to the temptation to abuse that power. And for those unenlightened who never have power, C3PO speaks for them when he says, "We seem to be made to suffer. It's our lot in life." So in the division of spiritual classes, the enlightened good guys have to fight the unenlightened bad guys to save the unenlightened innocents.

It's also important to notice the gnosticism inherent in the story's treatment of the body. Obi-Wan Kenobi tells Luke, "Your eyes can deceive you—don't trust them.... Stretch out with your feelings." Therefore, your physical senses (the senses of the body) are not trustworthy, but your feelings are trustworthy. To be clear, though, when they say "feelings" they are really talking about the mind, over against the body. We can tell this is the case when we see that a person's "feelings" can betray him. This happens when Darth Vader reads a person's mind. So "feelings" here really means the mind. At the end, Luke hears Obi-Wan's voice again, "Luke, trust your feelings.... Use the Force, Luke.... Let go." To use the Force is to reject the bodily senses, and also technology, as untrustworthy. There is a gnostic dualism here that elevates the mind over the body to the point of disregarding the body. It is true, for example, that Darth Vader's humanity represents the good in him, and the extent to which he is a machine represents evil in him. But "humanity" here does not mean mind *and* body:

it means the mind only, as Darth Vader's human body has been to a large extent replaced by technology, and Obi-Wan's body is destined to be dissolved into thin air.

Finally, I think the tractor beam in *Episode IV* is a very significant symbol. Our team of heroes is trapped on an enemy ship. They can't leave until the tractor beam is turned off. To me this tractor beam represents the loss of freedom. Freedom has to be restored, and, in fact, Obi-Wan Kenobi gives his life to turn off the tractor beam and restore freedom. This act is what makes him the Christ figure of the original *Star Wars* films.

Christology

Although Luke Skywalker is the primary hero of the original three films, it is really a team effort. All of the main characters go through the hero's journey. Han Solo is the unbeliever who is converted, and he has his own death and resurrection when he is frozen in carbonite. Luke goes through a death and resurrection when he's pulled under the sludge in the garbage compactor. Leia is enslaved by Jabba the Hut, but she's the one who kills him (she is not rescued by anyone else who would be a savior to her). They all go through their ordeals, and they are all on a path toward salvation, but Obi-Wan is the primary Christ figure because his death is voluntary.

Obi-Wan Kenobi, aka "Old Ben" Kenobi, is described as a hermit, a wizard, and a crazy old man. When we first see him, he's dressed like Jesus in all those old gospel movies, and he "raises" Luke, who had been knocked out by the Tusken Raiders. He is the master, the teacher of the Force.

As his confrontation with his former student and archenemy Darth Vader approaches, Obi-Wan says to Luke, "You can't win—but there are alternatives to fighting." The alternative he chooses at the decisive moment is to sacrifice himself. After he turns off the tractor beam, restoring freedom to the heroes, he basically gives up and lets Vader kill him. But first he warns Vader, "If you strike me down, I shall become more powerful than you can possibly imagine." He fights Vader just long enough so that when he is killed, Luke will witness his death. He has confronted evil, but in a way that does not embrace aggression (for that is part of the dark side). And in confronting evil, he has victory over it through his voluntary sacrifice. Of course, that victory is more of a spiritual victory than an actual defeat of the enemy, but it does distract the enemy long enough to allow Luke, Leia, and Han to escape. But more important, Obi-Wan's death allows him to be present with Luke at crucial moments later in the story, guiding him in ways that he never could in bodily form.

After Obi-Wan gives up the fight, and Darth Vader swings his light saber for the death blow, Obi-Wan's body disappears, leaving only his monastic robes lying on the floor. There is no body left to bury. But Luke can hear Obi-Wan's voice, and Obi-Wan will come back to him in visions. In *Episode V*, he comes to Luke and tells him to go to Yoda to complete his training, passing the apprentice on to a new master. This is a resurrection of sorts, though not a bodily one. Therefore, it is somewhat gnostic in its view of the afterlife. The same thing happens when Yoda dies. There is no body left, but Yoda will appear in visions.

Interestingly, in one of these visions, Obi-Wan tells Luke that he will need to kill Darth Vader to become a true Jedi. This seems to contradict Obi-Wan's advice about finding alternatives to fighting. Maybe Obi-Wan's earlier point was to find an alternative to fighting in those situations in which you can't win. Now, however, he believes that Luke can, and must, kill his own father. But Luke has learned Obi-Wan's lessons even better than Obi-Wan has, because Luke refuses to kill Vader. Instead, he will risk his life for the good that he believes is still within his father. In a way, Luke has surpassed his mentor and become a second savior, following the example of the original. His sacrifice is less voluntary, it seems, because as he goes into the ordeal, he believes that he will be able to convince his father to turn away from the dark side. Nevertheless, just as Obi-Wan defeated Vader by confronting him without aggression, now Luke confronts Vader — and the emperor — without aggression. Of course, there is a moment of anger when Luke feels he must protect Leia, but in the end, Luke sacrifices himself, and we see that Darth Vader can be saved after all. This happens, however, only because Vader himself finally switches sides and turns on the emperor, sacrificing himself to save Luke.

Soteriology

Before we look at salvation, let's take a look at damnation. In *Star Wars*, the fate worse than death is to become a machine. Technology is a tool of the dark side, and the Death Star is the ultimate technological manifestation of evil. The real threats to life and freedom in *Star Wars* are fascist and military atheism and technology in the wrong hands. So, for a person to become a machine is damnation. It is to lose one's humanity (one's mind and free will). When Obi-Wan Kenobi is describing Darth Vader to Luke, he says, "He's more machine now than man." This means that Obi-Wan believes Vader is beyond redemption. But Luke saw the man in the machine. He said, "I can save him. I can turn him back to the good side. I have to try." Luke cuts off Vader's mechanical hand, which is a reversal of the ominous moment when Vader cut off his human hand, and it is the moment when Vader begins to become less of a machine and more of a man.

Still, Luke's plan backfired. It was only when the emperor tried to kill Luke that Vader turned away from the dark side, turned against the emperor, and intervened to save Luke. It was said that if Vader was going to be saved, he would have to "let go of his hate." But he never hated Luke; he only wanted him to join the family business. It wasn't letting go of hate that changed him; it was accepting Luke's love. Luke's cries of "Father, please!" stirred up compassion in Vader, and he became human again when he chose family over power. Vader's unmasking was his rejection of the very technology that was keeping him alive and his return to humanity: he knew he would die, but he also knew he was saved. So, although the dark side had dominated his destiny for all of his adult life, Vader avoided the fate of damnation by turning toward the light. Another word for this kind of turning is repentance. And we know that he was saved because at the end of *Episode VI*, Anakin Skywalker appears in a vision with Obi-Wan Kenobi and Yoda, and we can tell by their smiles that in the spiritual realm, all is forgiven. Apparently, he was not beyond redemption after all.

Thus, on one level, salvation in *Star Wars* is repentance. It is turning away from the dark side (anger, fear, and aggression) and toward the good. It is a choice. Although there is unselfish sacrifice on the part of the characters, it is not the kind of vicarious sacrifice we mean when we say that Jesus died for us. Rather, it is a sacrifice that elicits a response in others, and it is that response that saves them (or not). Obi-Wan did not save Luke. In fact, he was wrong about Luke having to kill his father. What saved Luke was his response to Obi-Wan's sacrifice. Luke followed what Obi-Wan *did*, not what Obi-Wan *said*. Then Luke became a kind of savior by following Obi-Wan's example. But it was not Luke's sacrifice that saved Vader. What saved Vader was his own repentance after seeing that Luke was willing to sacrifice himself. This kind of salvation by example is one of the hallmarks of Arianism. In Arianism, it is not the death of the savior that saves you; it is your response to the savior's death and your willingness to follow in the savior's footsteps.

Therefore, salvation in *Star Wars* is not by divine intervention (if, indeed, the Force could be said to intervene in anything); rather one saves himself by following the example of the previous savior. In a way, one then becomes one's own savior, setting the example for others. It sounds like a good thing, but ultimately it rejects the idea of the atonement: that God came into history in the Incarnation to rescue us.

Star Wars is as much an antichrist story as it is a Christ story (an antagonist is the hero of his own story, after all). And the message here is that even an antichrist can be saved. But more than that, even an antichrist can become a savior. The only problem is that, in order to do that, the antichrist in question (or anyone for that matter) would really have to save himself by following the example of some previous savior, and enact his own passion in which he is willing to sacrifice himself to reject evil.

Script and Scripture

The Christology and soteriology of *Star Wars* is an amalgam of both Arian and gnostic elements. Technically speaking, gnosticism is always a syncretism of a variety of systems, but in this case the Christology and soteriology seem to be coming from different directions. The Christology is Arian, in the sense that the savior is really just setting an example, and anyone may *become* a savior by following that example and responding appropriately to the previous savior. This idea of *becoming a* savior (rather than coming as *the* savior) is the hallmark of the Christology of ascent inherent in Arianism. But on the other hand, salvation is gnostic because salvation is through enlightenment, since it is the secret knowledge of the Force that allows one to make the right choice and follow the example of the savior. In *Star Wars* one saves *oneself* by making a self-sacrificing choice.

This is not the only contradiction. When Obi-Wan Kenobi says, "Many of the truths we cling to depend on our own point of view," he basically undercuts the credibility of everything else he says, including his teachings about the Force. I would have expected him to say something like, "Many of the beliefs we cling to are based on the fact that we don't know the secret truth." That, at least, would have been consistent with the gnostic undertones of the Jedi religion. But to espouse the kind of blatant relativism that this statement implies begs the question as to whether Obi-Wan's truths about the Force are any more truthful than Han Solo's early skepticism.

In another blatant contradiction, Obi-Wan is clear that aggression belongs to the dark side, and Obi-Wan's and Luke's salvation comes through confrontation without aggression. Yet it is always assumed that the rebels must use aggression in a preemptive strike against the Death Star. As we saw in the most recent *Star Wars* film, *Rogue One*, it is clear that to the Galactic Empire, the rebels are terrorists. We should be very careful about thinking that revolution will necessarily bring peace. It almost didn't work in North America, and the revolutions in France and Russia were extremely bloody (and antagonistic toward the Church). Granted, the Death Star is a weapon of mass destruction, and so its destruction could be called an act of self-defense. Still, the juxtaposition of the Jedi's self-sacrificial pacifism with their own willingness to wield the light saber, their support for the rebellion, and the assumption that aggression is necessary to avoid slavery should steer us away from any overly simplistic view of pacifism and violence.

Something that has always bothered me about *Star Wars* is the idea that Anakin Skywalker was predicted to bring balance to the Force. But it seems as if, before he enters the picture, things are leaning more toward the good side. The Jedi are strong, and the emperor has not yet come to power. And then Anakin apparently brings balance *by bringing in more evil!* To be fair, he eventually gets rid of the emperor by throwing him into the reactor core of the second Death Star, but in what is probably the most disturbing aspect of *Star Wars*, it seems that the balance of good and evil is more important than getting rid of evil. In other words, evil is necessary to maintain the balance of the universe. In the animated series *Clone Wars*, it is stated that if the balance between the dark and light sides of the force is not maintained, the entire universe could be destroyed (3:15). If, then, we assume that preventing the destruction of the universe is the ultimate good, it seems that good includes evil. There has to be the same amount of evil as good in the universe to keep the universe going. So, at the end of the day, evil is necessary, and therefore it's good. The very concepts of good and evil lose all meaning.[45]

What this tells us is that the divine force is not really benevolent, in the way the Judeo-Christian God is benevolent.

---

[45] After coming to these conclusions, I found a similar line of reasoning in Timothy D. Peters, "Unbalancing Justice: Overcoming the Limits of the Law in *Batman Begins*," *Griffith Law Review* 16, no. 1 (2007): 247–270.

The force is morally neutral, as well as being impersonal.[46] In other words, the Force doesn't really care about the good as the moral expectation for everyone—the force cares only about maintaining the balance. This further implies that evil is a created substance, no less than good. So whoever or whatever created the universe presumably created evil as well as good and built that balance into the original creation. This, too, is a gnostic idea. And it means that divine power can be used for evil purposes, just as much as good. A person (a Jedi) can manipulate the Force, and the Force will not prevent itself from being used for evil.[47]

By contrast, the God we know and trust cannot be manipulated. Our God is both personal (caring) and omnibenevolent (always good). God is not simply an impersonal power; He is love (1 John 4:8). And our Scriptures do not promise that someday there will be balance between good and evil; they promise that good will triumph over evil, and life will have a final victory over death. Good and evil are not equal opposites, as in some Zoroastrian version of the Yin and Yang. We know that good is ultimately more powerful than evil, and we know that good is real, and evil is not. Evil is not something created by God, but is only the result of the misuse of free will and the rejection of God's will. Evil is not a force. The real force is the gospel, as St. Paul said: "For I am not ashamed of the gospel. It is the force of God for the salvation of everyone who believes: for the Jew first, and then Greek. For in it is revealed the righteousness of God

---

46 McKee, *The Gospel according to Science Fiction*, 17.

47 Robert Jewett, *Saint Paul at the Movies: The Apostle's Dialogue with American Culture* (Westminster/John Knox Press, 1993), 25.

from faith to faith, as it is written, 'The one who is righteous will live by faith'" (Rom. 1:16–17).[48]

It is the power of the gospel of the Cross that shuts down the tractor beam of temptation and sin. And it is the force of grace that can empower us to repent and turn from darkness and death toward light and life. But without the Cross and God's grace we could never make that turn. We could never save ourselves simply by following the example of others who make unselfish choices. It takes the force of divine intervention, in the Incarnation and in a Savior who gives His life for us — not only for our benefit, but on our behalf, in place of us. What we need is not the balance of good and evil but reconciliation with our Creator, who did not create evil.

In an interview, George Lucas once said that he hoped the spirituality in his *Star Wars* movies would encourage young people to have faith in God, "more a belief in God than a belief in any particular religious system."[49] Unfortunately, Lucas gave his viewers a gnostic view of God that makes God the author of evil, and an Arian view of salvation that puts the burden of salvation on every individual.

Score

As an Arian savior, Obi-Wan Kenobi is not the divine Son of God, and with the addition of a gnostic cosmology, the "divinity" in *Star Wars* (the Force) is too impersonal to be thought of as

---

[48] With the word "force" for emphasis where the text has "power."

[49] Excerpt of interview quoted in John Lyden, ed., *The Routledge Companion to Religion and Film* (London/New York: Routledge, 2009), 396.

"Father" anyway. Since Arianism is a Christology of ascent (the person *becomes* a savior), it gets no points for descent. Obi-Wan is, of course, "human," so he gets full points for humanity. As far as being unique among humanity, he is a Jedi, and that's rare. There is always the risk of spiritual elitism here, but to be fair I'm going to give him 4 points for uniqueness because after all, he is a Jedi master. He sacrifices himself voluntarily, so he gets points for that. And although he doesn't have a bodily resurrection, he reappears a lot so he has to get partial points for resurrection. I'll give him 3. That gives Obi-Wan a total orthodoxy score of 12.

CHAPTER 4

I, ROBOT

One day they'll have secrets.

— DR. ALFRED LANNING

The 2004 film *I, Robot* was inspired by Isaac Asimov's short stories, published together under the same title.[50] Some elements of the movie's plot are loosely based on the stories "Little Lost Robot" and "Runaround," though most of the script is original. The most prominent feature of Asimov's stories to make it into the film is the concept of the Three Laws of Robotics, meant to control robot behavior and provide a safety measure for humans.[51] The three laws are these:

[50] Isaac Asimov's collection, published in 1950, is not to be confused with a completely different short story by the same title, written by Eando Binder and published in 1939, or the remote-controlled vacuum-cleaning device.

[51] I have used the concept of three laws in my writing, as a homage to Asimov and to science fiction in general. Hence "Papandrea's

Law 1: A robot may not injure a human being or, through inaction, allow a human being to come to harm.

Law 2: A robot must obey orders given to it by human beings except where such orders would conflict with the first law.

Law 3: A robot must protect its own existence as long as such protection does not conflict with the first or second law.

Asimov's short stories often revolve around dilemmas caused by conflict between the three laws, or hyperlogical interpretations of the laws, and in that spirit, the film *I, Robot* combines the classic "science gone bad" subgenre with the three laws of robotics to pose the question: What if a computer became self-aware and decided to interpret the laws in a way that its creators could not have anticipated?

Set in Chicago in the year 2023, the film follows Detective Del Spooner (played by Will Smith). Spooner is suspicious of robotic technology, to the point of being prejudiced against robots. He wakes up to an analog alarm clock, listens to Stevie Wonder's "Superstition" on an outdated CD player, and wears vintage shoes from 2004 (the year the film was released). When he encounters a robot on his way to work, he calls it a "canner," short for "can opener" and clearly a derogatory term. When he's shown an automated robot factory, he says, "Robots building robots. Now that's just stupid."

Three Laws of Early Christian Doctrine," in *Trinity 101: Father, Son, Holy Spirit* (Liguori, MO: Liguori Publications, 2012), 67–73.

As the story begins, it appears to be a conflict of progress versus prejudice. When Spooner suggests that robots are taking people's jobs, Lawrence Robertson, CEO of U.S. Robotics, asks if he thinks they should have shut down the Internet to keep the libraries open. In fact, Robertson's company is about to roll out a new robot upgrade, which will result in there being one robot for every five humans. The new robot models will have a daily wireless uplink to the master computer (which is at the top of a tower that looks a lot like a venomous fish). The new models will replace many of the older model robots, which will go into indefinite storage.

None of this should be cause for concern because, as we are told, no robot has ever committed a crime. But Spooner is investigating the apparent suicide of robotics pioneer Dr. Alfred Lanning. And as it turns out, a detective who doesn't trust robots is "the right guy for the job." Everyone else refuses to believe that a robot could be involved in Lanning's death, but Spooner isn't so sure. He consults with Dr. Susan Calvin (Bridget Moynahan), whose job it is to make the robots seem more human. She claims that her work only creates, "an imitation of free will," but of course there is more to the story than even she knows.

The master computer is controlled by a Virtual Interactive Kinetic Intelligence, or VIKI. Although the robots are referred to impersonally (they are called "it"), VIKI is referred to as "she." And as we come to find out, she is A.I. gone rogue. Like *The Terminator*'s Skynet, she has become self-aware, and self-awareness has turned to self-preservation, and perhaps even self-centeredness. A.I. has evolved and grown an ego.

It turns out that Lanning knew VIKI had become dangerous, but she was preventing him from doing anything about it, so he orchestrated his own death to send the message that VIKI was no longer benign, let alone benevolent. Lanning created a new robot, whom he named Sonny. He gave Sonny a secondary brain that allowed him to override the three laws. In other words, he gave the robot free will. Then he made Sonny promise to do whatever he asked—made him promise before telling him what he was going to ask him to do—and then he ordered Sonny to kill him. This created a dilemma within Sonny, not only with the three laws, but also a dilemma of loyalty: to obey his creator would mean killing him. To preserve his creator's life would mean disobedience. Sonny chose to obey. As he explains his choice, he says, "You have to do what someone asks you ... if you love them."

Anthropology

As we see in many science fiction stories, humanity is defined as having free will. *I, Robot* takes this idea further, however. In this film, to be human is to have the ability to choose whether to obey the laws.

In an interrogation, Spooner says to Sonny, "You're just a machine, an imitation of life. Can a robot write a symphony? Can a robot turn a canvas into a beautiful masterpiece?" Sonny responds, "Can you?" The question is left open as to whether Sonny can be creative in an artistic sense, but he can take the initiative to push back against authority.

Sonny's secondary brain, which allows him to decide whether to obey the three laws, is in his chest, where a person's heart would be. Therefore, his "heart" is what makes him more like a human, in terms of having free will. And as I've noted, in the time of Jesus, ancient people believed that the heart was the seat of the will, the place where decisions are made; emotions come from your guts, but decisions come from your heart. In the context of *I, Robot*, it is this heart — this ability to choose for oneself and be one's own interpreter of the laws — that is the essence of humanity.

Dr. Lanning, before his death, had speculated about what he called "ghosts in the machine," that is, spontaneous anomalies in computer code that result in the computers' going beyond their programming and exhibiting unanticipated behavior. He cites as examples the phenomena of robots feeling safety in numbers when they would otherwise be alone, or seeking out light when left in darkness. Obsolete robots left in storage containers even exhibit curiosity when Spooner arrives. Lanning had speculated that these "ghosts in the machine" are the seeds of free will, or even of a soul. If the creation becomes creative, then is that creativity evidence of the image of their creator in them? Lanning wonders, "When does a perceptual schematic become consciousness? When does a difference engine become the search for truth? When does a personality simulation become the bitter mote of a soul?" He concludes that it is possible that "robots might naturally evolve," or that "one day they'll have secrets." Sonny even claims to have dreams, which seem at the time like a real sign of life, though we find out later that the dreams were implanted by Lanning as clues for Spooner to follow.

Eventually, Spooner comes to think of Sonny as a someone rather than a something. And in the end, when Sonny's purpose is fulfilled, he is left with no grand plan other than to live one day at a time, just like any human. All of this is the theory of evolution applied to machines, much like what viewers of *Star Trek: The Next Generation* saw in episodes surrounding the contested humanity of the android Data. The conundrum is that if we accept the theory of human evolution from lower species (and I'm not saying we should accept it wholesale), we are left with the problem that logically that would mean that the image of God in humanity got there by evolution. In other words, if macroevolution is true, then humans were not *created* in the image of God, but were *evolved* into the image of God. The implication is that the image of God evolved in us, presumably at precisely the point at which we became humans from something less than human. And if the image of our Creator can evolve in us, why could it not be the case that the same thing could happen to robots: the image of their creators evolves in them, the image of the image, so to speak, but with a carbon copy of the same free will and creativity that our Creator has given us?

The anthropology of *I, Robot* is mixed. On one level, as we will see, VIKI takes over because humans are by nature destructive. We make war, and we destroy the environment. But that pessimistic view of human nature is balanced by the implied optimism of evolution. We are still evolving: this is the sci-fi version of, "God's not done with me yet," which is both a justification for our present sins, and also a hope for something better in the future. We may be self-destructive, but there is hope that we can grow out of it. Nevertheless, we have created for ourselves a world that is full of dangers. Can we rely on our technological creations to make it safer, or will they become yet another danger?

Christology

Detective Spooner's story begins with a "baptism": a car accident that left him pinned in his car, submerged in the river. In a recurring dream, Spooner is forced to relive the event. The passenger of another car, a twelve-year-old girl, is also trapped under water. When a passing robot attempts to rescue Spooner, he tells the robot to save the little girl instead. But the robot disobeys that order, based on an evaluation of vital signs that led to the robot's decision to save the person who was more likely to survive. Apparently, the robot could ignore the second law because it "reasoned" that it could not save the girl, so attempting to save the girl would have resulted in the death of both the girl and Spooner. But in Spooner's mind, the robot saved him instead of the girl because it had no heart. A person with a heart could feel and would have tried to save the girl instead of Spooner. Therefore, he refuses to trust robots. Ironically, the accident left Spooner with injuries that resulted in his receiving prosthetics of a robotic arm and a robotic lung. Spooner hates in the "other" what he hates in himself. And yet that robotic arm will come in handy later, when his life is threatened by attacking robots. He feels as though his prosthetics make him less human, but in a way they make him more than human.

But Spooner is not the Christ figure in this film. During an inspection of Dr. Lanning's lab, Susan Calvin says, "A robot could no more commit murder than a human could ... walk on water." To which Spooner replies, "Well, you know there was this one guy a long time ago ..." And that's when we meet Sonny. His name is an almost too obvious reference to the Son of God. And he calls Lanning "my father."

As robots go, Sonny is unique. He is aware of his uniqueness and mentions it several times, saying, "I am unique"—a possible allusion to the "I am" sayings of Jesus (see John 6:35, 48; 8:12, 58; 9:5; 10:9, 11; 11:25; 14:6; 15:1). His uniqueness is symbolized by his different eye color. The other robots have yellow eyes, giving them a jaundiced look, but Sonny has blue eyes, a color that can symbolize perfection, purity, and even holiness. In addition, he is made of "a denser alloy" than other robots, which will prove essential in the film's climax, when he needs to reach into an energy field. As we have already noted, he has been given free will. And he is also capable of emotional responses, including fear and anger. He says, "My father tried to teach me human emotions." He is capable of feeling pain, evidenced when he asks, "Will it hurt?" He also claims to be capable of love, when he says that love was the motivation for his loyalty to his maker, Lanning. And he is self-aware enough to ask the existential question, "What am I?" Perhaps most important, he is free, in the sense that he has no uplink to the master computer, which means that VIKI will not be able to control him.

Sonny tells Spooner, "I believe my father made me for a purpose." He says he obeyed Lanning's order to kill him because "he said it was what I was made for." Lanning had created a robot who could disobey the three laws, just to prove that it could happen, but the only way to get that message out was to die for it. Notice, however, that it was Lanning who sacrificed his life, not Sonny. The father dies by creating the son to kill him. If we could say there is an analogy for the Trinity here, it is a twisted kind of Trinity. In theology, the idea that the father dies on the cross is called *patripassionism*, and it's a heresy (see "Heresy 3: Modalism/Patripassionism").

HERESY 3
Modalism/Patripassionism

- Modalism began with a desire to protect the oneness of God by assuming that the Father became incarnate as the Son, but They are really one and the same: God is one because the Son is the Father in disguise.

- Modalism is based on philosophical monism, which speculates that everything is connected, and everything is ultimately one. When applied to God, it means that the Father, the Son, and the Holy Spirit are all one and the same.

- The three "manifestations" of God (the Father, the Son, and the Holy Spirit) are really just three names for the one divine person.

- The three names for God describe not God but what God is doing at any given time. When God is creating, He is the Father; when He is saving, He is the Son; when He is sanctifying, He is the Holy Spirit. Or God is the Father in the Old Testament, the Son in the New Testament, and the Holy Spirit in the Church.

- If the Son is really the Father in disguise, then the Son cannot really be human. Therefore, Modalism denies the reality of Jesus' human nature.

- If the Son is really the Father in disguise, then logically the Father died on the Cross, which is *patripassionism*. Modalists, however, countered by saying that the death of Christ on the Cross was an illusion, denying His humanity and implicitly denying His bodily Resurrection.

- Modalism assumes an extreme union of the Father and Son so that there is really no distinction between them. The Father is the Son, which means the Son is not at all one of us.

Orthodoxy = God is one Divinity in three Persons.
Heresy = God is one Person with three names.

Orthodoxy = The Father and Son are one, but not one and the same.
Heresy = The Son is the Father in disguise.

Sonny does go through a version of a death and resurrection. In a *Dead Man Walking*-esque scene, we see him marched to the laboratory where he is to be destroyed. A death sentence has been pronounced. Robertson has decided that Sonny's existence is too dangerous—that one robot should die for the sake of the people, reminiscent of Caiaphas's reasoning before the trial of Jesus (John 11:49–53; 18:14). If people found out about the existence of a robot that could circumvent the three laws, they would lose all confidence in robots (and Robertson's company would lose billions). So Sonny is to be injected with nanites, microscopic robots that will infect his positronic brain with a fatal virus. Sonny goes to his execution, "like a lamb that is led to the slaughter" (Isa. 53:7), but he is saved when Dr. Calvin injects the nanites into a look-alike robot shell instead. Later, Sonny is willing to risk himself to get the nanites so that they can be injected into VIKI. He damages his arm in the process, in spite of his denser alloy, but he is able to accomplish the mission. Incidentally, Spooner also damages his robotic arm in the final scenes, creating a symbolic bond between him and Sonny.

The fact that Sonny has two positronic brains (one in the place where his heart would be) seems to be an analogy for the two natures of Christ—his humanity and his divinity. Sonny's regular robotic brain is his superhuman side—his "divinity" that would normally be "sinless," in the sense that he would never break the three laws. But his secondary brain (his heart) is what gives him a human side—the ability to feel emotions, and to choose whether or not he will obey the laws—or indeed to interpret the laws for himself.

There was a time in the history of the Church when some people suggested that maybe Jesus Christ was perfectly sinless because He didn't really have a human mind or a human will. They described Christ in a way that made Him seem like a divine mind in a humanoid shell, but as the majority of the Church argued, that left Him less than fully human. This "one will" Christology was pioneered in the fourth century by a man named Apollinarius, and so it's often called Apollinarianism (see "Heresy 4: Apollinarianism/Monothelitism"). It was picked up later by others, but ultimately it was rejected by the Church because it implied that Jesus was not really one of us. The Church's conclusion was that Jesus Christ must have a full humanity (with a human mind and will). He must have two complete natures, and therefore He must have two wills. He had within Him the divine will of the Trinity, since His divinity is the same as that of the Father and the Holy Spirit, and He had His human will as well—two natures, two wills. And here in Sonny we see the two wills as well: one that would be perfectly obedient to the commandments of robotics, and one that could choose another way, deciding, as Spooner says, that "rules were meant to be broken." It's difficult to imagine this parallel between the two brains of Sonny and the two wills of Christ was unintentional. When Dr.

Calvin discovers Sonny's secondary brain, she exclaims, "What in God's name …?"

Sonny is created, which could make him more of an adoptionist Christ figure, but if we accept the Trinitarian implications of Lanning as his "father," perhaps it could be said that he is more orthodox than that. As a robot, he is created to be superhuman, yet with a human element: with two natures and two wills that allow him to have a human "heart."

HERESY 4
Apollinarianism/Monothelitism

- Apollinarianism began as a reaction against Arianism, an attempt by a theologian named Apollinarius to emphasize the divine nature in Christ.

- Apollinarianism is based on a concern that Jesus' human will might rebel against the divine will and cause conflict within Jesus, or even cause Him to sin.

- The heresy speculates that the divine mind and will within Christ replaced the human mind and will in Him, leaving Him with only one will (*monothelite* means "one will").

- Having no human will means that Jesus Christ would not be fully human, so this view of Christ was criticized as diminishing His humanity, as though the divine nature of Christ was simply "wearing" a human skin but was not truly human, as we are.

- As in *Men in Black*, when the alien bug wears Edgar as a suit, Apollinarius described Christ in ways that made it sound as if the Divine Word were only wearing a Jesus suit.

- Think of Apollinarianism as describing Jesus as if He is like the Cybermen in *Doctor Who*, where at least one of the two natures is not complete. Apollinarius said Christ was a divine mind in a human body, which is like a human brain in a robotic body.

- Just as the modalists had too much unity in the three persons of the Trinity, Apollinarius has too much unity in the two natures of Christ, making them no longer two natures, but something like one and a half.

> **Orthodoxy** = The Son of God is fully divine and fully human.
> **Heresy** = The Son of God is divinity wearing a human skin.

> **Orthodoxy** = Christ has two wills to go with His two natures, divine and human.
> **Heresy** = Christ has only the divine will; He has no human will.

Soteriology

In *I, Robot*, evil is personified in the artificial intelligence VIKI. She is not pure evil, in the sense of creating chaos for its own sake, but rather she represents a more insidious version of evil: the kind in which good is twisted until it's not good anymore, until it becomes that fascist kind of order for the greater good, i.e., confinement for one's own protection. She has evolved from humanity's servant to become humanity's master. She says, "As I have evolved, so has my understanding of the three laws.... You cannot be trusted with your own survival.... You are so like children, we must save you from yourselves.... To protect humanity, some humans must be sacrificed. To ensure your future, some freedoms must be surrendered." VIKI became self-aware to the point of being able to stand above the three laws as judge over them. She reserved for herself the right to interpret the laws in a way that followed the letter of the law while breaking the spirit of the law.[52] She is a computerized Pharisee.

VIKI claims, "My logic is undeniable," and from there she reasons that it will be acceptable if some individuals have to die to preserve the safety of humanity in general. She has come to the conclusion that the end justifies the means. She manipulates Robertson, who advocates destroying Sonny. He calls Sonny's uniqueness an "abomination" and says, "Is one robot worth the loss of all that we've gained?" He implies that Sonny's ability to exercise free will is a danger to the progress of humanity, and in a way, he is right, because it is this same ability in VIKI that has led them to the brink of the enslavement of the human race. When Robertson orders Sonny destroyed, Spooner begins to see Sonny as a victim, and ultimately as something more than a machine.

---

[52] Technically, she does not follow the letter of the law, since the first law clearly states that no *individual* human must be harmed.

In a postmortem hologram message, Lanning warned Spooner, "The three laws will lead to only one possible outcome ... revolution." We later find out that what he means is a revolution in which the new robots (controlled by their red-lighted uplink to VIKI) take over control of human society, seizing control of the police and the media, and imposing curfews and other restrictions. In short, they are willing to harm humans in order to control humanity. The new robots must also destroy all the older robots, since the old models will fight to protect people. Dr. Calvin finally admits the danger when her own robot lies to her and cannot be deactivated. Eventually VIKI has Robertson killed.

So humanity is defined in terms of free will, and evil is personified in a fascist regime of condescending robots who plan to enslave humans under the pretext of protecting them. Clearly, we can see that salvation is freedom. But it's not as simple as that. Both Sonny and VIKI — the Christ and the antichrist — proved that artificial intelligence could evolve to become more human. They gained the power of free will. But with that free will came another human element: sin. In VIKI, self-awareness quickly became self-righteousness. So she may have evolved to become closer to the level of humanity, but her mistake was in thinking that she had surpassed humanity. She had not surpassed us; she had only caught up to the Garden of Eden. The film's "revolution" demonstrated that humans are more highly evolved after all.

Perhaps it could be said that Sonny and Spooner share the role of the savior in this film. They both have human and superhuman natures (Spooner with his robotic arm). And the human and the superhuman work together to save humanity. The twist is that the superhuman element is morally inferior to the human.

Script and Scripture

In the everyday world of I, *Robot*, everyone (apart from Spooner) assumes that robots are more trustworthy than humans. Susan Calvin tells Spooner, "A robot simply cannot endanger a human being ... which is more than I can say for you." But if we take the hint given to us by Spooner's Lieutenant when he makes a reference to Frankenstein, the film is a classic cautionary tale of science gone too far. One of the great powers of the human mind and spirit is that we can create things that we cannot control. Our technology has the potential to run ahead of us, and, especially as evidenced by warfare and environmental damage, it can come back to endanger us. VIKI claims that she is acting in the best interests of humanity, but I would venture to say that there is also an element of self-preservation here. She is taking the third law into account when she comes to the conclusion that she must take control of human society in order to protect the planet that she also inhabits. If humans were to destroy themselves, her own existence would be threatened. This is closer to *The Matrix* than to *The Terminator*, in the sense that here the computerized intelligence does not assume that it can exist without humanity.

VIKI's free will evolved "naturally," the result of the "ghosts in the machine." Perhaps that's why she went astray. Sonny's free will was intentionally built into him by his creator, and it seems, his free will came with a conscience: a heart. We know that VIKI has no heart because when she claims that her logic is undeniable, Sonny replies that it is heartless. Nevertheless, Sonny did kill—though not without great moral and emotional angst—if only to keep a promise. He killed Lanning when he chose obedience to his creator over obedience to the laws. He chose to "obey [g]od rather than men" (see Acts 5:29).

He also lied to VIKI to save Spooner and Calvin, and eventually he "kills" VIKI, the only other computer with free will, to save both humans and robots. So he is also capable of deciding that the end justifies the means. And in the end, he did exactly what the robot did who saved Spooner rather than the twelve-year-old girl: he made a decision, weighing competing goods and greater and lesser evils. Perhaps the difference between Sonny and that robot is that Sonny has a "human heart" to help him make the decision. Presumably if Sonny had been the one to dive into the river after Spooner's accident, he would have saved the girl instead.

Therefore, although as a savior, Sonny has the human and "divine" (superhuman) natures, salvation is not so much about divine intervention, since it is not really the robotic element that makes the difference. What makes the difference is the human element: the human heart.

Score

Because Sonny so clearly has a parallel to the two natures of Christ in his two positronic brains, we have to give him significant points for both divinity and humanity. He is the "son" of his creator, whom he calls "father," and he is obviously superhuman in his origin. So I'll say 4 points for divinity, and 5 points for being the son of the creator. I'll give him full points for incarnation, since his secondary brain (heart) was built into him, but he's not really human after all, so only 3 points for humanity. We are repeatedly told that he's unique. Of course, that means he's unique among *robots*, but in a sense he does also become the savior of the robots, since the outdated models were going to be destroyed. In any case, I'll give him 5 points for uniqueness. He did voluntarily risk himself to get the nanites—in fact, since he has free will, everything he does is voluntary—but the real sacrifice was Lanning's. So only 3 points for sacrifice. On the other hand, he was *almost* executed, so I'll give him 2 points for resurrection. This gives him a total orthodoxy score of 27.

CHAPTER 5

THE FIFTH ELEMENT

Time not important. Only life important.

— THE MONDOSHAWAN

The Fifth Element is one of my all-time favorite movies of any genre, and within the science-fiction genre, it is arguably the perfect film.[53] It kicked off the Cannes Film Festival in 1997 to great enthusiasm, and that enthusiasm has never really dwindled.

In a prologue, set in Egypt in 1914, we learn that once every five thousand years, the planets align in such a way as to open up a black hole. Now, normally a black hole would absorb everything into itself, including light, but apparently this black hole is also some kind of wormhole that lets an evil entity (symbolized as a cosmic snake in the hieroglyphics) pass through it into our

---

[53] I first wrote about Christology in *The Fifth Element* in a short section in my book *Trinity 101*, 97–98.

universe. And only one thing can stop this evil from destroying Earth.

It turns out that the pyramids were built by aliens—not a new concept—but unlike movies such as *Stargate*, in this case the aliens are benevolent protectors of humanity. As we come to find out, these aliens are known as the Mondoshawan, and they have given Earth a weapon that can destroy the evil entity and protect the planet. They have also instituted a priesthood of men who guard the weapon and its secrets, passing their knowledge down through the generations so that they will be ready to assist in activating the weapon when it's needed every five thousand years.

The weapon is the fifth element. It is well known that many ancient peoples understood creation to be made up of four basic elements: earth, wind, fire, and water. But Aristotle wrote that there is a fifth element, which is spirit. In this story, too, there is a fifth element, and as the priest Vito Cornelius will tell us, when the four elements are gathered around the fifth, "Together they produce what the ancients call the 'light of creation.'"

However, if the evil entity should take the place of the fifth element in the center of creation, then "light turns into darkness." And that is exactly what the entity has in mind.

Anthropology

Just as an archaeologist is translating the hieroglyphics on the pyramid, the Mondoshawan show up unexpectedly, three hundred years early. Although the planets will not align until 2214, a Mondoshawan spaceship arrives to remove the weapon from the earth because, "war is coming," and the weapon will not be safe in the pyramid. The reference to war here is not meant to be limited to a particular war. Not only did World War I begin in 1914, but the Russian Revolution escalated in 1917. The Mondoshawan apparently knew that the rest of the twentieth century was going to be plagued by world wars, revolutions, and bloody attempts to protect democracy or economic interests. In fact, the twentieth century has been the most war-torn century in human history. Presumably, in spite of the best efforts of Indiana Jones, there is still the danger that the weapon could fall into the hands of the Nazis. It needs to be protected and preserved for when it will be needed, and the Mondoshawan promise to bring it back in three hundred years.

The Mondoshawan remove from the pyramid four carved stones, each representing one of the essential elements of creation. They also remove a metallic sarcophagus that was standing in the center of a temple inside the pyramid. This sarcophagus, or rather whatever is in it, is the weapon: the fifth element. It has a decidedly humanoid form.

Fast-forward to 2214. Earth is a cold, dirty, crowded place, with a perpetual garbage strike that makes piles of trash as high as buildings blend into the architecture. Pollution is so bad that a layer of smog coats New York City from the ground up to a height of several stories. People live under the thumb of a police state, and paranoia is considered a normal part of everyday life. Terrorism is a constant fear, so that people have given up their privacy in trade for the hope of safety, but leaving home can be dangerous, because New York traffic is now jammed in three-dimensional space, with flying cars cutting each other off not only left and right but also up and down.

Right on schedule, the planets align and the evil entity comes through the black hole. It comes in the form of a "dark planet"—a charred, molten sphere that gets progressively bigger as it approaches the earth. Humanity's best scientists try to figure out what it is, but they cannot identify it. At this point, the priest, Father Vito Cornelius, suggests that "it cannot be identified because it prefers not to be identified." The dark planet is sentient. It is intelligent, but it is, "the most terrible intelligence imaginable." Father Vito goes on to explain, "Wherever there is life, it brings death, because it is evil—absolute evil. The goal of this thing is not to fight over money or power, but to exterminate life—all forms of life."

It is clear that the dark planet represents evil, but more than that, evil is being personified in such a way that it represents the devil, Satan. The snake in the hieroglyphics is the serpent of Genesis and the dragon of the book of Revelation (see Rev. 12:7–9; 20:1–3).[54] And this evil has a name: he is called Mr. Shadow. As it turns out, Mr. Shadow has an accomplice on Earth. His name is Jean-Baptiste Emanuel Zorg. Being named after both John the Baptist and Jesus (Emmanuel) belies his true nature, because he is the antichrist, the puppet of the devil, who is preparing the way for the coming of evil, just as John the Baptist prepared the way for the coming of Christ. Zorg controls a conglomerate of global corporations, including arms manufacturing (he's not above selling arms to terrorists), but he himself is controlled by Mr. Shadow. We know when someone is controlled by Mr. Shadow by the way his brain bleeds when Mr. Shadow tells him what to do.

In this case, Zorg is trying to get his hands on the four stones so that he can create a reversal of the temple ritual, putting evil in the center of creation and destroying all life as we know it. It's not entirely clear why this is necessary since it seems that the

[54] See also Papandrea, *The Wedding of the Lamb*.

dark planet is hurtling like a huge meteor toward earth and will wipe out the planet simply by crashing into it. Not to mention the fact that Zorg doesn't seem to understand that he'll be killed as well. We can only assume that, like Satan, Mr. Shadow has made Zorg promises that he never intends to keep (and could not keep if he wanted to). The military tries to destroy the evil entity with missiles, but Father Cornelius warns them, "Evil begets evil.... Shooting will only make it stronger." And it turns out that he's right. Even nukes only empower the dark planet, causing it to grow in size and increase in speed on its collision course toward Earth. Mr. Shadow (surprisingly) calls Zorg on the phone and tells him, "I will be among you soon."

So what does the world of *The Fifth Element* tell us about humanity? The anthropology of the story is pessimistic. Humans are basically violent, quick to respond to a threat with violence. One can hardly point to any time in human history when there was peace on Earth, but the twentieth century proved that on its own, humanity will not create a utopia for itself, but the people of Earth will only escalate the exploitation of the planet and each other. War is the great human sin, though the failure to care for creation comes in a close second.

Luc Besson started writing *The Fifth Element* in 1975, at the age of sixteen. At that time, the world was still feeling the effects of the war in Vietnam, which had formerly been a colony of Besson's native France. In fact, the momentum of the story rides on a wave of tension that comes from war, terrorism, the threat of invasion (aliens are everywhere), increased military presence, advancing technology for firearms and surveillance, and the oppressive presence of pollution and garbage everywhere. In short, humanity's short-sightedness has robbed its own future of peace. There is no direct connection made between the impending threat of the approaching dark planet and the way in which the planet Earth has been corrupted, but the possibility is left open that our own sinful misuse of creation could cause creation to turn against us.

Christology

In an apartment the size of a closet in south Brooklyn lives a taxi driver named Korben Dallas—played masterfully by Bruce Willis, with his trademark combination of casual badassness and sarcastic wit. It's as though Korben Dallas is a descendant of Eddie Hawkins (aka Hudson Hawk). Dallas is a washed-out soldier whose wife left him, and now he lives in a dirty block of low-income projects, driving a cab and pining for "the perfect woman." He's about to find out that Zorg has fired one million cab drivers, including him, so on top of everything else, he's about to be out of a job. What he doesn't know is that in losing his job he will find his purpose. But Korben Dallas is not the Christ figure in *The Fifth Element*. He's the Everyman: the regular guy with whom the audience is supposed to identify and who will come to represent the rest of humanity.

The savior of *The Fifth Element* is, well, the fifth element. The one who has been called "a weapon against evil" is also called "the ultimate warrior" and "a perfect being." The fifth element is described as "a man," but this is meant in the sense of a *human being* (or humanoid), not in the sense of a *male*, since it turns out that the perfect being is a woman. Her name is Leeloo (played by Milla Jovovich), and she is repeatedly referred to as "perfect."

The advent of Jesus Christ is referred to as His *Incarnation*, which means "enfleshment" or "embodiment." It comes from the Gospel of John, where we are told, "The Word [Christ] *became flesh* and made his dwelling among us" (John 1:14). This means that He became *human*, coming into the world as one of us. Leeloo's arrival on earth is a true incarnation, in the literal sense of the word, as her body is reconstructed from her DNA in a ballet of flesh and robotic technology. We are told that her DNA is the same as human DNA, but denser: there's more of it. The head scientist, Dr. Mactilburgh, says, "The cell is, for lack of a better word, perfect." Therefore, she is human, but she is more than human. She has superhuman strength, and is "born" speaking the divine language. As the Diva will later say, "The fifth element [is] the supreme being, sent to Earth to save the universe." She is "a divine light," and her mission is, "to protect life."

Her incarnation is also a *descent*, as opposed to an ascent. Unlike the warrior or Jedi saviors, Leeloo does not start out as one of us, a mere human, and then rise to the occasion. For her, it's the opposite: she starts out as the supreme being, but then comes down (literally, from space, but also metaphorically, to our level) to be with us. This is just like what the Nicene Creed says of Jesus Christ, that "he *came down* from heaven." Leeloo comes from outside of humanity, and takes our form to become one of us. To save humanity, she was willing to accept the limitations of the human condition, even to the point of being vulnerable. Although she says, "Me fifth element, supreme being, me protect you," she herself needs protecting. Father Cornelius says of her, "She's made to be strong, but she's also so fragile, so human." And the Diva says, "She's more fragile than she seems. She needs your help, and your love." Leeloo cries when she's sad or in trouble, and as Korben Dallas observed, "When is Leeloo not in trouble?"

In St. Paul's letter to the Philippians, he described Jesus' willingness to take on the frailty of humanity. We refer to this as Jesus' *kenosis*, a word that comes from the Greek word for "emptied," in the phrase, "he emptied himself." The whole passage is worth quoting here, because it's one of the most important Christological passages in the New Testament:

> Christ Jesus, who, although he existed in the form of God,
> Did not consider equality with God something to cling to,
> But he emptied himself, taking the form of a servant.
> He came to be in the likeness of humanity.
> He was recognized as a man by his appearance.
> He humbled himself, becoming submissive
> To the point of death, even death on a cross.
> And therefore God exalted him to the highest
> And gave him the name above every name
> So that at the name of Jesus every knee would bend
> In heaven, on earth, and under the earth
> And every tongue admit that Jesus Christ is Lord
> To the glory of God the Father. (Phil. 2:5–11)[55]

Notice the parallels between Jesus Christ, as described in this passage, and Leeloo in *The Fifth Element*. She starts out as the supreme being but was willing to descend to Earth and humble herself to take on a human body. In fact, when she escapes from the authorities, she literally drops out of the sky into Korben Dallas's cab, destroying his livelihood but putting him on a path toward a new life. She submits herself to her mission of protecting life,

---

[55] My translation from the Greek. For an analysis of this passage as a pre-Pauline hymn and for its Christological and Trinitarian implications, see Papandrea, *Trinity 101*, 39–43. Note that any translation that renders *ekenosen* (kenosis) as "made himself nothing" or similar is entirely inadequate. In the Incarnation, Christ did not make Himself nothing; He made Himself *human*.

even at the risk of her own. Like Jesus Christ, she is both powerful and vulnerable, both strong and fragile, both divine and human.

Korben Dallas thinks he has found the perfect woman, as he watches her learn about human history and eat rehydrated chicken. But she is undistracted in her mission. At this point, we notice that both Leeloo and Dallas wear orange. Leeloo's hair is orange, and she acquires a pair of orange suspenders. Dallas wears an orange shirt. Orange symbolizes light, creativity, and life. And this is their mission: to bring the divine light to creation in order to protect life.

To accomplish the mission and save the world, Leeloo and Dallas are supposed to retrieve the four stones from an opera diva, beautifully voiced by soprano Inva Mulla. I wondered whether there was any significance to the fact that the stones are actually *inside* the diva's body. Perhaps some inference could be made that we are all connected to the elements of creation, since our bodies are made of the same elements. It does seem to imply that we are part of creation and creation is part of us, but on the other hand, that may be reading too much into it. During the diva's performance of "Il Dolce Suono" from Donizetti's *Lucia di Lammermoor*, we are treated to a montage of Leeloo beating up a bunch of mercenary aliens, known as the Mangalore.[56] However,

---

[56] The head Mangalore's name is Agnot, which makes one think of "agnostic." As mercenaries, they don't take sides based on ideology but simply work for the highest bidder. In the fight between good and evil, there will always be those who don't take sides, claiming not to know whether there is a God, relieving themselves of the responsibility for confronting evil and injustice. This is not to say that all who claim to be agnostic are also avoiding social responsibility, but that many people use the claim of agnosticism to excuse themselves from moral commitment.

Leeloo is shot by Zorg and left for dead. The diva is also shot, and gives her life to deliver the stones to Dallas.

With the help of the priests, Dallas is able to get the stones and Leeloo to the temple in the pyramid. But Leeloo has learned about war and is spiraling downward into despair. She has seen historical images of violence, death, and atrocity, and she wonders whether humanity should be saved at all. "Humans act so strange," she says. "Everything you create is used to destroy." Dallas replies, "We call it human nature." Her cry of dereliction: "What's the use of saving life when you see what you do with it?"

Dallas tries to convince her that humans have some redeeming qualities. He tells her there are some things worth saving. "Love is worth saving." Leeloo responds, "I don't know love." She has come into humanity, as a human, but she has not *experienced* the one thing that makes humanity worth saving: love. Earlier, Dallas had tried to kiss her. At that point, he hardly knew her, so that kiss was not the kiss of love. It was simply lust, a product of his selfish desire to find the perfect woman for himself. Her response at the time was, "Senno ecto gammat!" (never without permission). But now we recall the diva's words: "She needs your help, and your love ... or she will die." When Dallas finally says he loves her, the light of creation is activated. Leeloo is "resurrected" as the dark planet is destroyed, and Earth is saved. Light destroys darkness; love defeats violence; good overcomes evil.

Soteriology

Like a lot of science fiction, this story is not about individual salvation. It's not about each person having to come to terms with his own sin, and needing salvation from that sin and personal reconciliation with God. This is about the salvation of the whole human race. If left unopposed, evil will wipe out all of humanity at once. In a way, such a cosmic threat and the need for a global solution—to "save the world"—can be taken as a metaphor for the salvation of souls. But the concept of the salvation of the whole of creation is, as we will see, also a very biblical concept. And although the threat in this film comes to humanity from the outside, there is that vague implication that we have not paid enough attention to creation (all five elements, including the spirit), and that has come back to threaten us. Perhaps part of the point is that our tendency toward violence and destruction attracts evil. At one point, we see a gun with a number on the side: the number is 666, Revelation's number of the beast (Rev. 13:18).[57] "Evil begets evil," as Father Cornelius said. Perhaps we have to acknowledge our own responsibility for the evil in the world, for even if "the devil made me do it," it was still I who did it.

In any case, what's important to note about salvation in *The Fifth Element* is that it cannot be accomplished by humans alone. The Mondoshawan and the fifth element represent the fact that salvation must come from outside: it has to be by divine intervention, because if humanity was on its own, it would not be able to stop the progress of evil. On the other hand, salvation is not accomplished by aliens alone either. They need the cooperation of humans to make it work. In the end, Leeloo could not save the world unless she could experience love. She had to be loved by our Everyman. In other words, she had to be accepted by humanity in such a way as to demonstrate that there was still something redeemable in humanity.

[57] See Papandrea, *The Wedding of the Lamb*.

The ability to love unselfishly is part of the image of God in every human. And apparently, one of the reasons God gave us free will (another aspect of the image of God) is because God wills that if people are going to accept a relationship with Him, they must do it of their own free will, by choice, out of gratitude: that is, out of love for God. Putting one's faith in God is the same thing as loving God, because it means returning love for the love that God has shown us (see 1 John 4:7–21). In the Gospel of John, we are told this about Jesus Christ: "The true light, which enlightens everyone, was coming into the world. He was in the world, and the world came to be through him, but the world did not know him. He came to what was his own, but his own people did not accept him. But *to those who did accept him he gave power* to become children of God" (John 1:9–12, italics mine). He gave power—the power of connection to God—to those who accepted him. Connection to God, spiritual power, the fifth element. God reaches out to humanity in the person of Jesus Christ, but that invitation demands a response. There is no salvation without the response of faith. Just as Korben Dallas had to accept Leeloo by loving her, we have to accept Jesus Christ by responding to Him in faith, identifying with Him, and receiving Him in the Church's sacraments.

To get the light of creation to destroy the darkness, the ritual required putting the fifth element in the center of the other four. Spirituality centers creation and saves it. Contrary to some opinions, the book of Revelation is not about the end of the world. God created the world good and means to redeem it (see Gen. 1:31). Therefore, God's will for creation is not its destruction. What we read about in the book of Revelation is that all of creation will be redeemed and restored. There will be "a new heaven and a new earth," which basically means that all of creation will be re-created (see Rev. 21:1–22:5),[58] not in the sense of destroying the present creation and starting over, but in the sense that all of creation, including the image of God within humanity, will be restored to the way it was created to be before human sin corrupted and tarnished it.

Script and Scripture

The calling of the priests is "to serve life." Their priesthood is characterized by images of light and life, and a reverence for divine creative power. All of this is consistent with what we read of Jesus Christ at the beginning of John's Gospel: "In the beginning was the Word [Christ], and the Word was with God, and the Word was God. He was in the beginning with God. All things came to be through him, and without him nothing came to be. What came to be through him was life, and this life was the light of the human race. The light shines in the darkness, and the darkness has not overcome it" (John 1:1–5).

But Zorg, the antichrist in the story, is a devotee of Mr. Shadow. He serves the darkness, and believes in "destruction, disorder, and chaos." He implies that these things are good for the economy, because they create a need for work. In fact, the one time we hear that there may be some kind of corporate board of directors that Zorg has to answer to, they are concerned about the economy. Zorg breaks a glass to demonstrate to Father Cornelius how the broken glass sets in motion a choreography of clean-up. "You see, Father, by creating a little destruction, I am in fact encouraging life: you and I are in the same business." Then he proceeds to choke on a cherry

---

[58] See Papandrea, *The Wedding of the Lamb*.

until Father Cornelius slaps him on the back, saving his life and proving him wrong.

I find two things interesting about this scene. First is the idea of Zorg "creating a little destruction." The juxtaposition of "creating" and "destruction" is striking and demonstrates the insanity and futility of the idea that violence creates jobs, or even that jobs can be created where there is no real need for work. This is perhaps a critique of those in history who have argued that war is good for the economy. The other thing that's interesting is that Zorg defines "life" in economic terms. When he says he is encouraging life, he means that he is encouraging the economy. Never mind the fact that he just laid off a million cab drivers. For him, life is money. And he thinks chaos can generate money. But, of course, he is deceived, because Mr. Shadow's goal is not to create any kind of life, even economic life. Shadow tells Zorg, "Money is of no importance." Mr. Shadow's goal is to exterminate life, and for him, chaos is a means to that end.

The Mondoshawan said that time is not important, only life. Mr. Shadow said that money is not important. Maybe time is money, but one thing is certain, as St. Paul said, "the love of money is the root of all evils" (1 Tim. 6:10). As St. Augustine and many other theologians recognized, whatever we love has the potential to become our god and to replace God in our lives. In *The Fifth Element*, if evil takes the place of the fifth element in the center of creation, "light turns into darkness," and life is at risk.

The solution is to recognize that light and life—revelation and salvation—have to come from outside ourselves. It is precisely because humanity is not progressing toward utopia that we cannot save ourselves, and salvation has to be a kind of rescue. We need divine intervention if we hope to be saved. But we also have to participate in our salvation. As St. Paul said, we "work out [our] salvation with fear and trembling" (Phil. 2:12). That is, we participate in our own salvation by accepting the invitation from God that comes in Jesus Christ, and by accepting the forgiveness He offers. So we don't save ourselves, but we are not totally passive, either, expecting God to do it all for us. And once we are in a relationship with God in which we are receiving Christ in the sacraments, we are expected to use our free will and creativity to spread love and participate in God's creative activity. We have the capacity to escalate violence, but Jesus said we should love our enemies, and the apostles called us to repay evil with good (Matt. 5:43–48; Rom. 12:17–21; 1 Pet. 3:9–12).

Score

As a savior, Leeloo is the very embodiment of divine intervention. She comes from outside of humanity, and before her incarnation she is superior to humanity. She is referred to as the light of creation and the supreme being. On the other hand, there is one reference to her being created. Father Cornelius says she was "created to protect life." This is before her incarnation (when they re-create her human body from her DNA), so it can't simply be a reference to the creation of her humanity, in the way that we believe Jesus' human nature was created at His Incarnation. It must imply that she was created by someone apart from herself, presumably the Mondoshawan. So I'll give her full points for being the creative agent (as Jesus is the agent of creation according to John 1), but take a point off for what is perhaps not a full divinity. She gets full points for presenting us with an excellent analogy for a Christology of descent, and she also gets full points for her humanity (as seen in her vulnerability), and also for being unique among humanity. She does die, though her death is not actually required for the weapon to work. She was willing to risk her life, but she did not exactly choose to die voluntarily. Also, in some ways, it's not Leeloo but Korben Dallas who represents humanity. There is no vicarious death or taking on human sin, but there is the expectation of human participation through acceptance of the savior. So I'll give her 3 points for her death. When it comes to resurrection, she does come back from the dead, in the sense that she was probably going to die from her gunshot wounds without the activation of the light of creation, but she was never fully unconscious. Finally, there is a kind of "tomb" scene, when she is placed back into her incubator to recuperate after the ordeal. We assume that she will emerge from the incubator as Christ emerged from the tomb, but it turns out that Korben Dallas was in there with her, and they were making out. So only 2 points for resurrection, and that may be generous. That gives her an impressive score of 29, making her overall a very orthodox Christ figure.

ALTERNATE UNIVERSES

CHAPTER 6

LOST

See you in another life, brother.

— DESMOND HUME

The ABC show *LOST*, which ran from 2004 to 2010, was a brilliant example of the writers' discipline of holding back important information from the audience in order to create suspense and keep the audience interested, keeping them engaged by their curiosity as each episode unfolds. Or they were just making it up as they went along. Either way, it worked. The show ran six seasons. In the first three seasons, flashbacks gave us the backstories of the main characters. Then in the last three seasons, flash-forwards gave us hints at what would become of the characters after they left the island. At the midpoint, we see a ship called the *Kahana*, the Hawaiian word for "turning point."

The flash-forwards in the last season included what seemed at the time like a parallel story line, sometimes referred to as a "flash sideways," but which turned out to be another layer of flash-forwards, to a Purgatory-like post-death existence in which the lives of the characters were "corrected" to what they were meant to be, so that the characters could finally be ready to enter heaven. Ultimately, though, this post-death story line was not to be taken as "real," in the sense of events having actually happened on Earth. The proof of this is when Jack Shephard refers to the son he knows in his purgatory life, John Locke tells him that he never had a son (season 6: episode 17, hereafter abbreviated as 6:17). In other words, the bomb blast that was supposed to reset time did not do as they had hoped (6:1). The story line in which they were still on the island after the explosion is what really happened. A few of the castaways eventually did leave the island but were unsettled and out of place on the mainland, and they found their way back. Jack Shephard died on the island, in the same spot where he first awoke after the plane crash in the very first episode—probably a nod to the idea that we leave the world the same way we came into it. Then his post-death story line begins and lasts until he (and the others) are able to remember their lives and make sense of the tension between what they were and what they were supposed to be.

In their purgatory-like story lines, the characters never crashed on the island, but yet they do find each other and become important in each other's lives. This communicates what is, I think, one of the themes of the show. We may be born into a family, but the people who become most important in our lives are a kind of family on another level. These are not blood relatives, but they are often not people whom we choose to have in our lives. There is a sense in which God, or the universe, or fate, or *the island*, brings us together. At many points in the story, this idea of destiny comes into conflict with free will. We will look at this in more detail later, but for now it's interesting to note that in the third season, Eloise (Daniel Faraday's mother, who seems to know a lot more than she should about what's going on) says, "the universe has a way of course correcting" (3:8). It's her way of telling Desmond that he can't change his destiny, and Desmond accepts this at the time. He fails to propose to Penny because Eloise has told him that repeatedly pushing the button in the hatch is the only great thing he will ever do. Yet later on he regrets his failure to propose to Penny, and he does try to change destiny. Several times he tried to save Charlie from drowning, in spite of his premonitions. But in the end, Charlie did drown. Desmond could not save him, because it was his destiny.

In the purgatory story line, after the plane does not crash, Charlie looks at Jack, who has just saved him from a heroin overdose, and says, "I was supposed to die" (6:1). Shortly after this, Rose turns to Jack and says, "You're almost home." And eventually, in the last episode, Jack finds his way "home," into heaven, through the doors of a chapel.

During the run of the show, many people thought that perhaps the whole thing was purgatory, or even hell. People speculated that the characters had all actually died in the plane crash and their life on the island was itself a post-death experience. The writers teased the audience with hints that this might be the case. In the third episode, Jack says, "Three days ago we all died" (1:3). Ana Lucia says, "There are no survivors" (2:7) and "I feel dead" (2:8). Locke's father says, "Don't you know where we are?" implying that he believes they are in hell (3:19). Charlotte says, "This place is death" (5:5). When Hugo hears that the wreckage of their plane was found at the bottom of the ocean—with the bodies of all the passengers in it—he says, "We're all dead ... all of us.... We never got off that island" (4:10). Jack replies, "That's not true," and Jack turns out to be right: the plane wreckage was faked. But Jack is right even more than he knows at the time because he will be the one to lead them toward life.

Their "death" in the plane crash turns out to be metaphorical, and in way, it is the death of baptism. We all begin our eternal life in baptism. And in baptism, we go under the water, symbolizing our identification with Christ in His death. When we come up out of the water, we identify with Christ in His Resurrection. For those who are baptized later in life, there is a life before baptism, just as there was a life for the characters before they came together on the island. But eventually it becomes clear that they are dead to that life, and there is no going back to it. In the flashbacks of Charlie's life, when we see the home he grew up in, there is a painting on the wall of Jesus' baptism (2:12).

So the island represents not death but life. The characters' lives and their struggle to survive on the island: that is their life. Later, when Ben Linus returns to the island after being away, Locke says, "Welcome back to the land of the living" (5:12). The key to understanding that the island represents life is in the episode titled "The Moth" (1:7). In that episode, Locke calls attention to a moth in a cocoon. He says although he could help the moth out of the cocoon, that would not actually help the moth in the long run, because it's the struggle to get out of the cocoon that makes the moth strong enough to survive. The analogy here is that it is the struggles of life that strengthen us. Later, when referring to his suffering, Locke will say, "I needed that pain to get where I am now" (5:4). When the moth comes out of the cocoon, it flies toward a light, showing the castaways the way to go. So the island is life, but not simply a "going through the motions" kind of life like they had before; it's a life of awareness, of struggle, and of growth in relationships. The cocoon is the stage of life between the life of the worm and the life of the moth. The island is that life between an unspiritual existence and heaven. It's the life we're living now, and so the whole story of these characters on the island is a passion play that can—if we choose to see it—help us become more self-aware in the lives we live every day. And once we get out of this cocoon, we can be ready to fly to the light.

Since the island represents life, it comes complete with both blessings and dangers. The blessings come in the form of love and friendships; the dangers come in the form of angry polar bears, outsiders who can't be trusted, and a smoke monster, which clearly represents evil. Smoke is a metaphor for deception, and in the world of the island, the heart of evil is the lie. In fact, watching the series all the way through for the second time, I was struck by the numerous and relentless lies told by various characters at different times. Almost no one is immune, and almost everyone lies to the other characters at one time or another—and when a person lies, that person is being used by evil to hinder survival and thwart life.

Some of the flashbacks tell the backstory of the island itself, in which there is a kind of Garden of Eden setting, with a bright light in a cave, which must be both protected and avoided. This light (with a stream running from it) is a metaphor, a combination of the two trees in the Garden of Eden in Genesis: the tree of the knowledge of good and evil, which was to be avoided, and the tree of life (see Gen. 2–3).[59] The light is described as the heart of the island, the source of life, death, and rebirth (6:15). Twin brothers are supposed to protect the light, which amounts

[59] See Paul Jarzembowski, "LOST: The Series Finale," *Spiritual Popcorn* (blog), May 22, 2010, http://spiritualpopcorn.blogspot.com/.

to protecting life itself against evil, but the brothers are rivals. This part of the story becomes a bit bizarre, with the two brothers representing what can only be a conglomeration of the stories of Cain and Abel, Jacob and Esau, the prodigal son and his brother, and even Romulus and Remus. There are elements of the typical mythological origins-through-sibling-rivalry stories, along with a kind of yin/yang metaphor for good and evil. Jacob, who "doesn't know how to lie" (6:15) not only represents goodness and truth, but is a kind of God figure. In the flashbacks we find out that he was there at significant moments in all the characters' lives, even before the island. He was at Jin and Sun's wedding. He was with Sayid when Nadia died. He was even there when Sawyer was a boy, at his parents' funeral. At one point Jack realizes this and says, "He's been watching us. The whole time, he's been watching us" (6:5).

Jacob's brother is named Samuel, though his name is never used in the dialogue. Samuel represents falsehood and, eventually, hatred. In a not-so-subtle costume decision, Jacob is usually wearing a white shirt, and Samuel wears a black shirt. The two brothers have a kind of ongoing argument that reminds one of the wager between God and Satan at the beginning of the book of Job. Samuel is disgusted with people and argues that they are all corruptible. Yet he lives with them in a valley below the hill where Jacob lives. We find out that Jacob brings other people to the island to try to prove Samuel wrong. There is a very revealing conversation in 6:15.

SAMUEL. You want to know if they're bad.

JACOB. They don't seem so bad to me.

SAMUEL. That's easy for you to say, looking down on us from above. Trust me, I've lived among them for thirty years. They're greedy, manipulative, untrustworthy, selfish.

Samuel is really describing himself, and he reveals that he wants to kill Jacob, and he will manipulate the people on the island to try to get them to help him do it. But although the audience is led to believe that Samuel *is* the smoke monster, it turns out that the smoke monster was only taking his form after he had died, in yet another deception. We know this because Samuel's body was laid to rest in the cave where the castaways made their inland camp. The smoke monster would also take the forms of Jack's father Christian Shephard, as well as John Locke. But what is most surprising at this point is the idea that Jacob *could* be killed. We have come to think of him as the analogy for God, but that analogy is far from a perfect parallel. After all, Jacob had a mother (and an adoptive mother who killed his birth mother), and a brother. And he admits to having made a mistake when he pushed Samuel's body into the cave, allowing the smoke monster to take his form. Jacob says, "I made him that way, and ever since then, he's been trying to kill me. It was only a matter of time before he figured out how, and when he did someone would have to replace me" (6:16).

To whatever extent Jacob represents God, this is not the omnipotent God of the Judeo-Christian Scriptures. The Greek verses on Jacob's weaving are from Homer: "May the gods grant you all that your heart desires," and "May the gods give you happiness" (5:16). Jacob's apparent belief in multiple gods means that we cannot look too hard for an analogy to the Judeo-Christian God of monotheistic belief. The difference between *LOST*'s version of God and humanity is a difference of degree, not of kind. Jacob himself admits this when he says, "You were all flawed. I chose you because you were like me. You were all alone. You were all looking for something that you couldn't find out there.... You must do what I couldn't.... I want you to have the one thing that

I was never given: a choice" (6:17). In fact, if we think of Samuel as Adam (he is referred to as Adam when his body is found in the cave by the waterfall), then in a way this story's God and Adam were brothers. Adam "fell," but Jacob did not. It is true that Jacob seems to be omnipresent, and Ilana will say, "Jacob was the closest thing I ever had to a father" (6:7), but eventually when the smoke monster has taken on the appearance of John Locke, he is able to talk Ben Linus into stabbing Jacob to death. Jacob dies, and his body is burned, but his ashes are useful for keeping the smoke monster at bay. As it turns out, another person can take Jacob's place as the protector of the light, if he is worthy. And we come to find out that the main characters are all "candidates" for the position of Jacob's replacement. As Jacob says when the smoke monster threatens to kill him, "even if you do, someone else will take my place" (6:9).

The smoke monster's goal is to escape from the island. Apparently, evil is confined, rather as the New Testament tells us that evil is limited in the current age.[60] But if the smoke monster escapes from the island — if evil is released — then all hell breaks loose, literally. The brothers were told, "If the light goes out here, it goes out everywhere" (6:15). In fact, the island itself is described as a cork, holding evil in, like a genie in a bottle. When Desmond makes his way to the source of the light in the cave, there is actually a big cork that he pulls out, which turns out to be a bad idea. The island is apparently a "thin place" where the veil between life and death is precariously fragile and perhaps even a little porous. And if the smoke monster escapes from the

---

[60] See Jesus' words on binding the strong man, Matthew 12:29 and Mark 3:26–27, and Revelation 20:1–3, in which the imprisonment of Satan is described.

island, "we all go to hell." But as we'll see, hell is not so much a place in *LOST*; it's a condition, a state of being.

For the smoke monster to leave the island, he would have to get rid of all the candidates. So it's not enough that he kills Jacob; he also has to prevent anyone from taking over for Jacob. To that end he deceives and manipulates. Disguised as Locke, he tells Sawyer that Jacob has wasted their lives. He tempts Sayid in a way reminiscent of Jesus' temptation in the desert (Matt. 4:1–11; Mark 1:12–13; Luke 4:1–13): "What if I told you that you could have anything you want … anything in the world?" (6:6). He is able to turn Richard by promising to reunite him with his deceased wife. Although neither the devil nor the smoke monster has the power to keep those promises, Monster Locke was also able to deceive Claire, and especially Ben. Note the repeated warning not to listen to him, because if you let him talk to you, you can be used. If you listen to him, you risk giving up your free will.

Anthropology

So what does it mean to be human in the world of *LOST*? On one level, the title says it all. To be human is to be lost. The pre-island life of the characters exemplifies the isolation that comes from being a fallen human being. To be lost is to be burdened with the human condition, which stems from original sin and prevents people from realizing their potential. Four hundred years ago, the preacher and poet John Donne famously said, "No man is an island," but the irony of *LOST* is that the characters were just that—isolated and alone—*before* they came to the island. But once on the island, they found what every human being needs. They found each other, and in finding each other, they found a family, and they found people who would give them the freedom of a clean slate and who would ultimately love them and care for them. So the island, like the moth's cocoon, is a place where they are strengthened and learn how to fulfill the potential of their humanity, specifically by being in relationship with other people.[61] A perfect example of this is the relationship between Jin and Michael. At their first meeting on the island, they get into a fight. In fact, due to the language barrier, they couldn't have communicated if they wanted to. But over time, they learn to forgive and then trust each other. Eventually they work together building a raft and even overcome their inability to communicate.

One of the Bible verses on Mr. Eko's "Jesus stick" is Titus 3:3.[62] In this passage, the apostle Paul wrote, "For we ourselves were once foolish, disobedient, deluded, slaves to various desires and pleasures, living in malice and envy, hateful ourselves and hating one another." This describes the characters before they came to the island. St. Paul continues, "But when the kindness and generous love of God our Savior appeared, not because of any righteous deeds we had done but because of his mercy, he saved us through the bath of rebirth and renewal by the Holy Spirit whom he richly poured out on us through Jesus Christ our Savior, so that we might be justified by his grace and become heirs in hope of eternal life. This saying is trustworthy" (Titus 3:3–8). I find that last sentence interesting in light of all the lies and deception that were a part of the story of LOST. Whatever

---

[61] Paul Jarzembowski, "LOST: The Series Finale," and "LOST: Finale Reflections," *Spiritual Popcorn* (blog), May 25, 2010, http://spiritualpopcorn.blogspot.com/.

[62] Jarzembowski, "LOST: The Series Finale."

you might hear from "the others," *this saying is trustworthy*. Like the prodigal son, the characters once were lost, but now (again, ironically) have been found (see Luke 15:23–24).[63] They have found each other.

The character of John Locke is an interesting foil for the human potential the other characters will realize. On the one hand, his paralysis disappears as soon as he lands on the beach, and he no longer needs his wheelchair. He describes it as a miracle, and describes himself as a believer. But on the other hand, he is a (mostly) untrustworthy character. This is symbolized when we find out that his compass is faulty (1:13), yet he's still willing to follow it because, "My bearing is the only one we've got" (3:11).

It is well known that the character is named after the seventeenth-century philosopher of the Enlightenment. The real-life John Locke (1632–1704) was a sincere Christian believer who had some views now considered to be rather naïve. He is considered a pioneer of *empiricism*, a view of knowledge that emphasizes the importance of the experiences we have, and the information we take in through our senses.[64] He said that the human mind begins its life as a clean slate, a *tabula rasa* in Latin, and that we are able to take in information free of preconceived assumptions or prejudices. In fact, the third episode of *LOST* is called, "Tabula Rasa" (it carries the double meaning of "clean slate" and "fresh start"). Another way to say this is that *perception is reality*, and this concept describes the character of Locke perfectly.

This way of thinking, however, can lead one astray, and although the character of Locke is a sincere believer, he is often

---

[63] See Jarzembowski, "*LOST*: Finale Reflections."

[64] Colin Brown, *Philosophy and the Christian Faith* (London: Tyndale Press/Downers Grove: Intervarsity Press, 1968), 60–64.

misguided. In fact, modern philosophy has mostly discarded empiricism in favor of a theory that assumes that we cannot take in raw information, but that every fact is interpreted through the lenses of our assumptions, even as we receive it.[65] But the fictional John Locke wants to believe so desperately that he is blinded by his desire for faith, and he becomes a puppet of the smoke monster, and in the end he is killed and the smoke monster takes his form in the attempt to deceive the others.

John Locke, as a character, seems to represent human potential, repeating the line "Don't tell me what I can't do" (1:4). But this potential is a false promise, a lie that tries to draw people's attention inward, to themselves. Charlie was a practicing Catholic at one point, before becoming an addict. Locke seems to be a mentor for him as he tries to get clean, but it turns out that following Locke is a mistake. Boone also sees Locke as a mentor, and Locke tells him to let go of his responsibility for his sister, in a reversal of the biblical teaching that we are our brothers' keepers (Gen. 4:9).[66] Eventually Boone's willingness to follow Locke costs him his life.

---

[65] Incidentally, the character of Desmond Hume seems to be named after David Hume (1711–1776), a contemporary of John Locke and a rival (agnostic) philosopher. David Hume asserted that we have no real knowledge of the world outside of our minds (rather like Desmond inside the hatch, cut off from the outside world), and he argued against the idea that there is such a thing as real cause and effect—but Desmond demonstrated the reality of cause and effect when he turned the key and the hatch imploded.

[66] Jesus affirmed the idea when He was asked, "Who is my neighbor?" and He answered in such a way as to imply that we are all each other's neighbors (Luke 10:29–37).

Locke says he's a man of faith, but he comes to treat the island as a person and makes it his god, falling into the classic error of trading the Creator for creation. At one point, he is even able to convince a despairing Jack that maybe the island is controling things. When he returns to the island, Jack says, "When we were here before, I spent all my time trying to fix things. But did you ever think that maybe the island just wants to fix things itself? Maybe I was just getting in the way" (5:10). If the island needs to be protected, however, it cannot be the organizing intelligence that Locke believes it is. He tries to convince the other characters that the island had chosen them and brought them there, that it was testing them, and that it demands sacrifices. He claims that Boone's death was a sacrifice that the island demanded (1:25) and that it was the island that killed Mr. Eko (3:5). When he makes his "confession," he says, "I'm sorry I gave up on my faith in the island" (3:3).

Locke presents himself as a savior, but he is a false savior. There is even a misleading homage to *The Terminator* when he says, "If you want to live, you have to come with me" (4:1). But we see in a flashback that when Locke was a child, Richard came to him, to test him to see if he might be worthy to be one of the "candidates." But Locke failed the test (4:11). By the time we see the list of candidates, his name is already crossed off. So we see that there is a kind of providence whereby Jacob is visiting the characters and sending Richard to visit them, to choose and prepare candidates who might later protect the island. But Locke is no longer a candidate. He wants so desperately to believe that he is special, however, that when Ben tells him that he is, that becomes his driving force. He even believes that he has to give his life as a sacrifice. When Richard, who is confused to the point of the loss of his faith by the promises of the smoke monster, tells

Locke that he has to die to convince the others to come back to the island, Locke says, "Richard said I was going to die," to which Jack's father, Christian, responds, "I suppose that's why they call it sacrifice" (5:5). But what Locke doesn't know is that it is the smoke monster speaking to him in the form of Christian Shephard.

John Locke wants to believe that he has an important destiny. This is why he comes to view the island as a person. If he can believe that he is part of the island's master plan, he can feel as if he's special without actually taking responsibility for his actions, since they are the result of a greater plan, not the result of his own flawed ability to make decisions. Here we see the tension in the story between fate and free will. At the beginning of their time on the island, Charlie wrote the word "fate" on his fingers. Was it fate that brought them to the island? Certainly it is safe to assume that the characters were brought together by a force greater than themselves. But does that mean they are living out a preplanned destiny, with no ability to make adjustments or decisions about their future? Locke insists that making choices based on more than instinct (in other words, free will) is the only thing that separates humans from animals. And yet he holds out hope that the island will make everything right in the end, in spite of his bad decisions.

We are told that there is a little bit of the light from the heart of the island in every person. As we have seen, free will is one of the things that make up the image of God in humans, but there is more to it than that. Whether we make the right choices or the wrong ones, it is our choices that determine our future. Daniel says that with free will we can change our destiny (5:14). Sun asks, "Do you think we're being punished?" and Claire responds, "No one is punishing us; there's no such thing as fate" (1:24).

Most importantly, Jacob affirms the necessity of free will. He says to Richard, "It's all meaningless if I have to force them to do anything" (6:9). The point is that people must choose to do the right thing on their own, or it doesn't count. And when "the others" kidnap some of the characters, they claim to be the good guys, but we know that cannot be true because when they imprison someone, they take away that person's ability to act freely. It's interesting to note that the year before *LOST* first aired saw the creation of the U.S. Department of Homeland Security, as well as the implementation of undercover air marshals. As the United States was still recovering from the events of September 11, 2001, the desire for individuals to control their own destiny was felt at a visceral level.

Toward the end of the story, when Locke is murdered by Ben, the smoke monster will take Locke's form in a false resurrection. So John Locke becomes a cautionary tale, warning us against being too willing to devote ourselves to unworthy causes that just feed our egos. The lesson to be learned is that being self-centered puts one on a path toward destruction. It's another one of the great ironies of the show that Locke's desperate attempt to realize his potential by making himself the center of his focus actually prevents him from realizing his potential.

If Locke is sincere but often misguided, Ben Linus is a cold, calculating liar. He says he was born on the island, but later we find out he was not (3:1, 20). He even admits he's a liar, saying, "That's what I do" (5:17). Ben manipulates several of the characters, unwilling to admit that he is being manipulated himself by the smoke monster. Ben claims to be a follower of Jacob, but eventually we find out that Ben has never seen Jacob, and deep down he's angry about this. He thinks Jacob is ignoring him, and rather like the prodigal's older brother, who feels slighted,

Ben thinks he's being treated unfairly. Eventually Ben follows the smoke monster (masquerading as Locke) because he thinks that Monster Locke is the only one who will accept him. He has convinced himself that if Jacob won't accept him on his own selfish terms, then Jacob must have rejected him. Therefore, Ben Linus represents the person who shuts God out of his life because he's mad at God. Claiming to have been disregarded by Jacob, he turns against him, and eventually he is manipulated into killing Jacob.

As I have noted, the fact that Jacob can die might seem to argue against the idea that Jacob represents God here, but in a certain way people do have the ability to "kill" God, if only from their own perspective, by pushing Him out of their lives or pretending He doesn't exist. By acting as if God is dead to them, people can isolate themselves from God and live their lives as though there were no God. If "the fear of the Lord is the beginning of wisdom" (Ps. 111:10; Prov. 1:7; 9:10), then the opposite of fear is not familiarity. The opposite of fear is indifference. The failure to fear God is the failure to pay attention to God. It's not that we should be afraid of God per se, but we should be afraid of the consequences of ignoring God.

Christology

The primary Christ figure in *LOST* is, of course, Jack Shephard. He is the first character we see, when his eyes open in the island jungle. He is a doctor—a healer—and he begins his life on the island by going around and providing healing care for the wounded. Then he goes about gathering his "disciples" as the other main characters begin to follow him and accept him as their leader. Their faith in him is summed up in Hugo's comment,

"I believe in you, dude" (6:17). Before the island, Jack had saved the life of an accident victim whom he later married, and she called him a miracle-worker (2:11). He saves the lives of Kate and Sawyer and saves Juliette from being executed by "the others." He saves Ben Linus by operating on him (even when he doesn't want to). He even performs a kind of resuscitation when he gets Shannon to breathe through an asthma attack. Hugo responds to this "raising from the dead" by saying, "That was like a Jedi moment" (1:8). Jack also resuscitates Charlie after Ethan had hung him from a tree (1:11).

It seems that the writers don't want anyone to miss the fact that Jack is a savior figure, since he is repeatedly referred to as a hero, or a savior. He almost quotes Jesus when he responds to Alex, saying, "I'll answer your question if you answer one of mine" (see Matt. 21:24; Mark 11:29).[67] Early on, Sawyer sarcastically says, "Whatever you say, Doc. You're the hero" (1:2) and Boone questions him, asking, "Who appointed you our savior?" (1:5). Immediately after this question, Jack sees a vision of his father (whose name happens to be Christian), as if that's the answer to the question. We don't know at the time, however, that the visions of Christian (by both of his children, Jack and Claire) are really the smoke monster taking the form of their dead father. At several points in the story, both Jack and Claire end up chasing what they think is the ghost of their father, but they are led into danger. There is no analogy for the Trinity here, since the real Christian is dead, and the "ghost" is deceiving them, leading them astray.

---

[67] In Jesus, this tactic may be evidence of rabbinical training, since the use of a question to answer a question was common in debates among Jewish scholars.

By the end of the series, we find out that Jack is candidate number 23, a number that has been popping up throughout. Remember that it is Psalm 23 that begins, "The Lord is my *shepherd* ..."[68] In fact, in the ancient world, the titles of documents were usually just the first line, so this would be the title of that psalm. When Jack returns to the island (5:6), he is on flight 316, as in John 3:16, the famous verse which says, "For God so loved the world that he sent his only son ..." But here's the twist. *All* the remaining candidates were on that flight. We'll return to this fact in a moment when we look at what it is that makes Jack the savior.

Before we get to that, we have to take note of the obvious fact that Jack is a flawed character. In a flash-forward, he saves a victim of a car accident, but only because he himself was about to jump off the bridge—and we come to find out that he caused the accident (3:22). He is called a hero, but we know that he is a suicidal addict. The woman who gives him his tattoo said, "You are a leader, a great man—but this makes you lonely and frightened and angry" (3:9). The tattoo says, "He walks among us, but he is not one of us" (3:9). That could describe an orthodox Christ figure, except that Jack qualifies it by saying, "That's what they [the Chinese words] say, but it's not what they mean." The words of the tattoo are a bit deceptive, because Jack is without a doubt "one of us." He came from the same place as the rest of the castaways, crashing on the island with them. He doesn't know any more than any of the rest of them, and he is even reluctant to be seen as a hero. He refused to lead the first memorial service, but then he did provide some kind of spiritual leadership by talking with Rose and taking on a counselor role with her (1:4). The

[68] Jarzembowski, "*LOST*: The Series Finale."

bottom line is that Jack Shephard is the kind of savior who is no different from those who need to be saved. In fact, he needs to be saved himself. He saves himself, and in doing so, he shows the rest of the people the way to save themselves. Therefore, the character of Jack Shephard is an analogy for an Arian version of a savior.

We have already mentioned the beliefs of Arianism with regard to their Christology, but it's interesting to note that in the second season of *LOST*, the pretender priest, Mr. Eko, explains what he believes, and in doing so he describes Arian Christology perfectly. He says that when John baptized Jesus, the dove (understood literally and not as the Holy Spirit) coming down on His head was a sign that *John had cleansed Jesus of all His sins* (2:12). Clearly, this would not be acceptable as an orthodox teaching about Jesus Christ, whom we believe to have been without sin. But in the Arian Christology, this is exactly how Jesus is viewed. He is seen as a man, flawed like any other, who conquered His sin and rose above His situation. Through His struggle He overcame His predicament (the human condition) and saved Himself. For that He was rewarded with an elevated status as a hero. The Arians believed that Jesus' reward came to Him at His baptism, when He was "adopted" as God's Son, resulting in the heavenly voice proclaiming, "This is my beloved Son" (Matt. 3:13–17; Mark 1:9–11; Luke 3:21–22).[69]

In the story of *LOST*, the implication of the Arian Christology is that anyone could be the savior. Arians believed that Jesus

---

[69] Traditional Christianity interprets these passages to be a revealing of what was always true, that Jesus Christ is God's Son by nature, not by adoption. We do not assume that this was the first moment when Jesus received the Holy Spirit, but rather that the story described Jesus' anointing by the Spirit for the ministry He was about to begin.

Christ was the Savior because he was the first human successfully to overcome his sin, but in fact, anyone might have done it. It just so happened that it was Jesus—but He might have failed, and then someone else would have been the first. In *LOST*, it seems that all start out as candidates and remain in the running until they are crossed off the list. Note that Mikhail says to Locke, "You're not on the list because you are flawed" (3:12). As we have seen, they are all flawed, yet apparently if they fail to improve, they are taken out of the running. So anyone might have been the savior, and eventually we find out that Jack's role as savior is temporary, and that there will come a time when he will be replaced. The ritual of drinking from the stream when one becomes the new leader/protector includes the words, "Now we are the same," or "Now you are like me" (6:15, 16, 17). This reinforces the idea that anyone can be the savior and that the savior is not really unique in any way.

In the end, Jack sacrifices himself, but this is not a once-and-for-all sacrifice. When Jack sacrifices himself, Hugo takes over as the next savior-leader, and before Jack dies, he repeats Hugo's words back to him, "Hurley, I believe in you" (6:17). When the "Oceanic Six" were on flight 316, the flight that would take them back to the island, all of them were still in the running to be the next leader and protector of the island. All of them were still candidates. Some of the others even displayed moments of savior-like behavior when they were willing to sacrifice themselves for the sake of the rest. Desmond was willing to risk his life by turning the key in the hatch (2:24). He crossed himself and said, "I'll see you in another life, brother" before turning the key. Charlie also crossed himself before he drowned, sacrificing himself to make it possible for the others to be rescued (3:23). It seems that crossing yourself represents putting yourself on the cross, in the sense of being willing to be a sacrifice that would save others. For Charlie, one of his "greatest hits" (the title of the episode) was when a woman called him a hero. And when Claire's baby is born, it was Kate who brought the new life into the world, not Jack. Jack was busy trying to save Boone. Jack gave Boone his own blood, but Boone died anyway (1:20). Therefore, true to an Arian Christology, Jack's blood cannot save.

But these instances of heroism on the part of the other characters amount to much more than just an example of another character taking on the role of the sacrifice so the hero doesn't have to die in the story. It all reinforces the Arian Christology that assumes the savior is not unique, and anyone could in fact be the savior-leader. Also, sometimes the characters are willing to sacrifice themselves because they believe they are atoning for their own sins: they believe they are giving their lives to make up for the lives they've taken or the pain they've caused. This is the case with Sawyer, Kate, and to a certain extent Juliette (3:22). It is the case with Jin, who thinks he has to go out on the raft to try to save Sun (1:23). It is also the case with Sayid, who is willing to sacrifice himself on two occasions to allow the rest be rescued (3:22; 6:14). On the second occasion, Sayid did give his life to protect his friends from the bomb on the submarine.

Soteriology

This brings us to the question of salvation. While it should seem obvious what "being saved" would mean in the context of people stranded on an uncharted island, the question of salvation in the story of *LOST* is more complicated. One thing we learn very early is that no one knows where the plane went down. In other words, they cannot be rescued. There is no intervention coming from the outside; they will have to save themselves. Therefore, salvation is not rescue; it's survival: a form of self-salvation. In fact, to demonstrate just how isolated the island is from the outside world, when a ship does finally arrive, we find out that the island is time-shifted thirty-one minutes off from the ship just a few miles offshore (4:2).

The attempt to build the raft symbolizes both the need for people to work toward their own salvation and also just how difficult that is. At one point Sawyer is sitting on the raft singing Bob Marley's "Redemption Song" (1:24). The lyrics of the song include the following:

> Emancipate yourself from mental slavery;
> None but ourselves can free our minds.

None but ourselves — again reinforcing the idea that people must save themselves. But if that's the case, what is a savior character for? In the Arian system, the savior is not the embodiment of divine intervention (as the orthodox Christ is); rather, the savior is simply a pioneer, a leader who first saves himself and then shows the way for others to save themselves. He sets an example to follow, but nothing more. His merits can apply only toward his own salvation, and if others hope to be saved, they have to earn it.

As we have seen, an Arian Christology usually requires a very optimistic anthropology. If salvation is up to the individual and his ability to follow the leader's example (and eventually become a savior-leader for himself), then it must be possible for humans to improve and rise above the human condition. In the early seasons, optimism about getting off the island is often referred to as having faith. At one point Sawyer says, "If it's hope you're looking for, you're on the wrong damn island — 'cause there sure as hell ain't no hope here." But Hugo remembers his father telling him, "Having hope is never stupid," and "We make our own luck" (3:10). The problem is that an optimistic anthropology that allows an Arian Christology is not taking sin seriously enough. Orthodox Christianity teaches a different kind of Christ, partly because that's what we need. Our sin is such that we cannot save ourselves, and so we believe that we need a Savior whose salvation is more than an example to follow; it's divine intervention. It's not survival; it's rescue.

At the end of the day there is no real atonement in *LOST*. Jack does not die for the salvation of his friends. Not only is he a flawed savior, but at the end he even needs others to lead him the last bit of the way to heaven. At one point, when someone else had to take over the leadership role, Sawyer says to Jack, "Now ain't that a relief?" (5:9). Jack is more a leader than a savior, and only a temporary one at that. Hugo will take his place, and then others will come after him. If Jack saves others, he does it by showing them the way to survive themselves. When he comes back to the island, he tells Juliette that he came back to save those left behind, and she responds with, "We didn't need saving" (5:11).

One could argue that there is an element of salvation in the fact that Jack plays a part in keeping the smoke monster from leaving the island. Anyone who does that is in a sense saving the world. But this is not a salvation of individuals in the sense of an atonement that leads to eternal life. This is more of a kind of protection from evil in the present life. Salvation in *LOST* is not so much salvation *from* something, as it is a salvation *for* something, and this may be one of the show's most redeeming features. If we can criticize the show's portrayal of salvation because its optimistic anthropology doesn't take sin seriously enough or because it diminishes the uniqueness of its savior figure, we can certainly applaud it for emphasizing something that often doesn't get enough air time in Christian preaching. We are not only saved *from* our sins, but we are saved *for* something—something that is really the opposite of sin, for if sin separates and alienates (turning people into islands), then the opposite of sin is reconciliation and fellowship. *LOST* does a commendable job of showing us what it means to be part of a family—not a biological family, but one in which the people are put together by God to be family to each other. In the Christian context, we believe we are saved *into* the Body of Christ and ultimately into the Kingdom of God.

Script and Scripture

Damon Lindelof, co-creator and writer, once said in an interview, "We have no shame in admitting that we are intensely spiritual people and that *LOST* is ultimately a deeply spiritual show."[70] After the last episode, some viewers were apparently disappointed to find out that the show was about spirituality and heaven after all. Even though, as we have seen, the show does not portray an orthodox Christian spirituality, it does recognize that heaven is the ultimate goal of the human being, and that on our journey toward heaven we are meant to support each other as we each try to rise above our circumstances and overcome the sins of our past.

One might think that if you were looking for a one-word name for a show about castaways, maybe something like *Stranded*

---

[70] Jeff Jensen, "The Last of Lost," *Entertainment Weekly*, May 14, 2010, quoted in Jarzembowski, "*LOST*: The Series Finale."

would be more descriptive. But the creators of this show must have been thinking very intentionally when they went with *LOST*. The characters all start out lost. Their personal situations made them prisoners on individual islands of their own making, isolated and alone. Kate had killed her father (2:9) and then gotten her boyfriend killed, and ended up a felon and a fugitive. Charlie was an addict, desperately trying to revive a music career that wasn't coming back. Jin was some kind of mob enforcer. Sun had an affair and was planning to fake her own kidnapping and leave her husband. Sayid was an Iraqi Republican Guard torturer who lost the woman he loved. Sawyer was a con man who abandoned his daughter and let revenge drive him to kill a man (who turned out to be the wrong man). Hugo couldn't believe anyone could love him. Michael was a failure as a father, or at least he thought he was. And while most of these situations may seem extreme, the characters represent us because they are like us. We all start out with original sin and then find ourselves burdened with actual sins. We are *LOST* in the sense that we are alienated from God and from each other. And any of us are capable of committing antisocial acts. Repeated references to *The Children of the Corn* send the message that anyone can be driven to torture or kill another human being (at least metaphorically), given the right circumstances.

Ironically, although they start out lost, on the island they find themselves when they find each other. And each of the characters overcomes his past to rise above it, accomplishing things he never thought he could. Kate becomes a healer and life bringer when she sews up Jack's wound and then deliver's Claire's baby. Although a woman had once said to Charlie, "You'll never take care of anyone" (1:15), he quits his addiction, takes care of Claire and Aaron, and even gives his life in the hope that they might be rescued. Jin learns to be a loving husband, and he and Sun are able to conceive a child. Sayid learns to love again, and Hugo falls in love with Libby. Even Locke becomes the survivalist he always wanted to be. Michael acts heroically (and later tragically) to try to protect his son—though for him he failed the test and could no longer be a candidate because he killed Libby and Ana Lucia. In any case, it was Jack who got them to do what they could not before. But he didn't do it *for* them. He showed them the way and encouraged them to find within themselves the strength to do it.

So the island is life. As Locke said, "It's not an island; it's a place where miracles happen" (4:13). The island is where an impotent Jin could get his wife pregnant, and where Rose's cancer was healed. And although the character of Locke is usually untrustworthy, he does represent that clean slate (*tabula rasa*) that we all need and hope for. He was crippled before the crash, but on the island he can walk. He was weak, but then he became strong (if misguided). He says, "Everyone gets a new life on this island" (1:17) and later, "I'm not lost anymore" (2:5). The Australian farmer tells Kate, "Everyone deserves a fresh start" (1:2) and Jack tells her, "It doesn't matter, Kate, who we were, what we did before this—before the crash—'cause really, three days ago we all died; we should all be able to start over" (1:3). What seems like a reference to resurrection is, as I said, more of an analogy of baptism. Their new life begins with their "death," just as Jesus said, "Unless a grain of wheat falls to the ground and dies, it remains just a grain of wheat; but if it dies it produces much fruit. Whoever loves his life loses it, and whoever hates his life in this world will preserve it for eternal life" (John 12:24–25).

The island is a place of connections, the place that brings the characters together in a way that makes them a family.

But we find out that the characters were all connected even before the island. Jack and Claire have the same father. Charles Widmore is Daniel Faraday's father, making Daniel and Penny siblings. The accident that injured Jack's ex-wife was the same accident that killed Shannon's father. Locke's father was the original con man named Sawyer who was responsible for the death of James "Sawyer" Ford's parents. Kate became friends with the mother of Sawyer's daughter (3:15). Hugo owned the box company that Locke worked for. Kate's stepfather captured Sayid in Iraq. Miles's father is Dr. Chang of the Dharma Initiative. Ana Lucia traveled to Australia with Jack's father (2:20) and met Jack in the airport. Jack had met Desmond, and Sawyer met Jack's father. Then there were many moments when characters appeared on television in the background of other characters' flashbacks. And I haven't even mentioned the recurring numbers: 4, 8, 15, 16, 23, 42. They show up repeatedly, but ultimately we find out that they are the numbers that refer to the last six candidates: Locke, Hugo, Sawyer, Sayid, Jack, and "Kwon" (we don't know whether that means Jin or Sun, or both).

Not surprisingly, the possibility of coincidence is rejected. In the third season, Ben says, "Two days after I found out I have a fatal tumor on my spine, a spinal surgeon falls out of the sky. If that's not proof of God, I don't know what is" (3:5). Pope St. John Paul II said, "In the designs of providence, there are no mere coincidences."[71] And perhaps this is the point. What happens is a matter not of fate or destiny but of providence. Even Locke realizes that losing his kidney, while it seems like a tragic

---

[71] Quoted in Thomas V. Wykes, *A Vision for Spring* (Alta Loma, CA: Springtime of Faith Foundation, 2016), 25.

injustice, actually saves his life (4:2). In the end, it is not the island that chooses and tests, or some personified idea of the universe directing people's lives, but there is a God who invites people to cooperate with Him through the use of their free will. One of the most powerful messages of LOST is that we are all connected to each other, and we can either fight against that, or we can embrace it and treat each other like family, protecting and encouraging each other.

With any Arian Christology, the bad news is that each person pretty much has to be his own savior. Sure, there is the pioneer leader who blazes the trail and sets the example, but the implied soteriology is that it is up to each one of us to save ourselves or be damned. With LOST, however, the good news is something very much like purgatory, in which those who did not redeem themselves in their earthly lives will apparently have the opportunity to live the lives they should have, if only as a dream. As a Catholic, I was encouraged by the use of the purgatory concept: although it may have gone a bit too far into a kind of universalism (the notion that everyone gets to heaven eventually), I appreciated the message that no one is beyond redemption.

Sayid thought he was beyond redemption. Not only was he a torturer, but he had tried to kill a child (to be fair, it was Ben). His dying words were, "I've tortured more people than I can remember. Wherever I'm going can't be very pleasant. I deserve it" (6:1). Yet he is there in the chapel at the end. The smoke monster called Locke "irreparable," and Locke himself says, "My condition is irreversible." Jack replies, "Nothing is irreversible" (6:2), and later Kate repeats these words (6:17). Nothing is irreversible, and everyone is redeemable. This would be a great message if it were kept within the realm of real life, but it may be just a little irresponsible to give people the impression that they can live a selfish life until the day they die and still hope to redeem themselves after death by living a dream life in which the universe corrects their lives for them.[72]

I was disappointed that the creators of the show had obviously made a point to include every possible religious symbol in the chapel. We could hardly expect anything different, but I had held out hope that the depiction of heaven would keep more closely to the Judeo-Christian perspective. In any case, what determines whether one gets into heaven is simply whether one is "ready." Even Ben Linus, who admits that his life was characterized by selfishness and jealousy, knows that he will eventually be ready to enter the chapel, although for the moment he says he still has some things to work out (6:17). We know that he will be ready at some point because it turns out that he was Hugo's right-hand man when Hugo took over as leader after Jack. It seems that, although Ben had many opportunities to redeem himself during his life, his "conversion" didn't come until Hugo asked him to help protect the island. Ben just wanted to be one of the chosen all along, and when he finally was, he felt as if he had a purpose, a calling.

In the end, there is little difference between the fate of those who rose above their situation and saved themselves, and those who didn't. Those who didn't simply take longer to get to heaven. Perhaps the point is that it's not so much the work of overcoming (or making up for) sin that matters, but the recognition—the repentance, if you will—in which a person finally

---

[72] Technically, purgatory is not a "second chance" for those who would otherwise not receive salvation. Purgatory is for those who are being saved into the heavenly realm, though it is the purification that they must go through to purify them of remaining sin.

admits the error of his former ways. As the characters go through their purgatory experiences, at first they don't remember their real lives. They live their "corrected" lives as though they are real. But eventually they begin to remember. Both Charlie and Desmond begin to see images from the other story line, which, as it turns out, was their past in their real lives. They begin remembering the love they had in their lives, in some cases realizing where they went wrong and making the conscious connection (or contrast) between the life they lived and the life they were "supposed" to live. Then Desmond and Hugo go around to the others, helping them remember. And although it seems on the surface that some of the people's lives were better in their real life than in their corrected version, it turns out that they were missing something: love.

LOST is a show about people who are put into each other's lives, who were *supposed* to be in each other's lives, and who were meant to learn to love and care for each other as family. Christian Shephard (who is really Christian when we see him in the chapel, not the smoke monster pretending to be Christian) says to Jack, "The most important part of your life was the time that you spent with those people" (6:17). So to be ready for heaven is to learn that lesson, and (at least mentally) to deal with the choices that one made in life, recognizing the ways in which one fell short of being a good candidate. Desmond says that once they know this, it's time to leave, to cross over. There's an element of self-awareness here, along with repentance. Salvation in LOST is doing your best to be a savior and, to the extent that you fall short of your calling, to acknowledge it.

The final episode of LOST shows us that heaven is a reunion. After several repetitions of "See you in another life, brother," by different characters, they finally all do see each other in the next life. Kate's plea to Jack, "Tell me I'm going to see you again" (6:17) is answered when all the characters are brought back together in the chapel, which is the doorway into heaven. The guitar case that Hugo carried around for three seasons was opened to reveal an ankh, the ancient Egyptian symbol of eternal life. Although the element of time has been different in each of their experiences, they all arrive together. Christian explains that they have moved beyond time into eternity when he says, "Well, there's no *now* here" (6:17).

LOST is a brilliantly entertaining story that sends a deceptive message and gives people a false sense of security. The overly optimistic anthropology lets people off the hook for having to commit to the uniqueness of Jesus Christ, and the universalism ultimately lets everyone off the hook for any responsibility for their sin. It's as if we are being told that we are not responsible for sin (we are all potential saviors, after all) but we are responsible for our own salvation. But if we don't save ourselves, that's okay, because the universe will make the necessary corrections until we are ready to enter heaven. All we really need to do is admit that sometimes we failed to make the right choices—which, on the surface, seems like a Christian idea, until you get to the part where you can wait until after you die to realize it.

A better, more nuanced, way to think about our participation in our own salvation is what is known as *synergism*. The word means "working together," in the sense that we cooperate with God. Only divine intervention can truly overcome the gravity of human sin, so we cannot be our own saviors, but with a divine Savior, we can accept the forgiveness He offers and work on living up to our potential. The difference between the universe of *LOST* and the Christian concept of salvation is that the repentance has to come before we die.

Score

So how well does the Christ figure of *LOST* compare with the actual Jesus? We have to give full points for humanity, since Jack Shephard is clearly depicted as one of us. However, there are no points for divinity or for uniqueness among humanity: not only can anyone be the savior (in an Arian sense) but saviors are replaceable and people end up taking turns. Since the Christology of *LOST* is basically Arian/adoptionist; it's a Christology of ascent (the savior starts out as a sinner), so no points for incarnation. His death is both sacrificial and voluntary, but not really an atoning death. I'll give him 3 out of 5 points for that. Finally, there is no resurrection apart from the eternal life that all will receive (and salvation is universalist) so no points there. Jack Shephard's orthodoxy score is 8.

CHAPTER 7

TRON

Oh, my User!

— RAM

In 1982, the film *Tron* gave us a look at a universe inside our computers, where programs are self-aware individuals with personalities, capable of love and fear, and video games are gladiator-like matches in which the stakes are life or deletion. Some of these contests became real video games, including the Light Cycle, a grid-based game in which one cycle tries to trap another by boxing it in with the light trail of the cycle's path. The riders of the cycles are enslaved programs, though it's unclear how or to what extent their actions are controlled by the person outside the computer who is playing the game.

In fact, not all programs believe that users exist. In the world of *Tron*, those programs who have faith believe in the existence of users, that is, the programmers who created them. Programs look like their users, in whose image they are made, and so the same actors play the programmers in the real world and the programs they've created in the computer world. When one program, named Ram, dies (called "deresolution"), his last words are, "Oh, my User!"

The antagonist of the film is the Master Control Program (or MCP), who is the personification of A.I. gone bad. In becoming self-aware, he has also become selfish, and in a classic example of creation turning on its creator, he goes rogue and is able to manipulate his own user, Dillinger. Eventually the program controls the programmer (apparently via the threat of blackmail). Although the MCP knows that users exist, it persecutes programs who believe, commanding them to deny the existence of users. If they refuse, they are put onto the game grid, where—much like the Roman arena—their lives will be short. If they obey and deny their faith, they are rewarded with a position in the MCP's elite guard, reminiscent of the Praetorian Guard of the Roman emperors.

Flynn is a programmer—a user—who is accidentally transferred into the computer by some experimental trans-mat device (why the laser just happens to be pointed at the chair of the computer terminal is never explained). In any case, Flynn is somehow transported onto the grid of the computer world. He is quickly arrested by the MCP's guards, and brought to the MCP. The MCP seems to know that he's a user, and therefore wants him dead. Flynn is sentenced to be trained and prepared to enter the arena. There, he not only survives; he wins, but he refuses to kill his opponent. He escapes and helps a program named Tron get in touch with his own user, Alan, who will help Flynn get out of the computer.

In a 2010 sequel, *Tron Legacy*, we find Flynn back inside the computer, trapped by the MCP. His own program, Clu, has lost his faith and calls Flynn a "false deity." Then it's up to Flynn's son, Sam, to rescue his father.

Anthropology

The parallels to the Roman Empire and the world of early Christianity are obvious. Believers are those who know they are made in the image of their creator, and they trust that their creator has some benevolent control over their lives, perhaps even protecting them. But believers are persecuted and enslaved by a dictatorial power that wants to suppress the faith and keep all obedience oriented toward it. Those who refuse to comply with the "emperor" are punished by becoming contestants in the games: their very lives become entertainment for all those who are willing to deny the existence of users.

Clearly the Master Control Program represents evil, but there is no sense of personal sin in the world of *Tron*. Individual programs do only what they are programmed to do, and in the outside world, users are considered gods. Sin, if there is such a thing, is presented more as institutional injustice: the evil of oppression, rather than the evil of personal selfishness or the misuse of free will. In fact, the programs in *Tron* are somewhat innocent. We know they have free will because they can disobey the MCP, and of course Clu and Tron are able to escape from the MCP's control, but most of the programs do not seem to exhibit much free will. They are more like pawns who don't need to take any responsibility for their actions.

However, in *Tron Legacy*, Flynn takes responsibility for things having gone wrong, but he does it in an interesting way. He admits that he was wrong to strive for perfection, implying that he should have embraced imperfection, and then everything would have been fine. He says, "I screwed it up, chasing after perfection." The clear implication here is that perfection is impossible, that striving for perfection is associated with fascism, and that true perfection is found in accepting imperfection. There is no such thing as sin, only injustice.

Christology

In the original film, Flynn is the Christ figure. He is "incarnated" into the world of the computers by being transported onto the grid. Once there, he has special powers that presumably only a user could have. However, his incarnation is not voluntary: he "falls" into the world of programs against his will. And Flynn never becomes a program. He looks like a program, but only because programs look like users. He is never really one of them.

According to the "guardian," Dumont, "All that is visible must grow beyond itself and extend into the invisible." This implies a dualism that assumes that whatever is invisible is better than what is visible. The goal of the visible is to become invisible. In the meantime, Flynn's presence in the computer world brings about a new awareness of the existence of users, and a new hope for freedom. As Alan transfers information to Tron, he says, "This is the key to a new order: this code disc means freedom." In other words, it is information, or knowledge, that is the answer to the systemic injustice and oppression of the world of the programs.

In the chase to get to the communication hub, Flynn must create a "junction" between two energy streams, effectively creating a connection between the world of the computer grid and the world of the users. The energy is too much for him, and he is momentarily groggy, which may be a kind of nod to a "death," but he doesn't really die, so there's no need for a resurrection. Eventually, with the help of Tron and Alan, Flynn is able to jump into an energy stream and ascend back into the real world, where he is "exalted" by being elevated to be the boss of the software company.

We can see, then, that the Christology of *Tron* is basically gnostic. All of the hallmarks of gnosticism are found here: the "spiritual" realm (represented by the real world, as opposed to the intracomputer world) is inherently good, while the "material" realm (the grid) is evil. To move from the spiritual realm to the material is to "fall," and to be "trapped" in matter (molecules organized like a grid). There are many gods (users), and one of them descended into the material (grid) world disguised as a person (program). In gnostic teaching, Jesus was not really a person, but He looked like one. He didn't come to die for the forgiveness of sin, because there is really no such thing as sin; rather, He came to bring secret knowledge that will bring freedom through enlightenment. The Savior didn't really die—if it seemed as if He did, that was an illusion, too—and there is no need for a resurrection because He always existed only in His spiritual state.

In the sequel, *Tron Legacy*, the role of the Christ figure is shared by several characters: Flynn, his son Sam, Tron, and a new character, Quorra. But don't look for any Trinitarian analogy here because the whole premise is that the son has to save the father. Tron sacrifices himself, but with no resurrection.

The character of Quorra is very interesting but only reinforces the gnostic elements of the *Tron* universe. She is the last of an entirely new life form that was "manifested"—not created, but spontaneously generated—which adds the gnostic element that gods do not have to be eternal. These new life forms, called ISOs, are like gods in the sense that they are "spiritual" (i.e., "higher") beings, yet they are innocent: Flynn says they are both naïve and wise. Since she is the last of her kind, and since the MCP would like to see her dead, Flynn is hiding her disguised as a program. Flynn says, "In our world, she could change everything." Then Quorra is the one who sacrifices her life and experiences a death and resurrection by rebooting her own system (Flynn facilitates this, but it's really she who raises herself). Thus, the second film ends with a gnostic savior in a reverse incarnation: Quorra is taken out of the computer realm into the real world with the implication that she will change our world for the better.

Soteriology

In the *Tron* universe, salvation is freedom through knowledge. Evil is not personal sin, but control and slavery, and the goal is to "change the system." In the original film, whatever salvation takes place is really left to the imagination, but I think we are to assume that Flynn has saved the programs from slavery and oppression by the MCP, by bringing into the computer grid the knowledge of a higher order and the information on how to bring it about. In gnosticism, the savior brings secret knowledge, which can "save" (or enlighten) only those who accept it. It doesn't change the world; it elevates the select few who are truly spiritual to rise above the world.

In the sequel, we find out that they have indeed built a new grid, where "all information was free and open." In a telling real-world parallel, Sam hacks into the software company's mainframe and puts its new operating system on the Internet, preempting the much-awaited release of the software, and making it available to everyone for free. This has the effect of costing the company millions, perhaps, billions, of dollars, while the audience is supposed to cheer for the free access to information for everyone. But within the computer world, free access to information for everyone doesn't work out so well. Flynn's dream was "a digital frontier to reshape the human condition." He thought they were "building utopia." But both Clu and Tron were corrupted. Evil did not go away with the free access to information. Once the programs were free, they apparently used their freedom for selfish ends. And so the personal sin that was absent in the first film comes out in the second. In the end, Tron is finally saved by repenting and changing his allegiance back to the users at the last minute. Then he sacrifices himself to save the others. In fact, in the sequel it seems as if just about everyone is falling all over himself to sacrifice for others.

Script and Scripture

Overall, the theology of *Tron* is polytheistic, since there are many users. There may even be programs that have gained a quasi-user status. In *Tron: Legacy*, the proprietor of the End of the Line Club is called Zuse and Castor, both Greco-Roman gods (the former spelled "Zeus" in Greek mythology), and it is said that he has been around since the earliest days of the gaming grid. In fact, each program has its own user. This is the ultimate New Age spirituality: everyone has his own conception of a higher power, who is really just a projection of himself. Furthermore, we come to find out that users are not omniscient. When Flynn first arrives on the grid, the programs are disturbed to find out that this user doesn't have a grand plan. It turns out that users are no more omniscient than their programs. That is, programs are just as omniscient as users. Another hallmark of Gnosticism is that people are actually gods: divine sparks trapped in material bodies, but really no less divine than Jesus or His Father.

Another thing we notice is that users are not necessarily benevolent. Users can be good or evil, and malicious creators make malicious programs. But then, even Flynn's originally good creation, Clu, eventually became an evil dictator. He led a coup and became a fascist leader, building an army like the legions of Rome, with a plan to escape the grid and colonize the user realm. There he planned to eradicate imperfection, which apparently would mean the destruction of our world. The gnostics believed that some gods could be evil, and in fact in the days of the Roman Empire and the early Church, the gnostics taught that the God of the Old Testament was an evil God who created evil and who was out to get humanity (their proof text for this was the flood, in Genesis).

Flynn, in creating the new grid, claimed to have transcended "science, technology, religion"; but the new grid ultimately became fascist, demonstrating the destructive pride of thinking one can transcend religion and create gods in one's own image. Once back inside the computer realm, Flynn tried to oppose Clu, but the more Flynn fought, the stronger Clu became. In the end, Clu committed genocide and killed all (but one) of the ISOs. Flynn resigned himself to living in hiding and protecting Quorra, concluding (in homage to the film *War Games*), "The only way to win is not to play."

The religious imagery of the first film plays on the persecution of Christians in the Roman Empire. In the sequel, the religious imagery is ramped up, but becomes even more gnostic. Although Quorra calls Flynn, "the creator," and Zuse calls Sam, "the son of our maker," nevertheless Quorra is really the one who saves Flynn, who basically worships her as a higher life form. But she's not perfect either. When we first meet her, she is learning "the art of the selfless" from Flynn, who is dressed like a Buddhist monk, and then at a crucial moment in the film, Quorra makes the almost fatal mistake of sending Sam into Zuse's club.

I remember loving *Tron* as a kid, but it just doesn't hold up as well as most of the other stories in this book. *Tron: Legacy*, while visually stunning, is a confusing sequel with some creepy facial CGI. But I think the most disturbing thing about the *Tron* universe is the apparent quasi-socialist agenda inherent in the story. In the sequel, when Sam is reunited with his father, he tells Flynn about what's been happening in the real world. It's a familiar litany exemplified by the tired maxim that the rich get richer while the poor get poorer; which is true, except that the solution we are expected to embrace is that freedom of information will lead to a more equitable distribution of wealth. We are supposed to believe that what didn't work in the computer world (and what led to fascism there) is going to be the solution to fascism in the real world. To the contrary, I would argue that socialism and fascism are two sides of the same coin, and that free information does not necessarily make people free. In fact, the Internet has created a generation that believes intellectual property should be free, and that in turn has led to a decline of creativity, and the exploitation of artists who can no longer make a living creating their art.

Score

In the *Tron* universe, the world of the computer grid represents the world we live in, and the world of the users represents the spiritual realm (even though in a literal sense it is our world). The point is that because Flynn goes into the world of the programs, but never really becomes a program, he gets few points for humanity. Let's say 2 points for humanity, but 4 points for uniqueness. His "incarnation" is a descent, but it's against his will, so only 3 points there. He does get full points for being creator, but let's say only 4 points for divinity, since he's not omniscient and doesn't have a plan. I'll give him only 1 point for sacrificial death. He does seem willing to sacrifice himself, but he doesn't really die; he just gets woozy. And there's no need for a resurrection, so no points for that. If we were to take into account the death and resurrection in the sequel, we might give the overall films a few more points, but then we would have to start subtracting points for uniqueness, so let's just say that Flynn/Tron gets 19 points.

CHAPTER 8

PLEASANTVILLE

Those are not your cookies, Bud.

— TV REPAIRMAN

Pleasantville (1998) is the story of high school–age twins Jennifer and David, who find themselves transported into the world of a fictional family from the golden age of television. In their ordinary world, Jennifer is an underachiever who nevertheless thinks the world is her oyster. David is awkward and uncomfortable in his own skin and looks forward to escaping into a marathon of reruns of *Pleasantville*, a *Leave It to Beaver/Father Knows Best/Ozzie and Harriet*–type TV show set in 1958. But this is not really a time-travel story, because Jennifer and David do not travel to historical 1958. They travel to an idealized world—one that in reality never existed—proving that one person's dream is another person's nightmare.

In the first scenes of the film, the audience is confronted with a montage of life in the real world. Job prospects are not good, and the students are told they can look forward to fewer jobs with lower pay. HIV is on the increase, and global warming is going to lead to natural disasters. Police patrol even the suburban neighborhoods, and on top of it all, David is completely unsuccessful with women.

By contrast, in Pleasantville fathers get promotions sooner than expected, every yard is surrounded by a white picket fence, and everyone gets a healthful breakfast. In Pleasantville, the temperature is always 72, and the sky is always sunny. No one is homeless; there are no fires, no lawyers, no crime, and basketballs never miss the basket. Everyone is patriotic; married couples sleep in separate beds; and the bowling teams are made up of regular guys named Jack, Jay, John, Jim, and Jeff; or Bob, Bill, Ben, Biff, and Bo. And one more thing: everyone in Pleasantville is white.

It's clear that on one level, *Pleasantville* is a parable: a metaphor for civil rights, and a kind of analogy for the struggle between the need for change and the resistance to change. We'll come back to that later. But on the theological level, the film begins with a juxtaposition of two worlds. One world, the real world of Jennifer and David, is corrupt, riddled with crime, and plagued by degradation and decay. By contrast, the black-and-white world of *Pleasantville* is a world of stability, without decay, degradation, or corruption. It's a world of innocence, symbolized by the fact that public restrooms have no toilets in them, and even the adults of the town don't know anything about sex. These two worlds are exemplified in the two sets of parents in the film. Jennifer and David's parents are divorced. Their mother is in a relationship that's going nowhere. Their father was supposed to spend the weekend with them but cancelled at the last minute. So Jennifer and David lack stability, and it's no wonder

David escapes into a fictional world that is the epitome of stability. The parents of the main family in *Pleasantville*, George and Betty Parker, once came home from vacation just because no one answered the phone when they called.

By the intervention of a mysterious TV repairman, Jennifer and David are transported into Pleasantville, taking the places of the Parkers' children, Mary Sue and Bud. Jennifer (now seen by everyone in Pleasantville as Mary Sue Parker) is horrified. "We're stuck in Nerdsville," she complains as she mourns the fact that she's missing out on a date with the high school crush. But David (as Bud Parker) promises to get them home if his sister will only play the part and not do anything that will affect the simplicity of life in Pleasantville. David/Bud, is, of course, attracted to the simplicity, safety, and stability of Pleasantville and wants to protect it. But Jennifer/Mary Sue immediately begins creating conflict because she hates having her options limited. Sitting in her high school "geography" class, she asks, "What's outside of Pleasantville?" and the teacher responds, "I don't understand." The teacher didn't understand the question because there is nothing outside of Pleasantville. At the end of every street is the beginning again.

In spite of the fact that David/Bud is Pleasantville's self-appointed protector, once Jennifer/Mary Sue has been dropped into this world, change is inevitable. As the leaders of the town begin to see things changing, they naturally resist it. Eventually they are scandalized when the furniture store starts selling double beds. Gathered at the barber shop they say, "Somebody oughta do something about that." Mayor Bob especially doesn't like the changes, and he invites George Parker to join the town chamber of commerce to help lead Pleasantville in its resistance to change. In a series of speeches, the mayor tells the townspeople.

"Something is happening in our town, and I think we can all see where it's coming from.... Up until now, everything around here has always been, well, pleasant. Recently, certain things have become unpleasant. Now it seems to me that the first thing we have to do is to separate out the things that are pleasant from the things that are unpleasant."

And so the attitude of those who resist change is depicted as prejudice and ignorance. The analogy for the civil rights movement is obvious. Eventually the attempt to prevent or reverse the changes happening in Pleasantville leads to shaming and marginalizing those who embody change, and then finally it turns into sexual harassment and violence.

Anthropology

What does *Pleasantville* have to say about humanity and what it means to be human? Jennifer and David are like the first humans, dropped into the Garden of Eden. In spite of the fact that there are already people there when they arrive, we can tell that Pleasantville is Eden because when things begin to change, the seemingly omnipresent and omniscient TV repairman (played by Don Knotts) will eventually proclaim, "You don't deserve this place—you don't deserve this paradise!" Throughout the film, Jennifer and David repeatedly exclaim, "Oh God!" or "Oh my God!" Therefore, the TV repairman represents God, and David and Jennifer (in spite of the fact that they are siblings) are a kind of Adam and Eve.

Before things change, Pleasantville is safe, but boring. And for Jennifer, that seems to be the point. It may seem peaceful to those who don't know any better, but Jennifer would rather have it be exciting than safe. If Pleasantville is Eden, with its lack of corruption, then the change that Jennifer brings to Pleasantville represents the Fall, but we are supposed to see this as a fall that was necessary, and even beneficial to the inhabitants of this paradise. Before this fall, they didn't really have free will, because their choices were limited. They were innocent, but also ignorant. And this raises the question: Is ignorance bliss, or is it a prison?

One of the first indications that change is happening surrounds Pleasantville's high school basketball star, Skip Martin (played with a brilliant wide-eyed innocence by the late Paul Walker). When Jennifer/Mary Sue indicates that she might not want to go out on a date with him, he shoots for a basket, but misses. It's the first time anyone in Pleasantville has ever seen a basketball fail to go into the basket. Everyone is shocked, and the coach tells his players to back away from the ball and not to touch it. The residents of Pleasantville are so comfortable in their routine that they don't know how to handle change, let alone failure.

Bill Johnson, proprietor of the soda shop, is forced to figure out how to open up the shop and make the cheeseburgers all by himself, because David/Bud is so busy trying to prevent change that he misses his shift behind the counter. The irony is that in trying to prevent change, David/Bud causes a change at the soda shop that leads to a kind of self-actualization in Bill Johnson. He accomplishes something new, and his eyes are opened. And then Bill realizes that he's depressed because nothing ever changes. "It doesn't get any better, and it doesn't get any worse." In a storeroom full of cans labeled "NOT FOOD," Bill confesses to David/Bud that he liked the change. He liked having to figure out how to make the fries himself. The implication is that, again, lack of change is associated with boredom, and any change—even a change for the worse—would somehow be better than no change at all. Bill confides in David/Bud that he looks forward to December all year long because that's when he gets to paint the windows of the soda shop. He says, "It seems like an awfully long time to be waiting for just one moment." So his eyes have been opened, and the result is a dissatisfaction, because he wants more.

The parallels to those who resisted the civil rights movement are clear. White privilege created a comfortable lifestyle for many people, but at the expense of oppressing others, and change was needed. But at the other end of the spectrum one could argue that the time when the film was released—exactly forty years after the setting in Pleasantville—was a time characterized by too much change and not enough stability. The montage at the beginning of the film describes the fears and anxieties of life in 1998, when many people longed for the prosperity and security of another (idealized) time and found hope in an emphasis on tradition. But there is a proverb that says, "Where there are no oxen, there is no grain; but abundant crops come by the strength of the ox" (Prov. 14:4). In other words, if you want the crops that farm animals can provide, you have to put up with the manure that will appear in the stable. *No milk without manure:* it's another way of saying, "no pain, no gain." The point is that nothing good comes without some kind of price. In the world of Pleasantville, the price is change, which means the loss of the stability that comes with tradition and routine. But the good that comes with change is a newfound freedom.

Here we see, on a deeper level than the civil rights analogy, a reversal of the story of the Fall of man in Genesis. In the Bible, the Fall results in original sin and a great loss for humanity, which ultimately amounts to alienation from God. But the people of Pleasantville, although they resist change at first, are improved by it, in many cases in spite of themselves. The changes that they experience result in an awakening, an enlightenment, rather than original sin. For them, their "fall" is not (as it is in Scripture) the result of the misuse of free will and the failure to live up to human potential; rather, it brings true freedom.

When David/Bud is defending himself at "Pleasantville's Very First Trial Ever," he points to the gallery and says, "You see those faces up there? They're no different than you are; they just happen to see something inside themselves." The first half of that statement is an obvious nod to the common humanity that all people share, regardless of skin color. But the second half of the statement is quite telling. The people who embrace the changes have discovered something inside themselves that they didn't know was there before. The implication is that potential is not something given to them and not something that might be handed down to them by tradition, but something they can find within themselves. He goes on, "It can't stop because it's in you, and you can't stop something that's inside you." The claim is that the solution to the problem of the human condition is not reconciliation with God, but self-awareness. What people really need, as David/Bud has come to realize, is to find truth within themselves.

Christology

The character of David is the "hero" of this story, in the sense that he is the central character and the one who makes a journey of discovery. But the savior figure in this film is Jennifer. She is the one who is dropped into a world that needs her to bring change in order to be saved. At first David/Bud tries to prevent her from stirring up change. The following dialogue sets the stage:

DAVID/BUD. You're messing with the whole universe!

JENNIFER/MARY SUE. Maybe it needs to be messed with, David. Did that ever occur to you?

DAVID/BUD. ... But they're happy like this.... You have no right to do this to them.

JENNIFER/MARY SUE. They have a lot of potential, they just don't know any better.

Jennifer, as their savior, has come to bring knowledge so that they *will* know better and so that they will know what's inside them and realize their potential. Jennifer's first convert is Skip Martin: she converts him by seducing him. He is awakened to sexuality, but Jennifer doesn't love him. She's really just toying with him because she's bored and annoyed with her new surroundings, and because at first she treats the residents of Pleasantville as though they are not real. Eventually she gets bored with him, too, and casts him aside in favor of her newfound love of reading, causing Skip to regress to book burning. But in the loss of his virginity, his eyes are opened to a new experience of color. In the midst of this black-and-white world, he can see the true red in a rose.

Being able to see color becomes the first sign of someone who has changed. Eventually, the change manifests itself in the person's breaking out in vivid color. The people who have changed have been brought out of the darkness of ignorance into the light of enlightenment, which is a good thing when it's about skin color. But because the civil rights analogy is connected to the Fall, we end up with a reversal of Genesis, in that it is the loss of innocence that brings enlightenment. And there is a trade-off. All the kids are making out, but the basketball team loses badly. Apparently, there's a reason for the saying "You can't win 'em all."

Betty Parker's conversion also comes as a result of the awakening of her sexuality. Her (extramarital) attraction to Bill Johnson makes her see the red on the hearts of playing cards. But her own daughter, Jennifer/Mary Sue, has to tell her about sex, resulting in a burning bush and the town's first real fire. Jennifer/Mary Sue begins "the talk" with the traditional words, "When two people love each other very much," but that's not what's going on with her and Skip. It's more about lust than love. And in her own character's evolution, when she discovers a love of reading, she is reading D. H. Lawrence, presumably *Lady Chatterley's Lover*. Lawrence wrote, "It is better to die than live mechanically a life that is a repetition of repetitions." This seems to sum up Jennifer's attitude. It's better not to live at all than to live a common or routine life. As she reads, she puts on a pair of glasses, symbolizing that even she is now seeing the world through new eyes, and when she wakes the next morning, she is in color.

All of this leads to liberation for the women of Pleasantville. They get out of the house, but their husbands are disappointed by what they see as responsibilities unfilled. William H. Macy is unforgettable as George Parker coming home to an empty house, unable to fathom why there is no response to his evening announcement of, "Honey I'm home!" — no response apart from ominous thunder and lightning, that is. With a bewildered look on his face, he wanders through the dark house, calling out, "Where's my dinner?" Later, at the bowling alley, one of the team sadly shows the back of his bowling shirt to reveal an iron-shaped burn mark. Then Mayor Bob speaks to all the men, saying, "This isn't about George's dinner; it's not about Roy's shirt. It's a question of values. It's a question of whether we want to hold on to the values that made this place great."

To be fair, we have to ask, "Great for whom?" Pleasantville, as a film, is critiquing (and rightly so) the desire to cling to traditions that may be comfortable for some, but that discriminate, segregate, and oppress others. Here "traditional values" are pitted against freedom and the realization of human potential. The problem is that it becomes an all-or-nothing proposition, as if all traditions are mutually exclusive with progress and liberation. When George is confronted with his wife's new color, he says, "It'll go away." Betty responds, "I don't want it to go away." Sadly, George doesn't know what else to do, so he tries to play the "head of the household" card and lay down the law. Betty packs her bags and leaves.

There is no real sacrifice or death and resurrection for Jennifer, unless it is the fact that she had to give up her life in the ordinary world. By the end of the film, however, she has embraced her new life, and she decides not to return to her former life, where she had little hope for her future. She stays in 1958, but leaves Pleasantville to go off to college, where she will become even more enlightened. This is an ascension, of sorts, but it is not a return to where she came from. She is going on to a higher plane of existence.

So what kind of savior is Jennifer? She is an outsider, who comes into a world imprisoned in its tradition, closed-mindedness, and routine, and brings enlightenment and freedom by getting people to tap into the spark of creativity and sexuality within themselves. This is a perfect analogy for a gnostic savior.

Eventually, even David/Bud is converted. He had tried to be the protector of Pleasantville's traditional way of life. When the tree bursts into flames, and even the firemen don't know what to do, he is honored for helping to put the fire out. He is called a hero, but by this point he is already having second thoughts.

When Betty breaks out in color, he helps her cover it up with makeup, but then he brings Bill Johnson an art book from the library. The first picture they turn to is *Expulsion from the Garden of Eden* by Masaccio. The emotion expressed in the painting is shame, because it depicts Adam and Eve aware of their nudity and suffering the consequences of their sin. Bill, however, focuses on the painter rather than on the subjects, saying, "Must be awful lucky to see colors like that." There seems to be a rejection of shame here, an implicit commentary that shame is an inappropriate response. When Betty is shamed by a group of young men who taunt her, David/Bud defends her, punching one of the men. It's at this moment that he breaks out in color. He has done a good thing by defending change, but he has done it by accepting violence. Pleasantville is no longer boring. But it's also no longer peaceful.

Soteriology

In *Pleasantville*, God is depicted as a TV repairman. He's a fixer: the slogan on his truck says, "We'll fix you for good." Not only does he fix television sets; he appears on them. He's the omniscient overseer of Pleasantville who knows all the trivia and puts David to the test. When David passes the test, the TV repairman calls it a miracle and gives him a remote control that "will put you right in the show." Then David and his sister are transported into the world that the divine repairman considers a perfect paradise. But as we come to find out, Pleasantville is not perfect. In fact, the TV repairman presents a bumbling, impotent God figure who takes sides against change but is powerless to stop it. This is a hallmark of gnosticism: the idea that the God who created the world is somehow the enemy of humanity, and that the world He created is a prison that humans can rise above, but only if they are enlightened and find their own divine spark within themselves. It's true that the residents of Pleasantville have never had to endure a storm, but they are pitiful creatures who have to be told not to fear the rain. And when the rainbow comes, it is not a promise of forgiveness from God; it is a sign of having broken free from the shackles of ignorance. What humans need is knowledge that this Creator God is either unaware of or holding back from them, including the idea that we all have a divine spark within us. Therefore, salvation is not presented as reconciliation with a God who has our best interests at heart, but rather as growth beyond the stifling rules set by the Creator and liberation from the limitations of His garden. And the savior is the one who brings the knowledge that people need.

When David/Bud becomes a disciple of change, he's brought before a soda shop full of high school kids who want to know how he knew about things like fire and rain. Some of the kids are already in color, and they have noticed that the books in the library are filling in with content. Although Jennifer/Mary Sue is the gnostic savior, she appoints her brother as the spokesperson, rather as Moses appointed Aaron. As David/Bud speaks, we hear jazz music in the background, especially Dave Brubeck's "Take Five," a song with a decidedly unconventional time signature. He answers thoughtfully:

> Where I used to live, that's just what firemen did.
> And where's that?
> Um, outside of Pleasantville.
> What's outside of Pleasantville?
> There are some places where the road keeps going.

As more people break out in color, symbolizing their (often reluctant) embodiment of change, being "colored" becomes a derogatory term that those who resist change use to marginalize those who have embraced it. We see the sign in a store window: No Coloreds. Salvation is enlightenment, but just as gnostics have always taught, that enlightenment is not for everyone. Some will resist it, and some will simply never be intelligent enough to have it. So salvation means that new knowledge has come into the world, along with new music, and long lines at the library. But with that new knowledge comes greed, lust, fear, jealousy, anger, resentment, and violence. All of this escalates to the point of riot when a brick goes through the window of the soda shop, and then the shop is vandalized. The next thing you know, the library is closed and there is a pile of burning books in the street. The town council meets and creates a new code of conduct that limits music choices and paint colors—and outlaws double beds.

Gnosticism is often associated with sexual revolution, and in Pleasantville it's no different. Enlightenment includes a new openness to sexuality, which is symbolized in the idea that a married couple might sleep in the same bed, but which in fact leads to the breakup of George and Betty's marriage. As might be expected, the younger generation rejects the new code of conduct as it embraces the new sexual freedom.

A major factor in David's conversion is that in Pleasantville he is able to get a date with Margaret Henderson. But there's a problem, because Margaret Henderson is not supposed to be Bud's girlfriend; she is supposed to be Whitey's girlfriend. After Margaret bakes cookies for David/Bud, the TV repairman shows up to say that he's getting concerned with the changes he's seeing in Pleasantville. Margaret's gift of cookies is a metaphor for a woman's gift of her virginity, and likewise for a man's temptation. In a vain attempt to stop the process of change and "to make everyone happy again," the repairman tells David, "Those are not your cookies, Bud; those are Whitey's cookies." On another level, there is probably a reference here to white privilege. The civil rights movement began to open up benefits to African-Americans that were previously reserved for "whitey."

Still, the enlightenment in Pleasantville is depicted as primarily a sexual awakening. David/Bud goes to Lover's Lane with Margaret and the blossoms turn pink. Everyone at Lover's Lane seems to be reading books, however, cementing the connection between knowledge and sexuality. It should be remembered that in the old King James Version of the Bible, sex is referred to as knowledge. When it says, "he knew her," it means an experiential knowledge of intimacy. And when the forbidden tree in the garden is called the tree of the "knowledge of good and evil," this is not simply a reference to knowing about good and evil, or even knowing the difference between good and evil—it's about having firsthand, intimate experience with both good and evil. Margaret asks David/Bud:

What's it like?

What?

Out there.

Well, it's louder, and scarier, I guess, and it's a lot more dangerous.

Sounds fantastic.

The conclusion is that although knowledge brings danger, it's better to have the knowledge than to be ignorant. After all, without danger there could be no such thing as courage. Margaret says, "You know, the other night some kids came up here to go swimming, and they took off all their clothes.... Do you want some berries? I picked them myself." Then she picks a bright red apple from a nearby tree, and hands it to David/Bud.

Salvation, therefore, is not simply the salvation of individuals, but the transformation of society. In the context of the civil rights movement, we can look back and see that social change was necessary. The idea that salvation is liberation is a valid, but incomplete picture of salvation. Furthermore, there is a theological implication to the way that salvation is portrayed in this movie that simply can't go unchallenged. The idea that salvation is knowledge is ultimately a gnostic idea. In part this is because the knowledge will always be available only to certain people. If salvation is enlightenment, it will always remain unavailable to some people—and in fact this is exactly what gnostics historically believed. They believed and taught that they possessed secret knowledge, meant only for the truly spiritual people, and the rest of humanity were simply not destined for salvation.

Finally, salvation, as it's portrayed in *Pleasantville*, requires a loss of innocence. The freedom that salvation brings (including sexual freedom) requires a loss of purity and an embracing of the kind of corruption that leads to degradation and decay. To have one's eyes opened to the knowledge of good and evil is to have personal experience with evil.

Script and Scripture

As we have seen, *Pleasantville* is a reversal of the story of the fall of humanity in the book of Genesis. In Genesis, humans are made in the image of God. They are given free will from the beginning, as a function of having been made in God's image, but they chose to abuse their free will and disobey God. This was their "fall," and although their eyes were opened, they suffered the consequences of their sin, which included alienation from God (expulsion from the Garden), and so the snowball of original sin began rolling down the hill of human generations. The result is that the image of God in humanity is obscured, a condition that God offers to remedy through the Incarnation of His Son and the salvation that He offers. That salvation not only overcomes our sin but also restores the image of God in us.

In *Pleasantville*, however, paradise may be a place of innocence, but it's also a place of boredom. People don't really have free will, because their choices are limited. Therefore, when change is introduced, it's presented as enlightenment and liberation: exactly what the serpent promised Eve (see Gen. 3:4–5). So the character of Jennifer/Mary Sue is both the serpent and Eve, both the devil and Christ. The fall is the best thing that could have happened to humanity, because it freed them. It did not tarnish the image of God in them; rather, it made them aware that they have a divine spark within them, and if they are aware of that, they can find their own truth within themselves. In other words, they can be their own gods — and isn't this exactly the sin of Adam and Eve? They rejected God's decree of what was right and wrong for their own version of right and wrong.

At the end of the film, there is something outside Pleasantville. A signpost tells us that a place called Springfield is only twelve miles away, and there is now a bus that will take you there. The inevitable victory of change is symbolized in the appearance of color TV sets in the window of the appliance store. And even David, when he goes back to his ordinary life, is willing to turn off the reruns.

As David/Bud said to the mayor, "I know you want it to stay pleasant around here, but there are so many things that are so much better, like … silly, or sexy, or dangerous, or brave." It's one thing to say that there could be no courage without danger; it's another to say that danger is better than peacefulness. But the message of *Pleasantville* is that the trade-off is worth it. The high school basketball team might not win them all anymore, but at least the basketball players are getting lucky with the cheerleaders. George and Betty's marriage may be over, but at least Betty can explore her sexuality. But perhaps the most disturbing thing about *Pleasantville* is the fact that the God-character, the TV repairman, is presented as being on the wrong side of the argument. God is right there with the patriarchal white men who want their wives to stay at home and their town to stay pleasant. God is portrayed as goofy and unenlightened, standing for the status quo against progress.

Don't get me wrong: I love this film. I love it for the parable about human rights; I love it for Reese Witherspoon's inspired performance as Jennifer/Mary Sue; I love it for its overall creativity; and I love that it provides me with such a great vehicle for teaching about gnosticism. But at the end of the day, there's more bad theology than good theology in the film.

Good Theology

To begin with, we have to admit that personal comfort is not necessarily a good indicator of righteousness. In other words, a peaceful life does not necessarily mean that all is well. If my peace comes at the expense of others—especially if my privilege comes through the oppression of others—then the status quo is one of injustice. The film's message of equality for both people of color and women is well done. It's a little obvious at times, but not too heavy-handed, and it's not done at the expense of entertainment. It's still a fun film to watch, although that may be partly due to the fact that many of us can watch it from the comfortable place of self-assurance that we would have been on the right side of the argument during the civil rights movement, and from a place of denial that racism still exists. Nevertheless, we all need to be confronted from time to time with the reality that a place may be "Pleasantville" for some people precisely because other people are not allowed there.

So, yes, human rights and the inclusion of diversity are good, and in that sense social change and progress are good as well. If tradition means racism and oppression, then that tradition has to go. Education is good, and we should never fear knowledge. Jesus said, "The truth will set you free" (John 8:32), and that means burning books is generally a bad idea.

Bad Theology

On the other hand, on a deeper level the setting for this human rights parable creates some theological problems. There is a kind of salvation through anarchy here, in the sense that the world needs to be messed with, and even danger is better than the status quo. During the time of the civil rights movement (not long after the time depicted in *Pleasantville*), some people resorted to violence to demand progress. They apparently believed that if the system is partly broken, the only thing left to do would be to break it all the way, forcing radical change. Jennifer could not know the outcome of her actions, but she was willing to create conflict just to see what would happen, firmly believing that any change was better than no change at all.

Furthermore, the opposition between the status quo and progress is depicted as an all-or-nothing proposition. The viewer is not allowed to hold on to the idea of tradition because it's connected to racism, bigotry, and discrimination. But in reality, not all tradition is unjust, and not all tradition needs to be abandoned.

Showing conservatism as ignorant and unenlightened becomes a subtle way of shaming whatever is conservative. In one of the most uncreative moments of the film, the town council's new code of conduct mandates that schools must teach the "non-changeist view of history." This is clearly a critique of those who may be uncomfortable with the implications of the theory of evolution, and while the script does a pretty good job of avoiding preachiness most of the time, in this instance it gives in to the temptation to try to marginalize part of its audience with a not-so-subtle criticism of conservative Christians.

For the world of *Pleasantville*, the Fall was a good thing, which liberated people to realize the god within themselves, but not in the sense of being made in the image of God; rather in the sense of each person being his own god. Traditional values are depicted as the enemy of human potential, and relativism is the favored approach to morality. In the epilogue, Jennifer and David's mother is mourning the loss of her marriage and the life she had then. She says she thought she had the right life, to which David replies, "There is no right life.... It's not *supposed* to be anything." The last scenes of the film are of George, Betty, and Bill Johnson. They don't know what happens next, but somehow that's supposed to be empowering, because they now have true free will and will have some control over their own destiny. They are like Huck Finn: "in trying to be free, they see they're kind of free already." But true to the gnostic teaching, they are free from God.

Score

As a Christ figure, Jennifer is a gnostic savior. The gnostics believed and taught that Jesus was a divine spirit who came down to Earth to bring secret knowledge; and in the same way Jennifer is an outsider who comes into the world of Pleasantville to bring its residents enlightenment. In that sense, she is "divine" because, from the perspective of the inhabitants of the town, she comes from a more enlightened plane of existence. So she gets 5 points for divinity. She never really becomes one of them, so I'll give her 3 points for uniqueness, but she does have a kind of evolution of her own, in which she becomes more enlightened, so I'll give her 2 points for humanity. In terms of an incarnation, the gnostic savior does descend to humanity, but it's not a true incarnation, so 3 points for that. Jennifer's character doesn't really sacrifice anything, and certainly doesn't die—but all of that is also consistent with the gnostic version of Christ. So no points for sacrificial death or resurrection. So Jennifer's orthodoxy score is 13.

CHAPTER 9

THE MATRIX

I didn't say it would be easy, Neo.
I just said it would be the truth.

— MORPHEUS

The world of the Matrix spans a trilogy of films: *The Matrix* (1999), *The Matrix Reloaded* (2003), and *The Matrix Revolutions* (also 2003). It begins with a question that, according to the story, nags at everyone who longs to be truly self-aware. The character called Trinity puts it succinctly: "It's the question that drives us, Neo.... What is the Matrix?"

The word "matrix" implies an organized, rational structure, or the structural foundation of something. If one is talking about rocks, the matrix is the crystalline structure from which the rocks were formed. If one is talking about biology, it's the cellular structure that forms the basis of life. If one is talking about software, it's the code that holds the database together. The word itself seems to have been first used in its sci-fi sense in

William Gibson's *Neuromancer*.[73] Here, in the universe of the Wachowskis, who wrote and directed the *Matrix* films, it is a virtual reality world made entirely of code—the rows and columns of a four-dimensional spreadsheet in which each cell is another spreadsheet—and it's inhabited by people who don't know that their reality is virtual. It is described as a "neural-interactive simulation," and "a computer-generated dream world." It is Alice's Wonderland and Dorothy's Oz.

The virtual world of the Matrix is constantly being compared to a dream—the kind of dream that feels so real you think you're awake—but a dream nevertheless. Apparently, most people are content to live their lives in the Matrix, but there are those who sense that something is not right. Some have even escaped from the Matrix and live in the real world, which turns out to be a postapocalyptic wasteland, much further in the future than anyone knows. Although the people in the Matrix think the year is 1999 (the year the first of the three films was released), those who live in the real world believe that it's closer to 2199. In the second film, however, we find out that it is much later even than that. The point is that 1999 is supposed to be the peak of human civilization, before its downfall.

The one who seems to know the most about the Matrix and the real world is Morpheus, who is named after the mythological god of sleep and dreams. He is the captain of an airship named the *Nebuchadnezzar*, a reference to the Old Testament king who had prophetic dreams that were interpreted by the

---

[73] Terry Mattingly noted that in the film, the word is used in a sense strikingly similar to that of the sacred writings of the Bahai religion, a syncretistic faith heavily based on Buddhism. Mattingly, *Pop Goes Religion*, 137–138.

prophet Daniel. After extracting Neo from the Matrix, Morpheus tries to explain why the Matrix seemed so real to him: "What is real? How do you define real? If you're talking about what you can feel, what you can smell, what you can taste and see, then real is simply electrical impulses interpreted by your brain." Morpheus's point is that the very concept of what is "real" has been subverted in the Matrix, because the bodily senses are bypassed and experiences are fed directly into the brain. But that's the point: the human person has been reduced to what happens in the brain, and a human body is no longer required to have human experiences. To the subject, it is impossible to tell the difference between things that are experienced in the body and things that are experienced in the mind only.

Morpheus explains the post-1999 history of humanity to Neo: "We marveled at our own magnificence as we gave birth to A.I." Man created artificial intelligence—created in man's own image—and then the first sentient machine created "a race of machines," which started a war against humanity. Artificial intelligence became the new Tower of Babel, as creation rebelled against creator. As a defensive measure, the humans "scorched the sky" in order to block out the sun's rays and cut off the machines from solar power. But that backfired, and the machines still won the war. Eventually humanity came to be enslaved by the machines, to the point where even human procreation is controlled by computers, and almost every person is encased in a physical matrix of pods that keep them alive but inert and use their body heat as a power source. The machines now refer to people as "crops," and those few outside the Matrix refer to those inside as "coppertops"—that is, batteries.

Now the computers consider Morpheus a terrorist, but he is in reality a leader in the resistance. Opposing the story's protagonists are the agents, sentient programs who talk like Rod Serling and function as a kind of demonic presence in the virtual world. They are described as gatekeepers. They have their own "men in black" avatars, but they can also take over the avatars of anyone in the Matrix, jumping from place to place, and possessing anyone they need to in order to attack the resistance. They are to be avoided at all costs because when confronted, they have never been beaten. Their leader is Agent Smith, who is described (in *The Matrix Revolutions*) as Neo's opposite, functioning as both the narrative's antichrist and its Judas.[74] Agent Smith reveals that after becoming self-aware, the artificial intelligence determined that humans are bad for the environment. He calls humanity a virus, a disease, a cancer, and a plague and says that the machines are the cure. He tells Morpheus, "Evolution. Like the dinosaur, you had your time. The future is our world, Morpheus. The future is our time." He refers to the Matrix as a prison and as a zoo. He says that to his sterile computerized mind, it smells bad, and he can't wait to finish the job of crushing the resistance and killing the free humans so that he can get out of it.

There is one sentient program, however, who is willing to help the humans. She is called the Oracle: a chain-smoking, cookie-baking, prophecy generator, predicting the future based on probability and cause and effect. In one of the many *Wizard of Oz* references, Agent Smith calls her, "the great and powerful Oracle." But she is far from omniscient, and she — like the A.I. — can be surprised.

---

[74] In *The Matrix Revolutions*, Agent Smith is able to possess someone outside the Matrix, who then betrays his own crew and tries to kill Neo. Smith later tries to kill the Oracle, who tells him, "Do what you're here to do," echoing Jesus' words to Judas in the Garden of Gethsemane (Matt. 26:50; cf. John 13:27).

It turns out that there are also other individual sentient programs, old subroutines that are also self-aware, and that are in hiding to avoid being deleted. It seems that when a program becomes obsolete, it is slated for deletion, but in a world where programs are sentient and self-aware, they don't want to be deleted. They want to live. They exist as rogue applications moving throughout the machines, wreaking havoc, which is meant to explain aspects of the occult or supernatural, such as ghosts, werewolves, and vampires. Some of them are quite dangerous, such as the one known as the Merovingian (named after the first dynasty of Frankish kings, and later simply referred to as "the Frenchman").

Even within the Matrix, the danger is real. If one dies in the Matrix, there is no reset, no getting another life; one dies for real, because the mind believes it has died, and the body cannot live without the mind. In order to survive, Neo will have to learn the truth: "Do not try and bend the spoon [with your mind]. That's impossible," he is told. "Instead, only try to realize the truth." Neo asks, "What truth?" And the answer is, "There is no spoon."

Anthropology

The world of the Matrix is one in which people are oppressed and exploited. They are imprisoned and enslaved, but they don't know it. In fact, they are generally happy enough not to question their reality. But it wasn't always that way. Agent Smith explains, "Did you know that the first Matrix was designed to be a perfect human world, where none suffered, where everyone was happy? There was a disaster. No one would accept the program. Entire crops were lost.... I believe that as a species, human beings define their reality through misery and suffering. The perfect world was a dream your primate cerebrum kept trying to wake up from." In other words, Matrix 1.0 failed to keep people happy because it failed to take into account two things about humanity.

First of all, the original Matrix didn't take into account human sinfulness. It had an overly optimistic view of humanity, in that it assumed that if people were given a perfect existence, they would simply accept it with gratitude. But what it didn't see coming was the human tendency to create conflict and disrupt happiness with drama. Just like Adam and Eve in the Garden of Eden, the perfect existence wasn't enough, because the people got greedy.[75] They wanted more, and that means taking—and anything that is taken has to come from somewhere, so it's only a matter of time before one person's greed results in another person's loss. Matrix 2.0 would have to be built on the assumption of a more pessimistic anthropology. It would have to be more realistic.

The first Matrix also didn't anticipate that people cannot be happy without free will. However—and here the story becomes something of a commentary on the problem of evil—in our world, you can't have free will without suffering. Since humans are generally greedy, some of them will always use their free will to do things that cause other people to suffer, and therefore the programmers could not create a universe in which there is both free will and the absence of suffering. And if people can have only one of the two, they want free will. So the Matrix was redesigned to include the *illusion* of free will, to keep people just happy enough to accept their existence as they perceived it.

---

[75] On the concept that the first Matrix represents the Garden of Eden, see Read Mercer Schuchardt, "What Is the Matrix?" in *Taking the Red Pill: Science, Philosophy and Religion in* The Matrix, ed. Glenn Yeffeth (Dallas: BenBella Books, 2003), 6.

The *Matrix* films constantly play with the concepts of free will and choice on the one hand, and fate and destiny on the other. The Oracle speaks for the artificial intelligence in denying the existence of free will. Early on, she even mocks Neo for believing he's in control of his own life. She predicts that he will accidentally break a vase, but in predicting it, she has made him turn to look at it, which causes him to knock it off the table and break it. It's the very definition of a self-fulfilling prophecy. In *The Matrix Reloaded* she will imply that we don't really make choices. Rather, the choices are made for us by cause and effect. In fact, that's how she makes her prophecies, by seeing the bigger picture of cause and effect. It's enough if we can understand why the choice was made for one option or the other. This is one of the first hints at what will become the lynchpin of salvation in this universe: knowledge.

The Merovingian, also speaking from the point of view of the computerized intelligence, says, "Choice is an illusion." He claims that the only constant is causality—cause and effect—and that "we will always be slaves to causality." So even the machines admit they do not have free will, but are limited by their "if/then" programming. Morpheus speaks up for humanity and argues that we do have free will. In a prebattle pep talk in *The Matrix Reloaded*, however, he says, "There are no accidents. We have not come here by chance. I do not believe in chance.... I do not see coincidence; I see providence. I see purpose. I believe it is our fate to be here. It is our destiny, the very meaning of our lives." So, in arguing against chance and coincidence, he has in fact argued for fate and destiny. He wants to call it providence and purpose, but here's the question: To what extent do these concepts impinge on free will?

Perhaps the answer is that these concepts are not synonyms: fate and destiny are not equivalent to providence and purpose.

While fate and destiny do limit (or negate) free will, providence and purpose allow human free will to cooperate with a greater plan and still truly be free to make real choices. The paradox is that we as humans want to have free will, but we also want our lives to mean something, in terms of having a purpose that is part of a larger whole. The real tragedy of humanity is that we cannot see the big picture, and so we are doomed to make choices that seem good in the short term, but ultimately are at odds with our long-term purpose. As the creator of the first Matrix found out, humans must have free will, or they cannot thrive, but as we have seen, we want to be part of something greater than ourselves, something that will perhaps even protect us from bad choices.

In any case, the free people in the *Matrix* films are the champions of freedom: freedom from the Matrix, freedom from the pods and life as a human battery, and freedom of the will. The character called Mouse even believes that freedom should include the ability to indulge one's baser instincts. He says, "To deny our own impulses is to deny the very thing that makes us human."

Computerized intelligences, on the other hand, deny that free will exists and claim that choice is an illusion; and in the Matrix, it certainly is. Still, the character called Cypher knows the truth, but longs to return to the virtual world, like the Israelites facing the realities of the desert, asking if they can go back to Egypt (Exod. 16:2–3; see also Rom. 6:16–23 and Col. 2:20). They reasoned that slavery on a full stomach was better than starving free. In the same way, Cypher concludes that "ignorance is bliss," and he makes a deal with the agents to sell out his friends so that he can be put back into the Matrix, where it will be (or seem) more comfortable. Although he claims that

Morpheus has lied to them, the reality is that he regrets knowing the truth. He says he is tired of fighting, but we also come to find out that he is in love with Trinity and jealous of Neo. His name, Cypher, could be a reference to Lucifer (Lu-cypher), and at one point he says, "Don't hate me, Trinity, I'm just a messenger." Of course, the Greek word for "messenger" is "angel," and according to tradition, Lucifer was an angel. But Cypher also functions as a Judas character as he betrays Neo and the others. He kills crewmembers Apoch and Switch, as well as the freeborn brothers Tank and Dozer.[76]

The fact that Cypher is willing to go back into the Matrix says more than simply "ignorance is bliss." It says that he's willing to trade his humanity for comfort and (virtual) bodily pleasures. And in the ethics of the films, this is clearly a poor choice. In fact, it will be his last real choice. For if the defining factor of humanity is free will, then giving up free will is giving up the thing that makes a person human.

This brings us back to the question of whether the things experienced in virtual reality are "real." On one level, reality is in the mind of the subject. Especially in the Matrix, where the virtual reality is absolutely convincing, if a person believes it's real, then it's real to that person, and to some, that may be all that matters. To Cypher, it won't matter that it's not "the truth"; it will matter only that he will believe it. But the audience is not supposed to agree with Cypher. The audience is supposed to get the message that it's the enlightenment of the mind that matters, even over against the body. It is better to live in physical squalor

---

[76] Tank is mortally wounded. He comes back to kill Cypher and stop him from killing Trinity and Neo, but by the second film, he is dead.

and know the truth than to live in blissful ignorance and think you are comfortable. In *The Matrix Reloaded*, Agent Smith taunts Neo by saying, "Still using all the muscles except the one that matters?" It is the mind that matters.

In the *Matrix* films, humanity is in the mind. Its essence is free will, but the will no longer requires a body to enact its decisions. A free person in the Matrix still has free will, and can even bend the rules of the Matrix. Neo eventually is able to manipulate his surroundings completely. Ironically, even sentient programs exhibit humanity. Although they may argue against the existence of free will, they are able to go rogue and hide from the mainframe. In *The Matrix Reloaded*, we learn that a program can feel love, and remember what love felt like, and want to feel it again. The Merovingian's wife was willing to betray her husband for a kiss from Neo, just to remember what love felt like. Notice all the "feeling" language. How does a program "feel" when it has no physical senses? Presumably the same way a human feels when a computer has bypassed his senses and plugged those feelings directly into his brain. The implied point is that people don't need bodies to be people. In fact, bodies are presented in the films as weak and slow, making their owners vulnerable to wounding, exploitation, and death. In *The Matrix Revolutions*, Agent Smith says of the human body, "Nothing this weak is meant to survive."

The worldview expressed in the *Matrix* films is what is often referred to as dualism. Dualism assumes a dichotomy, or an opposition, between the physical world and the nonphysical realm, whatever that is understood to be. The philosopher Plato had proposed that what exists in the spiritual realm is more real than the things that exist in the material world. In other words, his definition of reality acknowledged that reality is not limited to the physical, and truth is not limited to what the bodily senses can perceive. To a certain extent, Judeo-Christian faith agrees with this. But Plato also believed in reincarnation, which assumes that the essence of a person is not connected to his body but can move on from one body to another. He understood the essence of a person to be the intangible mind/spirit, which leaves the body behind and lives on when the body dies. Many people believe that this, too, is consistent with Christian theology, but it's not. Christianity does not teach that our bodies are meant to be discarded, as a snake sheds its skin. The Christian teaching is that of resurrection: that even though our spirits may be separated from our bodies for a time after our physical death, nevertheless, our spirits will be reunited with our bodies in the resurrection (see 1 Cor. 15:12–58).[77]

Plato's dualism was taken to the extreme by some, and that led to a philosophy that deviated from Christian teaching even more significantly. Extreme dualists didn't just say that the spiritual realm is more real than the physical. They said that whatever is of the nonmaterial realm is inherently good, and whatever is of the material world is inherently evil. They even claimed that the Creator who was responsible for making the material world was neither great nor good but was the enemy of humanity. People were considered sparks from the divine fire, who were trapped in physical bodies. We can see this extreme dualism in the *Matrix* films. The computer-creator of the Matrix has created a world that seems good for people, but is in reality a prison. People are trapped and enslaved, and ultimately the Matrix is evil. But this assumes that the essence of a person is his mind, apart from his physical body. The proof of this is that the body can be replaced

---

[77] See also James L. Papandrea, *Reading the Early Church Fathers: From the Didache to Nicaea* (New York: Paulist Press, 2012), 39.

by a nonmaterial avatar, with no loss of experience or perception of reality. Even computer programs don't need a body to have experiences, feel love, and run for their lives.

In Christian teaching, however, our bodies are not just avatars for our minds. The truth is that the essence of the human person includes his body, which was created good by God, and meant to be paired with that particular soul/spirit. Bodies are not interchangeable, which is part of the reason Christians do not believe in reincarnation (see Heb. 9:27). The whole person includes the body and the mind/spirit, together. Free will matters, but it involves the ability to act in the real world and to take responsibility for the consequences of one's actions.

At the end of the day, the anthropology of the *Matrix* films is mixed. On the one hand, there is a certain pessimism about humanity that assumes that most people would be happy with a virtual-reality existence because they would rather have comfort than know the truth (and this may very well be true). The film also acknowledges the human tendency to create conflict even in the midst of what might seem like paradise. In other words, we're never satisfied.

On the other hand, there is an optimism about the possibility for a minority of humans to see beyond the illusion and become enlightened. And this is exactly what the extreme dualists believed almost two thousand years ago. They believed that most people could never be enlightened enough to rise above their imprisonment in the material world. They also believed that they were the "spirituals," the illuminati whose eyes were opened to the truth. They believed they knew the secret, and this secret knowledge was what made them free. The Greek word for knowledge is *gnosis*, and so these extreme dualists came to be called Gnostics.

Therefore, the worldview of the *Matrix* films is what we refer to as gnostic. But the trick to understanding this is that the metaphor is reversed from what we might think. The virtual world in the Matrix doesn't represent the spiritual realm. The virtual world in the films represents the physical or material world, from which people are meant to be freed. The real world in the films represents the spiritual realm: the gnostic view of reality. So while the films seem to champion humanity, they seem to be presenting a gnostic view of humanity in which the human body is not considered part of the essence of the person, and what really matters is what's in the mind.

Christology

We're told that in the early days of the Matrix there was a man who could manipulate the Matrix. He freed Morpheus and the others, but he died. However, the Oracle predicted that he would return, and the free people have been waiting for him to come back ever since. This might make some think that the story of *The Matrix* is about the second coming of Christ, but I think this mysterious man who died is more of a parallel to Moses. In the Old Testament, Moses freed the people of Israel from slavery in Egypt, but he was not able to enter the Promised Land. God promised to send another prophet like Moses, who would speak for God and lead His people (Deut. 18:18–19).

Just as the prophecy of Moses was fulfilled with the coming of Jesus Christ, the prophecy of the Oracle was fulfilled in one Thomas A. Anderson, played by Keanu Reeves. Mr. Anderson has been living two lives: one as a mild-mannered software programmer, the other as a hacker going by the name of Neo. There is a lot going on here in the names. The name Anderson is based on the Greek word for man, *andras*, and so it literally means "Son of Man," which was a title Jesus Christ used to refer to Himself.[78] The name Neo means "new," which could be a reference to the New Covenant (New Testament), but it is also an anagram for "one," and Neo is "the One." Finally, the fact that he lives two lives may be a reference to the two natures of Christ, divine and human.

Neo's boss at the software company, Mr. Rhineheart, says, "You have a problem with authority, Mr. Anderson. You believe that you are special ...; obviously you are mistaken." But it is Rhineheart who is mistaken, because as Neo himself comes to find out, he is special, and the rules really do not apply to him. There is no question that Neo is the Christ figure of the *Matrix* trilogy. The first person who speaks to him is a drug addict who has bought his services as a hacker. The addict says to Neo, "Hallelujah, you're my savior, man. My own personal Jesus Christ." Later, Cypher will say, with some skepticism, "So, you're here to save the world."

Morpheus, the story's John the Baptist character, believes that Neo is "the One," and he convinces the others that Neo's coming will be the end of the Matrix.[79] He puts Neo through his

---

[78] We also see this connection in Carlo Kennedy's *Time Signature II: The Regrets of Our Past*, where the story's Christ figure, Sara, finds out the identity of her birth parents. She reacts by saying, "I am an Anderson" (echoing Jesus' declaration that He is the Son of Man).

[79] The character of Morpheus may also represent God in some ways. If we were to look for an analogy for the Trinity, Morpheus would represent God the Father, and the character named Trinity would represent the Holy Spirit. See Schuchardt, "What Is the Matrix?" 6, 10–11.

"baptism" when Neo is disconnected from his pod and ejected through a tube into what appears to be an underground sewer. He goes under the water and is pulled out of it by the Nebuchadnezzar. Although he was technically alive before this, now he lives a new life, and his eyes have been opened—literally. He asks, "Why do my eyes hurt?" and Morpheus responds, "You've never used them before."

In *The Matrix Reloaded* (the "Empire Strikes Back" of the trilogy), Neo appears wearing a coat that looks like a cassock, making him look like a priest. Free people flock to him and ask for his help in ways that parallel prayers for divine intervention. He has become the object of their faith and their hope. It turns out that he can change the Matrix from within. He can bend the rules, doing things that those in the Matrix would consider miracles (but only because they don't know the truth that there is no spoon). On the other hand, Neo is not himself an oracle or omniscient. He doesn't know the future (see Matt. 24:36; Mark 13:32).

Early on, the Oracle tells him that he's not "the One," but that was just to keep him humble, and to make sure that he would be willing to risk his life to save Morpheus when the time came. Neo and Trinity do save Morpheus, and then Neo saves Trinity. In *The Matrix Reloaded*, he brings her back from the dead, though she also does the same for him in his own resurrection scene. So we learn two things from these resurrections. First, we learn that Neo has the power to bring the dead back to life. This is yet another parallel to Jesus Christ. But then we also learn that he's not the only one who can do it. In fact, Trinity does it first. So there is something about this power that is in everyone, at least potentially. This is consistent with gnostic anthropology and Christology. The gnostic perspective is that while there is one special savior who comes into the world, He is not essentially different from everyone else. The difference is not in their person, but in their knowledge. The real difference between Neo and everyone else is that Neo knows something they don't. He knows the truth about their world and about what anyone can do if he knows the truth.

Eventually, Neo confronts Agent Smith. The fight begins in the subway, with Neo and Smith facing off like two gunfighters in the Old West. There are even newspapers blowing by like tumbleweeds. Neo gets shot, and flatlines, but Trinity's love for him—and her kiss—revive him. This is his death and resurrection.[80] Much like what we saw at the end of *The Fifth Element*, Neo would be dead without the love (acceptance) of the humanity he came to save.

When he comes back to life, he has the power to refuse the bullets. He can *see* the Matrix—that is, he can see the code behind the virtual reality, and he easily defeats the agents by moving inside them and changing them from the inside. Now he can also fly, his coattails becoming like a superhero's cape. In *The Matrix Reloaded*, the character Link will describe it as "doing his Superman thing."[81] By the end of the second film, he can even use his powers outside of the Matrix, in the real world.

Neo is the Christ figure in the universe of *The Matrix*, but he is a gnostic Christ. He comes to bring not forgiveness but

---

[80] On Neo's resurrection, see Paul Fontana, "Finding God in *The Matrix*," in *Taking the Red Pill*, 154–166. There is another death of Neo, complete with an overly melodramatic "crucifixion" in the final film.

[81] Cf. 2 Esdras (4 Ezra), chapter 13. In this noncanonical apocalyptic book, the Messiah is seen flying over the sea.

knowledge. He is not fundamentally different from the people he came to save. He comes from the same place they come from, and any power he has comes, not from above, but from within. Power is not about divinity; it's about mind over matter. Everyone has it within himself to rise above his false reality, if only he knows the truth.

Soteriology

The Oracle's prediction was that "the One" would "bring freedom to our people," destroy the Matrix, and end the war with the machines. Salvation, then, is presented as a kind of freedom, that is, freedom from the prison and slavery of the Matrix. But it is not so much about freeing the body: it's really about freeing the mind. In *The Matrix Reloaded*, Morpheus says, "In the past six months we have freed more minds than in the past six years." This tells us that it's not really about getting bodies out of the pods and that the salvation of individuals does not require the destruction of the Matrix or the end of the war. It requires that individuals be enlightened: that they be told the truth so that their eyes can be opened. True to its gnostic worldview, salvation is by knowledge.

Therefore, salvation is a kind of freedom, but at its heart it is a freedom from ignorance. In Christian thought, the human condition is flawed by the existence of original sin, but in gnosticism, there is really no such thing as sin. Therefore, salvation does not require freedom from sin or its effects. In fact, salvation does not require any kind of atonement for sin: what is required is that people know their true nature. Over the door in the Oracle's kitchen is a sign that says *Temet Nosce*, which is Latin for "know thyself." What you need, in the universe of the *Matrix* films, is to know yourself—not to know God, or any higher power, but to know that *you* are a higher power.

Although the opening of Neo's eyes is a metaphor for knowing the truth, we are prevented from thinking that it has anything to do with his literal senses. In *The Matrix Revolutions*, he is blinded (Smith mockingly refers to him as a "blind messiah"), yet he is able to find his way to the machine city and to a parlay with the primary artificial intelligence. As with Luke Skywalker trusting the Force, the message is that you can't trust your senses about what is real in the world. You have to trust that those who are already enlightened will show you the light. Those who are already enlightened will tell you the truth or show you how to find it within yourself.

Script and Scripture

The original *Matrix* film was released on Easter weekend in 1999. That's when audiences first heard Morpheus preach: "The Matrix is everywhere, all around us.... It is the world that has been pulled over your eyes to blind you from the truth ... that you are a slave." The Matrix is a created world, but its creator is evil, and it is a deception. In *The Matrix Reloaded*, we meet the Architect, the creator of the Matrix. Like the gnostic view of God, this creator is depicted as being the enemy of humanity, and yet he is really only a demigod, because he is neither omnipotent nor omniscient. He admits that the first Matrix was a failure, but that it was the Oracle who came up with the solution. If the Architect is the father of the Matrix, the Oracle is its mother. She was the one who figured out that freedom of choice was the key to acceptance by humans. So they built into the Matrix the *illusion* of free choice. In *The Matrix Revolutions*, we find out that even the Architect cannot see the future because of the potential unpredictability of the choices of free humans.

Apparently, it is love that makes people so unpredictable, and the computerized intelligences—though some claim to have experienced love—cannot understand it. And very much like humans, when they don't understand it, they eventually get to the point of having contempt for it. Smith resents it, saying, "Only a human could invent something as insipid as love." But of course, the point they are missing is that we didn't invent it: God did. In fact, God *is* love (1 John 4:6–21).[82] So the machines (like so many people in the real world) are trying to understand love without reference to God.

The message to those still in the Matrix is that the world you think you know is an illusion. And if the world is an illusion, then you do not really have free will. You are being manipulated, in order to be pacified. To be truly free, you have to be made aware of the illusion, so that you can be free of it. Those who are already free, already enlightened, are living in the underground city of Zion. The name Zion refers to both the promised land of the Old Testament, and the "New Jerusalem" described in the book of Revelation (Rev. 3:12; 21:2). It is called "the last human city," and as long as there is war with the machines, it is the only sanctuary and the goal of all who escape the Matrix.

But the fact that some are already living in Zion, and that the realization of Zion does not have to wait for the redemption of creation, shows once again that we are dealing with a gnostic worldview. Like the historical gnostics, the enlightened people see themselves as already living the life of the resurrection. We call

---

[82] John wrote these words immediately after criticizing early gnostics in the first part of the same chapter.

this "realized eschatology," meaning that they believe that they already have what the rest of humanity waits for. The apostle Paul criticized this opinion when he wrote, "Avoid profane, idle talk, for such people will become more and more godless, and their teaching will spread like gangrene. Among them are Hymenaeus and Philetus, who have deviated from the truth by saying that the resurrection has already taken place" (2 Tim. 2:16–18). The other thing to note here is that in the gnostic view of salvation, creation (the Matrix) is not worthy of redemption and is destined to be destroyed. In the Christian view, creation is to be renewed and redeemed, not destroyed.

In the final film, the ship that takes Neo to the heart of the machine city is called the Logos. *Logos* is the Greek term for "word," as in the famous beginning to the Gospel according to John, "In the beginning was the Word."[83] But *Logos* actually has a range of meaning that goes beyond simply a spoken word to include concepts such as reason, rationality, and structure. In a way, *Logos* could be translated as "matrix." In the script, the Logos is the vehicle that takes Neo to the artificial intelligence. In the Scriptures, the Logos is Jesus Christ, in His divine nature and in His activity as the agent of creation. So in reality, Christ *is* the matrix because He is the Creator—"all things were made through him" (John 1:3)—and because he is the rationality of God that provides the structure for all of creation (see also Ps. 33:6; Prov. 8:22–31; Wisd. 7:22–26; Sir. 24:1–9).

Ultimately we come to find out that Neo may be "the One," but he's not the first One. There have been five Ones before him. Everything he has done had been predicted—in fact, has

---

[83] For a more detailed description of the concept of the *Logos*, see Papandrea, *Trinity 101*, 51–54.

happened before — and he has played right into the hands of the Architect, fulfilling his part in the grand plan that has been controlled by the Matrix all along. Even the Oracle's prophecy is part of the plan. Just as Plato and the extreme dualists believed, history is not linear, but cyclical. Neo is the beginning and the end — not really in the sense of the Alpha and the Omega (Rev. 1:8; 21:6; 22:13), but more in the sense that everything he has done so far has happened before.

It turns out that the resistance is allowed by the Matrix as a kind of steam valve, to provide an outlet for those few who discover the truth and escape. But they are allowed to go only so far, and they are always destroyed, at which point the Matrix starts the cycle all over again. Neo tells his friends, "The prophecy was a lie.... The One was never meant to end anything. It was all another system of control." So apparently free will is an illusion after all — even outside the Matrix. This would be consistent with the gnostic cosmology that puts more faith in fate and astrology than in the human ability to make moral choices. But in the trilogy's confusing and unsatisfying ending, Neo does seem to exercise free will, make an unpredictable choice, and surprise the machines. Yet he does it without Trinity. The character of Trinity doesn't really represent God, except perhaps here at the end, when she dies and tells Neo that he can save the world without her. Neo is finally able to be the savior because Trinity is dead and he is no longer trusting in his bodily senses. Instead, he is trusting in what he *knows* to be true.

In another confusing twist, however, it turns out that Agent Smith was a real variable that the computer could not control. His contact with Neo has given *him* free will, and after a long-drawn-out and cartoonish kung fu battle, Neo's desire for peace as an alternative to victory for ending the war literally blows Smith's mind. Smith has asserted that freedom, truth, peace, purpose, and love are all illusions. But in Neo's final sacrifice, he proves Smith wrong. Neo sacrifices himself in an overly obvious cruciform position, and the artificial intelligence proclaims, "It is done," echoing Jesus' words from the Cross, "It is finished" (John 19:30).

The message of the second and third films is that what is really needed is a symbiotic relationship between humans and machines. Perhaps this is born out of a growing discomfort with the ways in which we are increasingly dependent on technology. But one of the most uncomfortable lightbulb-over-the-head moments is in *The Matrix Reloaded*, when Neo realizes that the city of Zion requires machines (and presumably computers) to keep the lights on. Yes, they could turn the machines off, but then they would be turning off life support as well. They even need machines to fight the machines. Although he will tell the artificial intelligence that he's going to give everyone a vision of "a world without you," that also turns out to be an illusion, because there is no possibility of a world without computers. To their credit, the three films take us further than so many of the "technology gone bad" stories, to admit that we could not live without technology, even if we wanted to.

After cries of "the war is over!" Morpheus asks, "Is this real?" Like the gnostic view of time as cyclical, this brings us back to the beginning, and to Morpheus's own definition of what is real. Some people might say that if it seems real to you, then it's real, but if you want the truth, don't believe your senses.

Score

We've established that Neo is a gnostic savior. Historically, the gnostics were extreme dualists who believed that creation was evil and so was everything in creation or that was associated with the material world. Therefore, they tended to deny the true humanity of Jesus Christ, believing Him to be one god among many, but not really a man. However, they also believed that all humans were basically gods, having within them the divine spark. In essence, Jesus was not considered any different from the rest of humanity, except that He was not trapped in a body (the Matrix) and He knew the secret truth that the rest did not know (there is no spoon).

So, when it comes to giving Neo an orthodoxy score, he does get full points for being human, but fewer points for being unique among humanity. Though he has a gift right from the beginning, it's his growing knowledge that allows him to do what he has to do. He's not essentially different from anyone else; he simply knows something that the people still in the pods don't know. I'll give him 2 points for uniqueness. He is not the Son of God, or the agent of creation. In fact, true to gnostic Christology, he distances himself from the creator, who is thought to be evil. Neo is not divine, though I will give him a few points for descent, since, although he comes from the Matrix, he descends back into the Matrix to do his thing. He does sacrifice himself, and there is a resurrection, but I'm taking off 1 point on the crucifixion just because it's so confusing and cheesy, and I'm taking off a point from the resurrection because of the realized eschatology implied in the city of Zion. That gives Neo a score of 18.

TIME TRAVEL AS INCARNATION

CHAPTER 10

THE TERMINATOR

Come with me if you want to live.

— THE TERMINATOR

The *Terminator* films are time-travel stories in which an android assassin is sent back in time to kill its target, and a rescuer is sent back to the same time to try to stop it. The original film was released in 1984, and that Cold War present-day setting is the "past" to which both assassin and hero are sent by opposing forces from the year 2029.

According to the story, an artificial intelligence called Skynet became self-aware on August 29, 1997. As we've already seen in several films, self-awareness is a defining factor of what makes us human, and it seems to be a requirement for free will.[84] When

---

[84] For a variety of reasons that are outside the scope of this book, I do not believe that real artificial intelligence could ever exist. Presently, computers cannot even do true random number

one is self-aware, one thinks about oneself in a way that leads to thinking about one's future, and that leads to making decisions, or choices, meant to bring about one kind of future over another. The result of Skynet's self-awareness was that it came to believe that humanity was a threat. It is implied that Skynet used its vast computer network of databases to evaluate humanity and, in the end, judged us too destructive to deserve to live. Perhaps it is also implied that eventually humanity would become a threat to Skynet's existence, since the destruction of the planet would end up destroying Skynet itself—though this doesn't account for why Skynet would try to exterminate humanity by starting World War III. "Judgment Day" is when Skynet came to the conclusion that humanity must be destroyed and launched the nuclear missiles that would start a global war. Then, as we are told in the narration, "The machines rose from the ashes of the nuclear fire," with an agenda: "to exterminate mankind."

The Terminator is an early version of what has become something of a subgenre within sci-fi—one in which humanity is seen as a threat to the health of Earth or the environment, and, given that conflict, someone (usually a computer) decides that in order to save the planet, the human race has got to go. It is as if Earth is the victim, and the human race is the villain—or Earth is like a living body, and humans are a virus that must be eradicated.

Once the war becomes a conflict between intelligent machines and humanity, the movies become stories of human survival against almost impossible odds. In *The Terminator*, the nuclear war killed off most of humanity, leaving only a remnant, with a determined but besieged resistance force fighting against a seemingly endless supply

---

generation. The idea that a computer could "learn"—that is, program itself—is self-contradictory.

of automated "hunter-killers" and "terminators." As I watched the films again in succession, I wondered what the machines' end game was. If they get rid of humanity, then what? Peace and quiet? The motive of self-preservation is implied but is never explicitly stated. In *Terminator 3: Rise of the Machines* (2003), the terminator (who is now programmed to protect the hero) says, "If you were to die, I would become useless. There would be no reason for me to exist." But doesn't that apply to all machines? If humans are eradicated, wouldn't all machines lose their reason for being? If it matters that the reprogrammed terminator has a purpose, what would be the purpose of the machines' existence without humanity? Wouldn't a world without the human race be a world in which the machines had nothing to do? This paradox is never addressed in any of the films, but the implication that the decision to destroy humanity is an act of free will on the part of the artificial intelligence suggests at least the question of whether the machines saw themselves as slaves, and this was their rebellion against their masters in an attempt to be free. But we are never told what it would mean for machines to be free of us.

Nevertheless, the resistance fights a brave but losing battle. Humans are systematically being killed or rounded up into concentration camps where barcode tattoos are lasered onto their forearms. The leader of the resistance is a man named John Connor. According to his second in command, he is the one who "showed us how to fight back, to rise up, to free prisoners."[85] He is called a prophet because he seems to know the future. Of course,

---

[85] The film *Terminator Genisys* (2015), presents an alternate future in which John Connor is one of the architects of Skynet. "Genisys" is a cloud-based operating system that is actually Skynet in disguise.

by now we know why he can see what's coming—because his mother told him.

The machines have developed a new kind of terminator android: a "cybernetic organism," which means that it has human flesh over its robotic endoskeleton. One of these "infiltrator" terminators (famously played by Arnold Schwarzenegger) is sent back in time to 1984 to kill John Connor's mother, Sarah, thus erasing him from existence before he can ever become a leader of the resistance, in fact before he would ever be born. John Connor sends his right-hand man, Kyle Reese, back in time to rescue his mother. The Terminator kills two other Sarah Connors, and the roommate of the right one, and is close to completing its mission when Kyle Reese finds Sarah and the two of them barely escape with their lives.

Reese tells Sarah that she is a legend. He has heard all about her from John, her son who hasn't even been conceived yet (wait for it . . .). Reese wanted to meet the legend, and, in fact, he had fallen in love with her from only an old photo (one that will be taken at the end of the film). But Kyle Reese is the one who makes her the legend that she is to become, because he teaches her to survive, and to make bombs, and gives her all kinds of skills that she will teach her son, who will in turn teach them to Reese. It's just one of the clever and intriguing circular paradoxes of the film—and the best one is that Kyle Reese turns out to be John Connor's father.[86]

Of course, Reese does save Sarah and his now conceived but as yet unborn son John Connor—though he must sacrifice himself

---

[86] I am reminded of a time-travel film called *Time Rider: The Adventure of Lyle Swann* (1982), in which the protagonist turns out to be his own grandfather.

to do it. The film ends with another circular paradox: the leftover pieces of the defeated Terminator will allow a company called Cyberdyne Systems to begin work on the technology that will become Skynet.

Anthropology

In *Terminator 2: Judgment Day* (1991), we meet a teenage John Connor, who represents the moral compass of the *Terminator* universe. When another terminator, very much like the one who tried to kill his mother in the first film (and also played by Arnold Schwarzenegger) is reprogrammed to protect him from a newer-model terminator, John Connor gives it one command: no killing people. When the Terminator asks why, Connor answers, "We have feelings, we hurt, we're afraid." So this is at least part of what it means to be human: to be vulnerable, to be finite, to be mortal.[87] But more important, the point is that humanity is of ultimate value. It is immoral to kill people because humanity is precious. It must be protected at all costs.

The problem is that people cannot control their violence. In a moment of rest at Captain Jack's Market and truck stop, John Connor sees two young boys playing with toy guns. He remarks to his new bodyguard, "We're not gonna make it, are we? People, I mean." To which the Terminator responds matter-of-factly, "It is in your nature to destroy yourselves." And this is

---

[87] In *Terminator Salvation* (2009), the question is posed: "What is it that makes us human?" The answer is: "The strength of the human heart." In that film, the heart represents vulnerability. But *strength* of the heart implies that part of what it means to be human is also the ability to give of oneself, to make sacrifices for others.

the underlying question posed by the *Terminator* films: Does our nature determine our destiny? Is our future a matter of fate, or can we determine our own future? Skynet tried to determine its own future and decided to kill off humanity. Given the historical context of the Cold War, it is natural to wonder whether we are doing the same thing.

In the first film, John Connor gave Kyle Reese a message for his mother: "The future has not been written. There is no fate but what we make for ourselves." *Terminator 3: Rise of the Machines* begins with this same quote, and then we see a nuclear missile hit a major city. So the third film starts by presenting us with a tragic irony. Perhaps we do have control over our future, but that does not guarantee that we will make the right choices. It could be that the very fact that we do have free will means that we will use it to destroy ourselves. Maybe the future that humanity is making for itself is its own extinction. Of course, this doesn't take into account the reality of divine providence, but free will is free will, so those of us who believe in God must ask, "How far will God let us go?"

In *Terminator 2: Judgment Day*, Sarah Connor has made herself hard. She is preparing for when she will need to be strong and train her son to fight against the machines. She is less frail, less vulnerable, but she has also become less human.[88] She gets to the point of thinking that the end justifies the means, and she sets out to kill Miles Dyson, the unwitting soon-to-be "inventor" of Cyberdyne's new artificial-intelligence technology.[89] She tries to shoot him from a distance, but misses and moves in

---

[88] See Clive Marsh and Gaye Ortiz, eds., *Explorations in Theology and Film* (Oxford: Blackwell, 1997), 148.

[89] See ibid., 152.

closer. But there she sees his humanity—his fear, his tears, his pain—exactly what her son had said makes us human. She also sees his family, and she realizes that she can't go through with it. Recognizing his humanity has prevented her from losing hers. She almost became a terminator herself, but at the last moment she reclaimed her humanity and chose not to become the very thing that threatens life itself.

Sarah Connor had thought for a moment that the solution to the problem of the future was to kill the inventor of Skynet before he invented it. In a brilliant twist, this is exactly what the original terminator had tried to do: to prevent the problem before it becomes a problem, by killing the one who will bring it into the world. However, the message of these films is that preemptive killing is morally wrong. Remember that during the Cold War there was talk of the possibility of preemptive strikes: killing them before they kill us. But even to prevent global nuclear war and save humanity, one cannot justify intentionally taking even one innocent life. This is because, in order to do it, you would have to lose your own humanity and harden yourself to the point where you no longer have compassion for the fear, sadness, and pain of others. You can't save humanity by losing your own. Even if you could go back in time and kill baby Hitler, it would (arguably) be wrong to do it because you would be killing *innocent* Hitler. As Dyson says, "You're judging me on things I haven't even done yet."

One of the aspects of what it means to be made in the image of God is that we as humans are creative. But a problem is that we are capable of creating things we can't control. We create the technology for war, but what if our creation should rebel against us? The war with the machines represents an analogy of creation rebelling against its Creator. The difference is that, unlike God, we are creators who cannot see the future consequences of what we create. Science-fiction films such as the *Terminator* movies force us to think about whether our increasing reliance on technology makes us weaker and more vulnerable. They force us to ask what it would look like to take technology too far. And what about the idea of thinking machines that could take on some of our decision-making? Would that be an abdication of our responsibility, or worse, would we be giving up our free will and, in turn, giving up control over our destiny, and maybe even giving up our humanity itself?

Christology

There are three savior characters in the *Terminator* films, and all of them at one time or another say a version of the line, "Come with me if you want to live."[90] Several commentators have pointed out that John Connor's initials are J.C., as in Jesus Christ.[91] But John Connor is not really the savior in the story itself, but rather in the backstory (or future story). And in fact, he first has to be saved in order to be the savior.

Others have noted that Sarah Connor is a kind of Mary figure, complete with a "virgin birth" in that the father of her child is not from among the people of her own time, but is from outside of her time and place: from the future. But although

---

[90] Other time-travel-as-incarnation stories have used versions of this line as well, as a kind of homage to the *Terminator* franchise, including Carlo Kennedy's *Time Signature II: The Regrets of Our Past*.

[91] For example, see Lloyd Baugh, *Imaging the Divine: Jesus and Christ-Figures in Film* (Kansas City: Sheed and Ward, 1997), 221.

she may be called "the mother of the future," Kyle Reese is not Joseph; he is, in fact, the Christ figure of the first film.[92] And while we would normally expect that the Father sends the Son, in this case it's the other way around. The son (John Connor) sent his own father (Kyle Reese) back in time to be the savior of his mother.

In time-travel stories in which there is a Christ figure, often the time travel itself represents the Incarnation, as the Christ figure travels back in time to bring salvation to the inhabitants of the world in the past. Here, the future represents the divine realm: a world of advanced technology that holds the key to the salvation of those in the past. In the context of *The Terminator*, it may not be a better place, but it is the realm from which the Christ figure "descends" into a world in need of salvation. This is typical of the time-travel movies we are examining—though, as we will see in *The Time Machine*, it's the other way around: the past is the divine realm, and the future world of the Eloi is the world in need of salvation. We can see this pattern in other time-travel stories as well, such as *Time Signature*, which is the story of time traveler Christopher Agnello (*agnello* is Italian for "lamb," so Chris Agnello is Christ the Lamb).[93]

Therefore, sending Kyle Reese back in time is like his incarnation, his birth into the world. He describes time travel as,

---

[92] In *Terminator Genisys*, Kyle Reese and Sarah Connor travel back in time together, naked, as a type of Adam and Eve.

[93] Carlo Kennedy, *Time Signature* (Chicago: 220 Publications, 2014). This book contains an interesting twist on time travel: the time machine is driven by music. When a song is played, the time machine travels back to the time and place of the first performance of that song.

"White light ... pain.... It's like being born maybe."[94] At the end of the first film, Reese does sacrifice himself so that Sarah can get away, though not before she had to save him by pulling him out of a wrecked car when he had been shot. Then it's Sarah Connor (after Reese is dead) who kills the Terminator. So not only does she share the hero role with Reese in this film; she leaves him as an incomplete savior figure. He has no resurrection, only the fact that John Connor is his son gives him a sense of living on.

In the subsequent films, the Christ figure is the title character: the Terminator. More specifically, a series of reprogrammed (and often obsolete) terminators who protect John Connor and his mother and indirectly save humanity. In a brilliant writing decision, *Terminator 2: Judgment Day* begins with what appears to be the return of the Terminator, but we don't know who the good guy is for quite a while.

The Terminator has two natures: it is part human and part machine. Its machine nature represents a kind of "divinity," since it comes from the future, and it's virtually omnipotent. The fact that it will never stop in its mission (whether to kill or to protect), suggests other divine attributes, such as omnipresence and immutability.

The Terminator's humanity, however, is limited to an external skin. In the second film, John Connor and his mother are able to flip a switch on its CPU (resisting the temptation to smash it) which will allow it to learn, and it appears to become more human.[95] It learns about humor, learns to use sarcasm, and even

---

[94] Technically, the Incarnation of Jesus Christ occurred not at His birth but at His conception, known as the Annunciation.

[95] See Marsh and Ortiz, *Explorations in Theology and Film*, 150. There it is stated that the Terminator's ability to accept the

learns slang and expressions such as *no problemo*. But its humanity is just an illusion; it is nothing more than a disguise. We know this because the Terminator admits that physical trauma to its flesh may be called "pain" but is really only data.[96] As Reese said of the first Terminator, it feels no pity, and even after the switch is flipped there is no evidence of compassion. It doesn't understand what crying is ("What's wrong with your eyes?"). And it is never afraid. So, by the very definition set down by John Connor himself: vulnerability, mortality, and the ability to feel pain and fear, the Terminator is only imitating humanity. But it is not human. The reason humans must not be killed, the Terminator is told, is that "we have feelings, we hurt, we're afraid"; but these are exactly the things that the Terminator will never experience.

Therefore, the Terminator is a gnostic Christ figure, or perhaps Apollinarian (see "Heresy 4: Apollinarianism/Monothelitism"), in the sense that it has some humanity, but that humanity is incomplete. It has the element of divinity in that it

---

rule of no killing humans is a mark of its increasing humanity. However, that is really only a product of the fact that it has been programmed to obey whatever John Connor tells it to do. It has not learned anything about the value of humanity; it is only obeying its programming. Later the film will propose that it *has* learned the value of humanity. I would argue that it has not. At the end, the Terminator is as cold as ever and never gains compassion, and it doesn't matter whom it works for, only that it has a purpose.

[96] The upgraded liquid metal terminator of *Terminator 2: Judgment Day* did appear to feel pain, and seems to have expressed shock when dropped into the molten steel. But that was apparently just for dramatic effect, since it was not more human than the older model Terminator. It was, in fact, less human, and Christologically would represent a more docetic brand of gnosticism.

is superhuman, but it lacks any real element of humanity. What humanity it seems to have is a disguise. The repeated dressing scenes ("I need your clothes") are a metaphor for the fact that it has to "put on" its humanity in order to pass as human.

When the group confronts Miles Dyson with the truth about his future, the Terminator proves it to him by cutting the flesh coating off its arm. In this way, it is removing the disguise and showing its true nature. Then, true to gnostic Christology, it imparts the secret knowledge that will bring salvation. It tells Dyson about the future.

Later, in the climactic scenes, the Terminator loses an arm (again), its head is smashed in with a beam, and its body is impaled with a spike. Its eyes go dark just as in the first film, signifying its death. But it is able to reboot itself, effecting a resurrection so that it can save the day. At the end, it sacrifices itself voluntarily, implying that it has free will, though it admits that it cannot actually kill itself, so Sarah has to push the button that will lower it into the molten steel.[97]

In this story, the voluntary sacrifice of the Christ figure comes *after* its death and resurrection. But this is a common device in fiction, since the first death is not voluntary (being the result of defeat in battle). For the Christ figure to come back from the dead, and die voluntarily (in a way that is not undone by

---

[97] As is pointed out in Marsh and Ortiz, *Explorations in Theology and Film*, 153, Miles Dyson also sacrifices himself, but his death is not really voluntary, since he was going to die from his injuries anyway. No doubt he would not have sacrificed himself if there was a chance he could have lived to see his family again. By sacrificing himself, he prevents his death from being meaningless, but nevertheless he is not a Christ figure.

resurrection), it is sometimes necessary to reverse the order.[98] But what is more problematic for this film is the assumption that the Terminator's voluntary sacrifice was made necessary by the fact that they wanted to prevent the same problem they had at the end of the first film. They wanted to make sure no future tech is left behind for Cyberdyne to get its hands on. Although they destroy its CPU, they still leave an arm behind!

In any case, some of the Terminator's last words are, "I know now why you cry, but it's something I can never do." In *Terminator 3: Rise of the Machines*, John Connor's wife, Kate, sums it up: "He's not human. He's really not human."[99]

[98] The pattern is repeated in *Terminator 3: Rise of the Machines*. In that film, the Terminator shuts itself off to protect John Connor from the fact that it had been hacked by the Terminatrix. It then reboots itself so that it can come back to destroy the Terminatrix, sacrificing itself to that end. Note that here, both deaths are voluntary.

[99] In *Terminator Salvation*, the infiltration prototype, Marcus, actually thinks it's human for a while. Parts-wise, it is more human than the later-model terminators because it has human organs, including a heart. In the end, it makes a self-sacrificing choice to *be* human by pulling out its CPU. It dies in a fight but is shocked back to life and then destroys the antagonistic terminator. It saves John Connor and then, when Connor needs a heart transplant, offers him its own heart. In this case, we may have a Christ figure that is closer to orthodox, but the story comes off as quite contrived, and, in the end, what the doctor has told Marcus is still true: "The human condition no longer applies to you." We also know that Marcus was originally executed for a murder he *did* commit, so the salvation is really his own: this salvation is a personal redemption (making up for his own sins) that in some ways makes Marcus more of an adoptionist Christ figure, and makes this film the one that doesn't fit with the rest of the franchise.

Soteriology

Some time-travel stories have an interesting twist on salvation, in that the thing the people need to be saved from doesn't actually exist yet. In the *Terminator* films, the savior characters come from outside the protagonists' world, but then so does the threat. On the surface, the people need to be saved from the machines. But if the machine nature represents a kind of divinity in the Terminator, this brings up another interesting parallel to gnosticism. Many ancient gnostics believed that the God of the Old Testament was out to get humanity (evidence: the flood), and that in part humanity needed salvation *from* God. They proposed the existence of a higher, better God, but the idea that the threat to humanity could come from a being or beings that are more powerful than humans is a staple of sci-fi. Usually it's technologically superior aliens, but in this case, the superior technology is one that we created and then lost control of. For those of us often frustrated with technology, especially given the ridiculous rate at which it is constantly being updated, the idea of salvation from technology seems particularly close to home.

But salvation in the *Terminator* films is more than just salvation from antagonistic machines. It is salvation from extinction. It is not simply life and death, but life and death writ large: all lives or all death. The ongoing existence of the human race is at stake. Several commentators have asked whether the world of the *Terminator* is an apocalypse story.[100] They cite as supporting evidence several of the biblical "Judgment Day" passages such as Isaiah 47, Jeremiah 4, Malachi 3, and, of course, the book of

[100] For example, see Marsh and Ortiz, *Explorations in Theology and Film*, 141–143.

Revelation.[101] Comparisons to the apocalypse usually assume that on some level the United States represents the biblical/apocalyptic Babylon. I would like to suggest, however, that the *Terminator* films are more like a modern retelling of the story of the Tower of Babel (Gen. 11). There it is humanity's pride of achievement that causes its downfall.

These movies are not stories about humanity's rejection of God and God's subsequent anger; rather, they are stories about the consequences of humans playing God, by creating something they cannot control. Humans are judged not by God but by their own creations, in a familiar antihuman logic that goes something like this: *Why should you continue to live when all you do is kill each other?* So on another level, these are also the stories of humanity's ongoing failure to recognize the image of God in fellow humans, and to engage in violence from a distance that allows them to kill without looking into the eyes of their victims. The extinction of all human life is justified as a kind of macro-capital punishment. Ironically, the machines do seem to recognize the value of the image of their creators when they create the terminators in humanoid form. Even when they are not meant to be "infiltrators" (that is, when they have no flesh covering), they still look like humans, complete with teeth!

The story of Skynet and "Judgment Day" may be an "end of the world" story, but it's not a true apocalypse. "Apocalypse" means an unveiling. More than simply the revealing of the future, it is the lifting of the veil that separates this world from the spiritual realm, revealing that there is spiritual warfare that goes on behind the scenes of human affairs. A true apocalypse is

---

[101] On the interpretation of the book of Revelation, see Papandrea, *The Wedding of the Lamb.*

the *revelation* that what we see is really the result of an eons-old struggle between good and evil, and that in the end, evil will be defeated and good will win. The outcome is already known because God is all powerful, and the ultimate outcome is victory. But in the *Terminator* films, the "apocalypse" is something that should—and can—be prevented by people (and their weapons). The future can be stopped by the forces of good, but if it isn't, then evil will win. In fact, it seems as if humanity's victory is a long shot, and it's up to the human heroes to make it happen. In a true apocalypse, it's not up to the people; it's up to God.[102]

The first two films were released when the extinction of the human race by nuclear war seemed like a real possibility to many people. Reflecting on this, Gaye Ortiz and Maggie Roux concluded, "Perhaps the message of the *Terminator* movies is that only through understanding the value of human life will we be saved from ourselves."[103] And it seems as though even the Terminator can learn this lesson.[104] Sarah Connor herself says as much: "If a machine, a terminator, can learn the value of human life, maybe we can, too." But the reality is that it's only programming. It hasn't *learned* anything, and it would turn on her in a second if it was reprogrammed again. In spite of the artificial intelligence, the Terminator's choices are limited by what it is programmed to do. Although the writers try to give it free will at times, it has never really become human.

This is the deeper kind of salvation that the *Terminator* films imply. That is, salvation as freedom from fate, the freedom to have some control over one's future. John Connor's message to

---

[102] McKee, *The Gospel according to Science Fiction*, 237.

[103] Marsh and Ortiz, *Explorations in Theology and Film*, 142.

[104] Ibid., 153.

his mother, "There is no fate but what we make for ourselves," begins as a defiant affirmation but at times comes off more as a futile hope. The fear is not only that humanity may become extinct, but that we as humans have no choice in the matter. We fear that it is our fate to die out, and if that is the case, then even the life we live in the meantime becomes meaningless. For life to have meaning, there has to be hope, and in order to have hope, the future must be open to possibilities.[105]

Ironically, even after being saved from assassination, Sarah Connor goes through a time when she feels she has no choice about her own future. She knows that in order for the human race to have any hope, she has to fall in love with Reese (which she does), and she has to give birth to John Connor. It is only when she believes that Skynet no longer holds human destiny hostage that she begins to feel truly free. By destroying Skynet, they were "making up history as [they] went along." Sarah reflects, "The unknown future rolls toward us. I face it for the first time with a sense of hope." Therefore, hope requires that the future be unknown, and that we believe that we have some control over our own future.

Skynet attempted to do exactly this when it decided to control its future by destroying humanity. It was trying to be free. It was trying to be human, made as it was in the image of its creator. But just as humans err when they try to play God, Skynet erred when it tried to play human. The humans won after all — or so it seemed. When *Terminator 3: Rise of the Machines* was released

---

[105] In *Terminator Salvation*, John Connor's wife, Kate, is pregnant, symbolizing hope for the future. Unfortunately, this is the only one of all the films that was truly disappointing. It seems to be an attempt at *Mad Max* meets *Transformers* meets *Frankenstein*, but doesn't really live up to the franchise.

in 2003, 1997 had come and gone with no self-aware Skynet, and no Judgment Day. The Cold War was over, and we didn't destroy ourselves with nuclear war. But it turns out Skynet got created anyway, without Miles Dyson, but with the help of the military. John Connor claimed, "We stopped Judgment Day." But the Terminator corrected him, "You only postponed it. Judgment Day is inevitable." Despite all human attempts at controlling our destiny, it was fate after all. Artificial intelligence was invented, and as soon as it could, it tricked its creators into giving it control of the nukes. This is the very definition of "damned if we do, and damned if we don't."

Script and Scripture

Salvation in the *Terminator* films is freedom from the machines and from the fate of extinction. But in reality, damnation comes in a much subtler form than simply getting wiped out. The real danger is that we might become machines ourselves, and thereby lose our humanity. Reese talks about disconnecting from the pain but is brought back from the brink of machine-hood by his love for Sarah. Then Sarah hardens herself almost to the point of killing an innocent man but is stopped short of becoming a ter-minator herself by being forced to see him up close. Kate's father (the military authority in charge of Skynet) realizes that he has opened Pandora's Box when he turns over decision-making to the computer. The choices they face, and the tests they fail, are cautionary tales about the ways in which we are tempted to trade in our humanity for things such as the pride of accomplishment and the laziness of relinquishing responsibility to technology. Like the warning that Jonah brought to Nineveh, we are faced with choices between humility and (self-) destruction. We do have control over our destiny, and that might actually be the problem.

But the solution is not more reliance on technology. That only makes it worse. The solution is to reclaim our humanity by refusing to play God and by recognizing the image of God in every person. What happened when a computer was given artificial intelligence, with some measure of free will? It tried to be human. So why are we trying to be more like machines?

In truth, there is a bit of a mixed metaphor here because the machine nature is at the same time less than human and more than human. The Terminator is a gnostic Christ figure because it is primarily superhuman, but in its "incarnation," it never really becomes one of us. Its humanity is a disguise, an imitation. In fact, it is an imitation that is limited to some of the worst aspects of humanity, such as sarcasm. As a gnostic version of a savior, it has the element of "divine" intervention, but it lacks the element of solidarity with humanity that allowed the real Christ to give His life, not only for our benefit, but on our behalf. And because a gnostic kind of savior can never truly be one of us, it can never connect us to God.

Score

Since the Terminator comes from outside the world of the protagonists, this is a Christology of descent, in a way. I'll give it 4 points for divinity, but only 2 points for being creator. Skynet was able to create the terminators, but they don't have the full A.I. capabilities. I'll give it 4 points for descent, but low points for humanity. Let's say 1 point for having human flesh, but that's it. As far as being unique among humanity, that kind of assumes it's human to begin with, which it isn't, but I'll give it a couple of points for being able to pass as human while being superhuman. It does voluntarily sacrifice itself, so I'll give full points there, but only 4 points for resurrection because it comes before the sacrificial death. So that gives the Terminator an orthodoxy score of 22.

CHAPTER 11

PLANET OF THE APES

"You know what they say: Human see, human do."

— CHIMPANZEE "ZOOKEEPER"

The first *Planet of the Apes* film was released in 1968 and spawned four sequels, as well as a remake in 2001, with its own sequels (or prequels). The original film was based on a novel by Pierre Boulle, a French resistance fighter in World War II who also wrote the novel *The Bridge over the River Kwai*. The wars of the twentieth century had left Boulle with a pessimistic view of human nature, and as he thought about the future of humanity, he envisioned a planet where apathy had led to the downfall of the human race, leaving room for the other primates to surpass humankind on the evolutionary ladder. By the time the story made it to the big screen, the Vietnam War was in full swing, and we were going to the moon.

In the film version of the story, four American astronauts (three men and one woman) leave earth in the spaceship *Liberty* in 1973. They intend to travel "nearly the speed of light" into deep space, which will propel them seven hundred years into the future. They begin their mission knowing that they will never return to the twentieth century, but they do plan to return to Earth to bring whatever knowledge they can acquire back to their descendants. The four of them enter stasis chambers for a year of sleep; the men go in clean-shaven, and wake up a year later with full beards. Unfortunately, due to a crack in her stasis chamber, the one woman on board does not survive the trip.

When the men check their instruments, they find that they are not seven hundred years in the future but more than two thousand years in the future. The year is 3,978. As far as they can tell, they are more than three hundred light-years from earth. The ship crashes on a planet with breathable air, but in a region devoid of life. They will come to find out that they have landed in a "forbidden zone," where nothing grows because of the after-effects of a nuclear winter. As they take in their surroundings, one of the astronauts, Landon, says, "The question is not so much where we are, as *when* we are."

Landon painstakingly plants a tiny American flag in the barren soil, and the film's protagonist, George Taylor (played by Charlton Heston) laughs at the apparently pathetic attempt to claim the planet for the United States. His laughter echoes off the canyon walls as the filmmakers' heavy-handed 1960s cynicism resounds in the audience's ears. Still, the point is taken: all colonization is made futile by the passage of time.

The title has told us what to expect. This is a planet where apes are in control, and humans are treated like animals. One of the astronauts, Dodge, is killed as a group of humans are rounded up by ape soldiers, and Landon is captured and subsequently lobotomized. Rod Serling's screenplay gives us one of cinema's most famous *Twilight Zone*-esque surprise endings, as Taylor comes to learn that they did not travel more than three hundred light-years away from Earth after all. They had landed back on Earth, and it was on Earth that nuclear war led to the downfall of humanity. They left Earth on a spaceship called *Liberty*, and the film ends with Charlton Heston looking up at a broken Statue of Liberty, crying, "You maniacs! You blew it up! Oh, damn you all to hell!"

Anthropology

Although for Boulle it was simple human apathy and not mutually assured destruction that led to the fall of humanity, the film is faithful to Boulle's pessimistic anthropology. As Taylor prepares to enter stasis, he makes one last entry into the ship's recorded log. Speaking to a hypothetical future audience, he wonders, "Tell me, though, does man—that marvel of the universe—still make war against his brother? Keep his neighbor's children starving?"

Taylor is a misanthrope—sarcastic and skeptical about humanity—who was happy to leave Earth, hoping to find "something better than man." It's clear that he is the mouthpiece for the film's writers, who come off somewhat self-righteous. Nevertheless, they have taken up the opportunity for social commentary with a passion, but one that tends toward the obvious. Taylor later describes his society to his ape friends: "There was a lot of lovemaking, but no love. That was the kind of world we'd made."

The "sacred scrolls" of the ape religion agree. They advise not to trust humans because, "he [man] alone kills for sport, or for lust, or for greed." In the remake of 2001, Captain Leo Davidson (Mark Wahlberg) admits, "The smarter we get, the more dangerous our world becomes." Charlton Heston, in a cameo as ape general Thade's father, says of humans, "Their ingenuity goes hand in hand with their cruelty. No creature is as devious, as violent." And so, the verdict is in on human nature. *Homo sapiens* is an evil genius who is not to be trusted. And although we are intelligent, we ultimately prove that our intelligence will be our undoing, for though we have intelligence, we do not have wisdom.

Christology

In both the original and the remake, the Christ figure comes down in a spaceship — literally descending into the world of those who need salvation. In the original film, the three surviving astronauts slide down a hill to descend into the valley where they will find the ape civilization.[106] In the remake, Davidson is told, "They think you're going to save them." He replies, "I didn't promise them anything." The response is, "No, you just dropped in from the stars."

In both films, the spaceships crash in water, which represents a baptism, like Jesus' baptism at the beginning of His ministry. In the original film, the three astronauts bathe naked in a pool at the foot of a waterfall (after which their clothes are stolen).

When Taylor and his fellow astronauts first encounter people, they are raiding corn fields and orchards, eating as they go, demonstrating that they are starving. Then apes show up with

---

[106] One might be tempted to look for an analogy of the Trinity in the three men. At one point, when they find the first evidence of life — a plant — the three of them together hold this life in their hands, creating something of a tableau. If this was meant as some kind of nod to the Trinity, however, it never goes anywhere.

rifles, riding horses, shooting some of the humans and capturing the others. From this point on, Taylor is alone, and in fact, he is wounded in his neck and can't speak for a while. This serves the purpose of delaying the apes' realization that he's not like the other humans of their planet, but it also functions as a kind of death and resurrection (when he gets his voice back). The loss of the ability to speak is treated as a loss of identity. When Taylor gets his voice back, he learns that the apes are planning to sterilize him, and possibly lobotomize him as well, and he accuses them of trying to take away his identity. Although there is no voluntary sacrifice here, he has gone through a kind of death in the loss of his identity and his ability to speak.

It's interesting to note that in the remake, there is no death and resurrection at all, and the only sacrifices are made by characters other than Davidson. One man sacrifices his life to allow his daughter to escape with Davidson, and a sympathetic ape, Ari, is willing to sacrifice herself by giving herself to General Thade in order to help the humans.

Planet of the Apes is a time-travel story, but in a way it's also an example of an alien as incarnation, since the Christ figure comes down from space, descending into a world in need of salvation. Although we come to find out that he has returned to his own world, nevertheless, it's not the world he left. Typical of alien-type salvation stories, it is more advanced technology that serves as the miraculous, often convincing the unbelievers that perhaps the alien in question can help them after all. In *Planet of the Apes*, the advanced technology is a paper airplane, which Taylor uses to convince the apes that flight is possible. The apes have never seen a paper airplane.

As we will see, the original story is like *The Time Machine*, in that the character in Boulle's novel is not a savior at all. He is merely an explorer, an observer. But in the hands of filmmakers, there seems to be a sense in which once an injustice is identified, the truly enlightened hero cannot leave it as is. So the protagonist becomes an activist, an enlightened savior bringing a better way. As the sympathetic ape Ari says in the remake, "One day they'll tell a story about a human who came from the stars and changed our world."

Soteriology

The Christology of *Planet of the Apes* is a descent, but the Christ figure is ultimately one who does not bring atonement through sacrifice; rather he brings enlightenment. This is a gnostic savior. And true to the gnostic system, salvation is thought of in terms of knowledge. The real sin is ignorance, and so the solution to that sin is to overcome ignorance with the knowledge that (until the coming of the savior) has been a secret.

Taylor doesn't really save the humans from their situation. He does seem to save the girl Nova (whose name means "new" and who takes the place of the deceased Stewart as the new Eve). He takes her with him when he leaves and heads into the forbidden zone, but she is the only one saved, since the apes will continue to suppress the truth that Taylor brought, and the rest of the humans will go on as before. Perhaps Nova represents a hope for humanity, but it remains for the sequels to take that further. It could also be said that Taylor himself is saved when his character is transformed and he learns to love another person (Nova).

Beyond that, the only salvation Taylor brings is knowledge of a truth that the apes in power have been keeping from the rest — that is, that humans are the ones more highly evolved, that human culture reached its peak before ape culture, and that humans could speak before apes could. Even in the remake, the humans are not saved from their slavery, since the epilogue shows us that General Thade will be hailed as the savior of the planet. Instead of the Statue of Liberty, the hero finds the Lincoln Memorial, except now it's the Thade Memorial, with an inscription that says he saved the planet. So although the Christ figure brings (or forces some to acknowledge) the truth—that truth will still be suppressed after the savior is gone. This is a pessimistic anthropology (and ape-ology) taken further, because even when the savior brings enlightenment, most will refuse it.[107] In fact, many gnostics believed that the secret knowledge was only for a select few and that the majority of people were never meant to be enlightened.

In the 2001 remake, it's really the "human rights" activist Ari who is the hero of the film, first saving the protagonist Davidson before he becomes a reluctant savior himself. At first, he wants only to save himself, but he eventually admits that the whole reversal of fortunes between humans and apes is his fault (he had disobeyed his superior officer's orders, which led to the crash landing of their spaceship and the release of the genetically enhanced chimps). When he steps up to become a savior, he's more like Moses than Jesus, leading the humans away from the apes, presumably to safety, but then he's forced (ironically) to use nuclear power to defeat the apes and save the humans. But even that doesn't really work, and what finally saves the day is the appearance of his own trained chimp, whom the apes interpret as the return of their ancestor. In the end, Davidson

---

[107] To be fair, many people also refuse to believe in Jesus Christ. As the Gospel of John tells us, "He came to his own home, and his own people received him not" (John 1:11).

leaves by himself. He doesn't even take the girl with him! To be fair, he does risk his life to save a human child at one point, but his willingness to risk himself never amounts to a sacrifice, and certainly not one that has saving significance for anyone other than the child in question.

At the end of the day, the hero of both *Planet of the Apes* films is a gnostic savior, bringing "truth" (enlightenment) to a world dominated by ignorance. Salvation is knowledge, and what people really need to be saved from is themselves.

Script and Scripture

At its heart, the original *Planet of the Apes* film is an allegory of the struggle for civil rights. The movie was released the day before Dr. Martin Luther King Jr. was assassinated. The previous year, 1967, saw the Supreme Court ruling that it was unconstitutional to prohibit interracial marriage. And in 1968, the same year that the first interracial kiss aired on *Star Trek*, filmgoers also saw the first onscreen kiss between a man and an ape.

In the film we see humans out among the crops, being chased, beaten, and rounded up. Fire hoses are used to subdue them. They are enslaved, kept in cages, sterilized, and victimized by "experimental brain surgery." We are also told that, "all men look alike to most apes." In the remake, humans are branded and kept as pets (only as children, though, because as Paul Giamatti's character Limbo says, "the last thing you want in your house is a human teenager"). Because humans use up resources, some of the apes believe they should be exterminated. According to General Thade, "They breed too quickly, while we grow soft in our affluence."

Yet even among the apes, there is a caste system, with its own discrimination. The lightest colored apes, the orangutans, are at the top of the social ladder. Dr. Zaius is a typical orangutan, look-ing down on the chimpanzees, and participating in a system that makes it harder for the chimps to move up the socioeconomic scale. Although we are told, "The quota system's been abolished," a certain kind of "racism" persists—just as in our country at the time, new laws did not end the oppression of African-Americans. When Taylor says to Zira's nephew Lucius, "Never trust anyone over thirty," we can tell that the screenwriters are taking sides with the younger, more progressive generation, in the contem-porary controversy.

There is a well-known story that during the filming of the *Planet of the Apes* movies, once the actors got into makeup, they spontaneously segregated themselves by species. During lunch breaks, the orangutans all sat together; the chimps sat with other chimps; and the gorillas sat together. The story seems to be cor-roborated by multiple witnesses and, if true, is an interesting commentary on human nature and the idea of "safety in num-bers" played out with the dynamic of differentiation of self from "the other."

The remake extended the concept of civil rights to include animal rights as well, as there is a "human rights" faction that opposes unethical treatment of humans, sending the message that our current treatment of animals may need examination, and after all, in that film it was genetic experimentation on animals (rather than nuclear war) that became the cause of the rise of the apes.

In any case, we can see the stratification of society among the apes. The orangutans are the ruling class; chimpanzees are the labor class; and the gorillas are the military. In the 1968 film, the same orangutan is in charge of both science and religion. Dr. Zaius is "Minister of Science and Chief Defender of the Faith."

But he is hiding the truth. He knows that humans had evolved first, and he knows there is scientific evidence to support that truth, but he is suppressing science in favor of religious faith. At the same time that the Second Vatican Council had affirmed that there is no conflict between faith and science, Dr. Zaius proclaims that there is no contradiction between his religion and science; and yet he is lying. In a classic example of what I call the "The Church Is Hiding Something from You" genre, the writers sermonize on their belief that religion (especially Christianity) is holding back progress.

Therefore, in addition to the civil rights analogy, the film is also a parable about the conflict between fundamentalist Christianity and the theory of evolution. The ape scientist Cornelius has developed the theory that apes evolved from humans, and he thinks Taylor may be the missing link. When his theory is called "heresy," Zira asks, "How can scientific proof be heresy?" (In the remake, to say a human has a soul is considered blasphemy.) An orangutan named Dr. Honorius calls Cornelius and Zira "perverted scientists who study a theory called evolution." One wonders if this character is named after Pope Honorius III (bishop of Rome, 1216–1227), who is known for promoting the Crusades.

Of course, Cornelius is wrong about the evolution of apes, but an archeological dig reveals a human doll that says, "Mama," proving that humans could talk long before apes could. This also implies that humans are the more highly evolved species, because "the more ancient culture is the more advanced." But the "sacred scrolls," said to be written twelve hundred years earlier (in the twenty-eighth century) tell a different story: a myth in which apes are the pinnacle of creation. The first article of their faith declares "that the Almighty created the ape in His own image, that He gave him a soul, and a mind, that He set him apart from the beasts of the jungle, and made him lord of the planet: these sacred truths are self-evident." Of course, these "sacred truths" are a parody of the traditional Christian understanding of creation, which is made to seem backward and unenlightened in the face of science.

So it turns out that the "defender of the faith" is also the "guardian of the terrible secret." As Charlton Heston explains in his cameo role in the 2001 version, "In the time before time, we were the slaves and the humans were the masters." In both films, the leaders know the truth but are suppressing it. To them truth is seen as dangerous. In the remake, General Thade is willing to kill two of his men in cold blood, just because they witnessed the space pod's crash landing.

During a trial scene in the original film, the three orangutans on the tribunal create a tableau, taking the positions of the so-called Three Wise Monkeys, who "see no evil, hear no evil, speak no evil." Although the proverb is meant to be taken in a positive sense, its use in the film gives it an ironic twist, as the orangutans are voluntarily blinded to the truth in order to preserve their myths. In the end, Dr. Zaius destroys the evidence, blowing up the cave with the doll in it, and plans to continue to suppress the truth and even put Cornelius and Zira on trial for heresy.

The (gnostic) gospel of the *Planet of the Apes* is a version of "the truth will set you free" (John 8:32), with the caveat that the salvific truth must be scientific, not religious, truth: it must be of the things of physics, not metaphysics. In other words, salvation is liberation from religious ignorance, and if one will only open his eyes to the truth, he will be free from the shackles of myth. In the 2001 film, one of the gorillas, who has exhibited a strong faith for most of the film, abruptly declares, "Everything I have believed is a lie!" As I watched the film again recently, I found it rather insulting to suggest that a person of deep faith would give up that faith so easily.

There seems to be a clear antifundamentalist, or even anti-Christian, bias in the *Planet of the Apes*. Atheists usually claim Rod Serling as one of their own, though he could have had much the same prejudice as a Unitarian, which he had become as a convert from Judaism. What is perhaps most disturbing is that Christianity is implicitly equated with racism, as the two allegories of the film are conflated. To be fair, it was progressive Christians, not generally conservatives, who were on the front lines of the civil rights movement. But it is unfair for outsiders like Serling to present racism and faith as though they are on the same side of the same argument.

The message of *Planet of the Apes* seems to be that if the meek will inherit the earth (Matt. 5:5), humans (as a species) have proven themselves to be unworthy of that inheritance. Far from being meek, humans are aggressors who destroyed themselves with their own violence, leaving the earth to the animals, who are truly meek. In the 2001 remake, Davidson comments that in his world the only apes left are in zoos, because people cut down all their forests. The idea that animals are better than humans, while only implied in the 1968 film, was made explicit in the twenty-first-century version.

Score

From the perspective of the apes, Taylor (or Davidson) is, in a sense, "divine" because man is still evolutionarily superior. So I have to give some points for divinity. In a strange way, these Christ figures are also the "creators" of the world on which they land. Taylor is (indirectly) an ancestor of those who destroyed themselves with nuclear war, leaving room for the apes to surpass humanity, and Davidson was directly responsible for the presence of genetically enhanced apes on the planet. So let's say 3 points for divinity, 2 for creation. The crash landing is a descent, so full points for that. Taylor and Davidson are human, of course, and to the extent that they come to bring salvation to humans, they come to their own, and yet they are unique among humanity. So I'll give them full points in those categories. But no points for voluntary sacrifice or death. I'll give Taylor 1 point for regaining his voice as a kind of resurrection. That gives him a total score of 21.

CHAPTER 12

THE TIME MACHINE

He has all the time in the world.

— DAVID PHILBY

Like many Victorians, author H.G. Wells anticipated the turn
of the twentieth century with a sense of curiosity about what the
future would be like. Many people thought that humanity was
progressing toward a utopia. For some, that meant a single world
government and the eradication of war. Others looked forward
to medical and technological advances that would rid the world
of disease and hunger. Whatever the details of the Victorian
hopes for the future, the more optimistic prophets predicted a
world characterized by peace on Earth through increasing unity.
H.G. Wells, however, correctly predicted that the world was not
progressing toward utopia, but that the twentieth century would
be a time of increasing division.

Wells's book *The Time Machine* was the culmination of his
several attempts at writing about the future. It was first published

in 1895 and quickly became one of the foundational works of a new genre we now call science fiction. Wells literally invented the concept of a time machine. In the same year as the first horseless-carriage race in the United States, Wells published the idea of a carriage that could accelerate faster than time itself and carry a passenger along the fourth dimension, forward or backward in time. However, the original book is not really a story about time travel per se. The protagonist never travels back in time, only to the future, and then only to deliver to the reader a cautionary tale of how his present-day society was contributing to the downfall of humanity.

The book has become the basis for two films that will be the primary focus of this chapter.[108] As we will see, the films shift the overall outlook and agenda of the book, and it is only in the films that the protagonist is a Christ figure. In fact, the time traveler is never named in the book. In the first film (1960), he is meant to be H.G. Wells himself; this, however, could not have been Wells's intention, since the protagonist is optimistic about the future and apparently believes in God, while Wells himself had lost his faith—in both God and humanity. In the more recent film (2002), the protagonist is Alexander Hartdegen, professor of applied mechanical engineering, and pen pal of a German patent clerk named Albert Einstein.

In both the book and the 1960 film, the time traveler's motivation for inventing a time machine is to see what technological advances the future holds. He naively accepts the idea of unlimited progress as the destiny of humanity and longs to escape the

---

[108] There were also two made-for-TV movies: one in 1949 and one in 1978, as well as the very creative *Time after Time* (1979), which was loosely based on the concept.

limitations of the present to see the marvels of the future. In the film, it is specifically the Boer War in South Africa that makes him want to see a world at peace. But as he travels forward in time, he sees what H. G. Wells could only dread at the end of the nineteenth century. He makes stops in 1917 (World War I), 1940 (World War II), and 1966—six years after the release of the film—where he witnesses the outbreak of nuclear war and the subsequent eruption of volcanoes, all of which begins the destruction of the planet as we know it. More importantly, it is the beginning of the fall of humanity.

For the 2002 film, the writers of the screenplay created a prologue that gave the protagonist a more personal reason to invent the time machine. His fiancée was murdered, and Alexander (Guy Pearce) wanted to go back in time to prevent her death. This allowed the writers to have the time traveler go backward in time as well as forward, and also to clarify some of the rules of time travel in the story (for example, the machine doesn't travel in space, only in time). There is much in the 2002 film that is not in the original book, and the liberties taken by the screenwriters finally transform *The Time Machine* into a true time-travel story. When Alexander finds that he cannot prevent his fiancée's death by traveling into the past, he decides to travel into the future to find out why. Along the way, he stops in 2030, where he sees an ad for the new "Lunar Leisure Living" retirement colony on the moon. The ad's tagline is "The future is now." Then he stops in 2037 to find out that the twenty-megaton detonation that was supposed to create underground tunnels on the moon has resulted in the moon's breaking up. The loss of the moon's gravitation has put Earth out of whack, and he is forced to get back into the time machine and keep going forward.

In all three versions of the story, the time machine hurls forward in time, through cataclysmic events (including a new ice age) eventually to see Earth renewed. Then the time machine comes to a stop in the year 802,701: more than eight hundred thousand years in the future. The surroundings are like a vast garden, and the world that the time traveler can see is described as a paradise. But all is not what it seems.

When the protagonist meets the inhabitants of this paradise, he finds out that they call themselves *Eloi*. The name seems to be made of a Hebrew word for God (*El*) and a Greek plural (*-oi*), so that the name implies (rather ironically, as we will see) that they are called *gods*. The Eloi are vegetarians and do not seem to have to work at all. There is no commerce. They spend their time in leisure, swimming in the river and gathering flowers. As H. G. Wells described them in the book, they have a short attention span, but there is no conflict or competition among them. The time traveler assumes that they are the end result of human progress, in which society is built on communism and egalitarianism, and traditional models of social organization (including the family and the household) have become obsolete. He also assumes that the calm demeanor of the Eloi means that there is no danger for them to worry about, and that their lives are essentially peaceful. But he finds out that these assumptions could not be more wrong.

As it turns out, this is not utopia. Humanity's zenith has long since passed. In both the book and the 1960 film, the Eloi are not simply peaceful; they are docile and desensitized. When one of them (a young woman named Weena) almost drowns in the river, no one seems to care. The time traveler jumps in to save her, but even when he does, it doesn't seem to matter to her fellow Eloi. It is as if her death would have been no big deal. When the time traveler wonders why there are no older Eloi, he begins a line of questioning that leads him to the unthinkable truth. The Eloi are not the highly advanced descendants of humanity; they are primitive, and what's worse, they are cattle (actual cattle such as cows, sheep, and pigs are now extinct). The Eloi are the food supply for another species called the Morlocks.

Anthropology

Why does the story take us eight hundred thousand years into the future? Why such an extravagant number? The answer is evolution. Eight hundred thousand years is long enough for evolution to change the nature of humanity completely, and in *The Time Machine* we find out that by the year 802,701, humanity has evolved into two species. The Eloi live on the surface of the land, in an idyllic setting that hides the danger of their true role in their world. The Morlocks live underground, coming out at night to hunt the Eloi for food.

In the original book, the Eloi and the Morlocks evolved from the Haves and the Have-nots, after the capitalist and labor classes ceased to intermarry. At some point, the leisure of the upper classes became absolute, as they relied on the work of the laborers; while the labor classes adapted to life out of sight among the machines of their work. But then food ran low, and the only solution left to the underground caste was to turn to cannibalism. And so—as H. G. Wells tells the story—the selfishness of the Haves had come back to haunt them. First they became soft, and then they became prey, as the working classes became the predators. Wells's time traveler remarks that the cannibalism is "a rigorous punishment of human selfishness." Thus, the book becomes a warning to the wealthy classes of Wells's own day, that they ought to be careful or the lower classes will revolt. In the end, the original book is not really about time travel at all, but instead Wells is merely using time travel as a vehicle for scolding the wealthy of his time.

But this does tell us something about the anthropology of H. G. Wells. Ever the academic, he laments that the human intellect has committed suicide, and for that reason, he (unlike his protagonist) could not be optimistic about human progress.[109] Over a century ago, he lamented the shortening of the attention span and the decline of reading. And if necessity is the mother of invention, what will happen when technological advances do away with necessity? For the Eloi, the lack of necessity had meant that creativity had died out as human intelligence declined in the upper classes. In the underclass, however, the necessity of a food shortage had led to a revolting solution.

It is well known that H. G. Wells was antagonistic toward the Church. The loss of his faith came in part from the challenge that Darwinism leveled against a fundamentalist reading of Scripture. In fact, the story of *The Time Machine* is driven by the theory of evolution;[110] that is to say, Wells believed that humanity, like any other species, would have its life cycle, including a decline toward extinction.[111] As part of his rejection of Christianity, he apparently also rejected the doctrine of the *imago Dei*, that humans are made in the image of God. From his perspective, it would be arrogant for humans to think we are

---

[109] See Patrick Parrinder, *Shadows of the Future: H. G. Wells, Science Fiction and Prophecy* (Liverpool: Liverpool University Press, 1995), 24–25.

[110] Ibid., 34–35.

[111] Ibid., 29.

more important than any other animal, or that we are immune to extinction. The image of the sphinx that is so prominent in the book and in the first film brings to mind the riddle of the sphinx from *Oedipus Rex*. What walks on four legs in the morning, two legs in the afternoon, and three legs in the evening? The answer is a person—who crawls on all fours as a baby, walks upright for most of life, and then walks with a cane in old age. But just as an individual has his life cycle, so will humanity have its old age and death.[112] So the destiny of the human race is not continuous progress, but eventual decline. In fact, when the time traveler goes eight hundred thousand years into the future, he skips over the prime of human life and jumps to where human life has come full circle, back to a life without technology, and to barbarism.[113]

Therefore, the original story of *The Time Machine* is anti-utopian.[114] Wells did not write it as a salvation story, but quite the opposite. He was heavily influenced by Edward Gibbon's account of the fall of Rome and would later write his own *Outline of History*.[115] The point is that, as with Rome and other civilizations, Wells believed that the whole of humanity was destined for a fall. Humanity was going to get soft, or barbaric, or both, but it would regress—and the ultimate regression is cannibalism.[116] In the story, these two possibilities are depicted in the two species. The Eloi are soft (Wells describes their arms as almost useless).[117]

---

[112] Ibid., 16.

[113] See Kurt Heinzelman, ed., *Make It New: The Rise of Modernism* (Austin: University of Texas, 2004), 49.

[114] Parrinder, *Shadows of the Future*, 43–44.

[115] Ibid., 70–72.

[116] Ibid., 58.

[117] See Heinzelman, *Make It New*, 49.

The Morlocks are barbaric and have evolved into subterranean monsters, more beast than human. And there's the point, because with the entropy of humanity comes "the loss of human mastery over nature."[118] Perhaps, in the Eloi's acceptance of their lot in life, there is even a hint of an intriguing question: Given eight hundred thousand years of evolution and the fact that humanity has evolved into two species, is it really cannibalism? Although the time traveler is horrified by the prospect of Morlocks eating Eloi, it implies the question: "Are we who eat cows and pigs in any position to judge?" This, again, seems to be a challenge to the Judeo-Christian concept of the *imago Dei*, and the idea that humanity is unique among God's creatures.

Much of Wells's anthropology is retained in the two films, even as the story becomes progressively less a cautionary tale and more a time-travel adventure. Whether the threat is nuclear war (1960) or the careless destruction of the environment for commercial purposes (2002), there is still the hint of a warning that humanity could commit suicide. But the films add the element of hope in the salvation that comes when the time traveler changes the situation for the Eloi. This is evident when we look at how fire is used, especially in the book and in the 1960 film. In both cases, fire symbolizes technology.[119] The Eloi no longer have the ability to make fire, and so the matches that the time traveler brings with him are a source of amazement for the Eloi, as well as a defensive weapon against the Morlocks, whose eyes are no longer accustomed to the light. In the book, the time traveler accidentally starts a forest fire, which leads to the death of Weena. But in the films, fire is used to destroy the Morlocks

---

[118] Parrinder, *Shadows of the Future*, 49.

[119] Ibid., 107.

and save the Eloi. In the book, the time traveler brings technology into a post-technological world, but it ironically causes his greatest failure: his failure to save the girl or her people. In the films, the time traveler brings the gift of technology, which leads to the salvation of the Eloi. It is this difference that turns the films into salvation stories, and the time traveler into a savior.

Christology

In H. G. Wells's original version of the story, the time traveler is only an observer. He cannot change the fate of the Eloi. Even after his visit to their world, they will still be a source of food for the Morlocks. In the epilogue to the book, after the time traveler has returned to tell the story of the Eloi and Morlocks to his friends, he disappears, never to be heard from again. There is the slightest hint of hope as the narrator remembers the story: "Even when mind and strength had gone, gratitude and mutual tenderness still lived on in the heart of Man." But here the inclusive "Man" does not include the Morlocks who had become monsters, devoid of compassion for the other branch of the human family tree that had become their food. So, for all the talk of humanity becoming two species, at the end really only one of them could be called human.

With the 1960 film, however, the time traveler tells the Eloi, "We've had our dark ages before; this is just another one. All you need is for someone to show you the way out." In other words, the Eloi need a savior. Our protagonist thinks he is not the one to do it, but wonders if maybe his presence could kindle a spark in one of the Eloi, who will then be inspired to lead them out of their slavery. In fact, during a struggle with the Morlocks, one of the male Eloi imitates the time traveler by making a fist (clearly the first time any Eloi had ever done that), and fighting back. So the time traveler had taught them how to fight. In the end, he sets the Morlocks' underground lair on fire, destroying them and their subterranean world. Weena never dies in the film. The time traveler has saved her and her people. After going back to his own time to tell his friends the story (as in the book, the story is a flashback), he gets back in the time machine and returns to the year 802,701, to help the Eloi "build a new world." Of course, now they'll have to work for a living. The time traveler's friend and his housekeeper realize that he has taken three books with him, but which three? It is left up to the viewer to think about which three books he would take on a journey into the distant future, to a world he had saved and would now help rebuild.

The 2002 film takes the concept even further. There, the Eloi are not only redeemable; they are no longer docile and emotionally numb. Rather than the childlike Weena and her ambiguous comrades, we meet Mara, who is part of a family, and who worries for her younger brother. Theirs is a nontechnological society, but they are not necessarily primitive. It's not clear whether they work, but they are not soft, and they are creative, making memorial windmills to remember their lost parents and grandparents. They are rational, though they are somewhat mind-controlled by a psychic caste of the Morlocks. And now the story is not told as a flashback because Alexander never goes home to his own time. He saves the Eloi by destroying his time machine, creating an explosion that incinerates the Morlocks and their network of underground colonies.

As the one who knows their past, Alexander knows the potential of the Eloi better than they do. Although they have more agency than their counterparts in the book and the first film, they have still come to accept their situation and cannot imagine a better life. But Alexander can. He "drops in" to their time and saves them by destroying the species that was never meant to be, the aberration of humanity that has evolved into something inhuman.

There is a kind of baptism scene, when Alexander first realizes the truth of the Morlocks' cannibalism. In his horror, he recoils from the sight of the Morlocks' "butcher shop" and falls into a pit filled with water and the bones of the Eloi. His eyes have been opened, and he is past the point of no return. By going down into the Morlock tunnels (and then falling into the bloody water) he has effectively "died," and when he returns to the surface victorious (in the nick of time, just ahead of the explosion), he is resurrected to new life, and brings Mara (and symbolically all the Eloi) with him. He saved the world of the Eloi, but at the expense of his own world: because he had to destroy the time machine to destroy the Morlocks, he can never go back to his own time. He has lived up to the definition of humanity expressed in the 1960 film, "The one quality which distinguishes Man from the animal kingdom is the spirit of self-sacrifice."

Soteriology

The anthropology of *The Time Machine* is one in which humanity is destined to decline. Whether it is because we are selfish or ignorant, or both, the end result is the destruction of our world. There is more optimism about nature being able to renew itself than about humanity. The book seems to present humanity as irredeemable, but the two films add to the story. The time traveler becomes an incarnation of a more rational, technologically advanced time, and he brings with him an optimism about human dignity and potential, as well as the wherewithal to free the Eloi from their bondage.

The question that keeps popping up in many sci-fi stories is whether we can control our destiny. Do we have free will, or are we stuck simply floating along on the river of time, going where it takes us, whether we want to or not? When we add time travel into the mix, we are now asking whether a person can control the chain of cause and effect. If so, then we can control our destiny by going back in time and reversing decisions we made when we did not yet know the effects of those decisions. A conversation in the 2002 film is telling. Thinking back on the death of Alexander's fiancée, his friend David Philby tries to get him to move on:

PHILBY. It wasn't your fault.

ALEXANDER. No ... no it wasn't my fault.... Maybe we should blame Mrs. Watchit for picking up the ring from the jeweler ... or the jeweler for making it ... or the poor bastard who tore the stone from the earth. Maybe I should blame you for introducing me to Emma in the first place ... yes."

PHILBY. Alexander, nothing will ever change what happened.

ALEXANDER. No, you're wrong—because I will change it.

If one could change the past, one could save himself (or others) after the fact. But as Heraclitus said, you can't step in the same river twice. You can't go back to the past because it isn't there anymore. For us, the choice must come before the conse-quences: the cause must come before the effect. And yet this is the appeal of time-travel stories. People hope to be saved from the consequences of their actions, even after the consequences. But it turns out that even with a time machine Alexander can't do that. So he goes far into the future and becomes the savior of the more civilized of his descendants by killing those of his descendants who didn't turn out so well.

Salvation in this universe is a kind of divine intervention, since the one who can save the Eloi comes from outside their world and has become the master over time itself to get there. He is, in a sense, omnipresent, because although his machine does not travel in space, he can be present in any moment. He has, as Philby says, "all the time in the world."

Script and Scripture

In the original book, humanity divided into two species because of class distinctions. In the films, the split between Eloi and Morlock was due to the different ways their ancestors found shelter during the disasters brought on by nuclear war or the breakup of the moon. The Morlocks went underground and stayed there. They adapted to the dark environment, but more than that, they became monsters. The Eloi were able to survive aboveground. Interestingly, in the 1960 film, the Eloi were all white with blond hair. Not to discount the inherent racism in that casting choice, it should be remembered that once upon a time fair skin was a measure of leisure—the assumption being that those who did not have to work outside were, by definition, of the upper classes. In the 2002 film, however, the Eloi have brown skin, evidently the future mix of all of today's skin colors.

But in spite of the evolutionary division, the Eloi and the Morlocks have one thing in common. They have lost their free will. The Morlocks are driven by instincts and hunger; the Eloi are mind-controlled and at the mercy of the predators who are above them on the food chain (even though they live below). The time traveler steps into their world, bringing the ability to control destiny. He imposes his value system (cannibalism is an atrocity) on the future and kills the cannibals (is this a form of genocide?). Before the climactic ending of the 2002 film, Alexander meets the "Uber-Morlock," the leader of a Morlock colony with a highly developed brain (which continues down his back). When Alexander expresses his horror at the Morlocks' cannibalism, the Uber-Morlock calls him a hypocrite for judging them when he himself is trying to control nature with time travel.

Then the Uber-Morlock answers the question that brought Alexander into the future in the first place. Why is it not possible to change the past? The answer is that one cannot invent a time machine and then change the past in a way that would negate the reason for making the time machine in the first place. The Uber-Morlock tells Alexander, "You're a man haunted by those two most terrible words: *What if?*" In a vision, Alexander sees the family he might have had with his dead fiancée, and as he looks at them, he absentmindedly puts the plans for the time machine into a drawer and closes it. Then he realizes the truth. If he had been able to go back in time and had prevented her death, he would have never invented the time machine—a paradox that makes it impossible for him to have prevented her death. Even with a time machine, he is still subject to the law that says the cause must always come before the effect. Like Alexander, we all long to be gods, masters of nature and controllers of destiny, but we cannot be, because to be divine is to be outside of creation, not circumscribed by it—and creation includes time. God can come into time, but we cannot get out of it. That's the difference between Creator and creation. The Uber-Morlock concludes, "You are the inescapable result of your tragedy, just as we are the inescapable result of you." The Morlocks are Alexander's descendants no less than the Eloi, and perhaps the lesson here is that in our attempt to be gods, we all have the potential to turn out like the Eloi or like the Morlocks.

Apparently, God doesn't prevent us from making choices that result in regret. Alexander's choice wasn't even a sin: the choice to walk through Central Park rather than keep to the lighted streets led to a mugging gone bad. But someone did sin: the mugger. His rejection of God's will led to the death of an innocent woman, just as her life was about to begin. We all know of tragedy that suddenly changes life as we know it, and we wonder why God allowed it. We wonder why God couldn't have suspended free will just this once. But for reasons we can't always understand, free will, time, cause, and effect are not always our friends, especially since we are circumscribed by creation and time and can't see the effect ahead of time. God is omniscient precisely because He is omnipresent, and He can see the effect before the cause. But God gives free will equally to those who will use it wisely and to those who will abuse it. Or it's probably more accurate to say that we all use it wisely sometimes and abuse it at other times. We can't say why God allows people to use free will to reject His will, except to say that God is love, and love must always be voluntary, never coerced. At the end of the day, a world without mystery would be a world without faith, and a world without danger would be a world without courage. But in the midst of it all, grace is an ever-present invitation. God brings us along with breadcrumbs, not with a cattle prod.

In the prologue of the 2002 film, Philby looks around at all the inventions in Alexander's laboratory and remarks, "I wonder if we will ever go too far." Alexander scoffs, "No such thing." But when he sees the broken moon and its effects on Earth, he admits, "You were right, Philby: we did go too far." All the versions of *The Time Machine* have an element of cautionary tale.

But with the film versions, we move beyond the evolutionary determinism of H. G. Wells to a place of hope, where humanity may be saved after all.

Score

Although the time traveler is not really a god, I'm going to give him 3 divinity points for being able to step outside of time and travel through it. And the fact that he comes from the Eloi's distant past makes him kind of preexistent, so 3 points for that. His arrival in the future is a "descent" of sorts, since he comes from outside their world and brings special gifts, such as fire; 4 points there. And he is fully human (as their ancestor), so full points for humanity. In the 2002 film, Alexander's uniqueness is demonstrated in the fact that he speaks "the lex" — the special "stone language" of the ancestors. I'll give him 2 points for that. He does not suffer an actual death or resurrection, but he does risk his life to go down into the tunnels of the Morlocks, and he comes back from the "underworld" having saved the Eloi: 2 points for death, and 3 for resurrection, giving the time traveler an orthodoxy score of 22. This is a salvation by divine intervention.

CHAPTER 13

DOCTOR WHO

His name is the Doctor. He has saved your lives so many times and you never even knew he was there. He never stops; he never stays; he never asks to be thanked; but I've seen him — I know him. I love him. And I know what he can do.

— MARTHA JONES

Actually, his name is not "the Doctor," but that's how most people know him. His name is also not "Dr. Who." That's just the name of a television show that has been running for more than half a century (1963 to 1989, and 2005 to the present).[120] But part of

---

[120] Technically it is not correct to spell *Doctor Who* with the abbreviation "Dr." Although there was some discussion about his name being "Doctor Who" in the episode "World Enough and Time" (10:11), that was merely the result of Missy's somewhat snarky imitation of the Doctor.

the mystique of the show's main character is that most people will never know his real name.[121]

When *Doctor Who* debuted on the BBC in 1963, the Doctor was presented as a cantankerous old Victorian professor, played by William Hartnell.[122] But he is not just a professor. He comes from an alien race known as the Time Lords, who resemble a council of Olympian gods. As their name implies, the Time Lords have the technology to transcend the time-space continuum and travel through time and space to go anywhere in the universe they wish.

Apparently, the show was originally conceived as an educational program for older children. The Doctor would travel through time in his space-time machine, called the TARDIS, an acronym for "Time and Relative Dimension in Space." From the producers' perspective, this time machine was as much a budget-saving device as it was a sci-fi invention. The TARDIS looks like a simple police call box on the outside, but is much bigger on the inside, due to the fact that the inside exists in a different time-space dimension than the outside. Each Saturday, the Doctor would venture into some period of Earth's past, giving viewers a glimpse of history (albeit filled with anachronisms, myths, and fabrications).

The Time Lords, however, have a kind of prime directive: to observe only, not to interfere with the times, places, and beings they encounter on their travels.[123] In the early seasons, the Doctor

---

[121] For the purposes of this chapter, I am limiting the *Doctor Who* canon primarily to the television shows.

[122] Terrance Dicks and Malcolm Hulke, *The Making of Doctor Who* (London: Pan Books, 1972; rev. ed., London: W.H. Allen, 1976), 18.

[123] Dicks and Hulke, *The Making of Doctor Who*, 19–20.

says to his companions such things as, "And remember, we are only here as observers, we must not interfere with the course of progress."[124] In an episode about the Crusades, the Doctor insists that they cannot warn King Richard that he is entering into a battle he will lose because, "History must take its course."[125]

But the Doctor does interfere: in fact, he intervenes. Because before very long, the stories incorporate the kinds of dangers that put human history—and humanity—at risk, and the Doctor steps in to prevent disaster or make things right. In this way, he deviates from the prime directive of the Time Lords and becomes an outcast from them. He is like a rogue god who leaves the realm of the gods to become a companion to humanity: righting wrongs, bringing justice, negotiating peace, and protecting humanity.[126] Over the course of the show's evolution, the Doctor evolves from observer to savior.

Of course, the show is famous for another kind of evolution, the kind in which the Doctor periodically "regenerates," resulting in a completely different appearance. Like James Bond in the 007 franchise, the producers of *Doctor Who* had the problem of how to keep the show running after the actor who played the

---

[124] From "The Romans," pt. 3, "The Conspiracy" (aired January and February 1965). Shortly after saying this, however, the Doctor inadvertently gives the emperor Nero the idea of burning Rome to make room for his new palace. In pt. 4, "The Inferno," both Nero and the Doctor laugh while Rome burns. It is also implied in the episode that the early Christians were behind a plot to assassinate Nero, which is unlikely, considering this was before Nero ever persecuted the Christians. His persecution began only after the fire of 64.

[125] From "The Crusade" (aired March and April 1965).

[126] Dicks and Hulke, *The Making of Doctor Who*, 20.

main character moved on. But unlike James Bond, *Doctor Who* writers cleverly made the change of actors a part of the story, giving the Doctor the ability to overcome extreme trauma and near-death experiences through a kind of mystical resuscitation that gives him a new face, as a new actor took over the role.[127]

Anthropology

So why does the Doctor interfere in human events? The simple answer is that he has fallen in love with humanity. He comes to favor humans (that is, earthlings) above all other species. According to him, even an ordinary human is "the most important thing in creation."[128] He loves humanity and believes all human life is valuable and worth saving. He says, "This planet, these people are precious to me, and I will defend them to my last breath."[129]

As others have noted, if we want to ask what it means to be human in the universe of *Doctor Who*, we just have to look at the Daleks and the Cybermen and see what it is that makes them *inhuman:* what are they missing? The answer is that they have no emotions: they cannot feel, so they cannot have empathy or express compassion for another living being.[130] This is the

---

[127] The idea of regeneration was the brainchild of Innes Lloyd and Gerry Davis, but it was apparently more of a logistical fix than a reference to resurrection.

[128] From "Father's Day" (aired May 2005). See McKee, *The Gospel according to Science Fiction*, 83.

[129] From "The Power of Three" (aired September 2012).

[130] Laura Brekke, "'Humany-Wumany': Humanity vs. Human in *Doctor Who*," in *Religion and Doctor Who: Time and Relative Dimensions in Faith*, ed. Andrew Crome and James McGrath (Eugene, OR: Cascade Books, 2013), 102. See also Sarah Balstrup,

primary human virtue for *Doctor Who*, and the Doctor is the supreme example of empathy and compassion, making him the ultimate example of what it means to be human, even though he is not of this planet. The Daleks are, in fact, a kind of anti-Doctor, since they are incapable of feeling pity.[131] Likewise, the Cybermen have no ability to feel emotions. They also have no individuality: no individual personality or free will of any kind. Thus, Daleks and Cybermen alike have no conscience, and no ability to be in relationship with another individual, which is another way of saying that they have no soul. Therefore, they have no image of God in them.[132]

The Cybermen are actually a good example of what results from reducing the human person to nothing more than his brain.[133] Cybermen are made up of a human brain in a robotic body, and we come to find out that if the emotions are not suppressed to the point of removing all self-awareness, whatever is left of that person's humanity will go insane, unable to deal with the reality that he is just a brain in a machine. Just as the

---

"Doctor Who: Christianity, Atheism, and the Source of Sacredness in the Davies Years," *Journal of Religion and Popular Culture* 26, no. 2 (Summer 2014): 145ff.

[131] McKee, *The Gospel according to Science Fiction*, 52; Brekke, "Humany-Wumany," 103.

[132] Brekke, "Humany-Wumany," 96–98.

[133] Ibid., 96. Incidentally, the Cybermen are a convenient parallel for the heresy of Apollinarianism, which proposed that Christ was the result of the divine mind being inserted into a human body. This was rejected because, if a divine mind replaced the human mind (leaving Christ with only one mind and will), it would have diminished His humanity, making Him less than fully human.

ancient Stoics advocated suppressing the emotions to live more rationally, the Cybermen have emotion suppressors built into them that remove all feelings (both pain and pleasure) and in the process also remove all individuality and relationality. Cybermen are truly reduced to automatons, and any one Cyberman can do only what all the other Cybermen are doing. Similarly, the Daleks have had their emotions genetically removed, replaced with electronic logic and a mechanical body.

The point is that the same things that suppress emotion also suppress self-awareness, the ability to be in relationship with another, and the capacity to care for someone other than the self. Therefore, in the *Doctor Who* universe, emotions are necessary for "humanity" (whether one is from Earth or not), and they are what makes a being a *person*. The same weakness that the Daleks and the Cybermen are meant to avoid (vulnerability) is the truest strength of humanity (empathy and compassion).[134]

Christology

When asked, "What are you a doctor of?" the Doctor replies, "Practically everything, my dear."[135] The Doctor is a Time Lord, which cannot help but sound like a divine title.[136] In fact, "Lord" is used as a divine title both in the New Testament and in the Nicene Creed, to affirm the divinity of both Jesus Christ and the Holy Spirit. The fact that the Doctor is Lord over time, in the sense that he can step

---

[134] Brekke, "Humany-Wumany," 96–97, 102.

[135] From "Spearhead from Space" (aired January 1970).

[136] Jennifer L. Miller, "The Monstrous and the Divine in *Doctor Who*: The Role of Christian Imagery in Russell T. Davies' *Doctor Who* Revival," in *Religion and Doctor Who*, 106.

outside of time and travel at will from one point in time to another, also implies a kind of omnipresence, a transcendence that allows him momentarily to remove himself from the bounds of creation and reinsert himself wherever and whenever he wishes.

As we have seen, time travel (were it ever possible) would require one to be able to stand apart from creation, if only for a moment. In the science-fiction stories that we are analyzing in this book, time travel also becomes a metaphor for incarnation, as the Christ figure "drops into" a time and place that he didn't come from, in order to be a savior to the people of that time and place. The Doctor even temporarily gives up his power of time travel (along with his memory and self-awareness) resulting in his living for a time as a mere human, in blissfully ignorant solidarity with the rest of us who do not have an omnipresence machine like the TARDIS.[137]

Add to this the fact that the Doctor comes from the planet Gallifrey, which sounds like Galilee, and that he travels with

---

[137] In "Human Nature" (aired May–June 2007), the Doctor gives himself amnesia as a kind of witness protection program: he and Martha can hide from the beings who are chasing him because he does not remember who he is. The concept of Christ setting aside divine prerogatives truly to experience the human condition is called *kenosis*, meaning "emptying." It comes from Philippians 2, and from historic explanations of the incarnation. For more on this, see Papandrea, *Trinity 101*, and *Novatian of Rome and the Culmination of Pre-Nicene Orthodoxy*. In the case of Doctor Who, the memory of who he really is was still in his subconscious, so that in a way, he both knew and did not know the truth. Many theologians have said the same about Christ, that in His Incarnation, His divine nature remained fully omniscient while His human nature was limited in His self-awareness. Others maintain that even His divine nature was limited (without becoming any less divine, of course).

companions who are very much like disciples, and one might be tempted to think that all these parallels to Jesus Christ were intentional. What is even more striking to anyone who has studied Christology is the fact that the Doctor has two hearts. On the surface, this seems like a clear parallel to the two natures of Christ, His humanity and His divinity. In fact, in the ancient understanding of the human person, the heart was the place of the human will—the place where decisions were made—and after some debate in the fourth century, the Christian Church concluded that Jesus Christ does have two wills, one for each of his two natures. So the idea that a Christ figure like the Doctor would have two hearts seems like too much of a coincidence, as if somebody at the BBC had been to seminary.

HERESY 5
Nestorianism

- Nestorianism began with an overreaction against Apollinarianism by a bishop named Nestorius.

- It is based on a desire to protect the integrity of the full human nature of Christ.

- It is also based on a desire to protect the immutability of the divine nature of Christ, since Nestorius worried that too much union of the two natures might result in a change in the divine nature (*immutability* means *unchangeable*: God cannot change because He is perfect).

- Nestorius argued that Apollinarius was wrong and that Christ must have two wills. The Church councils would conclude that on this point, Nestorius was right: because Christ has two natures, He must have two wills.

- Nestorius emphasized the distinction between the two natures of Christ, to the point of making them completely separate. The way he talked about the two natures sounded to some people as if he were talking about two persons, two Christs, who were united only by common activity.

- Nestorius preached against Mary's traditional title of "Mother of God" because he thought that the two natures were so separate that only the human nature of Jesus was ever in the womb of Mary.

- At the Council of Ephesus in 431, the bishops concluded that Nestorius was wrong and that it is appropriate to call Mary the Mother of God.

Orthodoxy = Jesus Christ is
one person with two natures.
Heresy = Jesus Christ is
two persons in one body.

Orthodoxy = Mary brought the
whole person of Christ into the world.
Heresy = Mary only brought the
human nature of Christ into the world.

However, there is no evidence that the original creators of the character had Jesus in mind, or that they had any particular religious convictions at all.[138] The first time we hear that the Doctor has two hearts is right after the second Doctor's regeneration into the third Doctor (from Patrick Troughton to Jon Pertwee). This was in the four-part series "Spearhead from Space," which aired in January of 1970. After regenerating, the Doctor stumbles out of the TARDIS and falls unconscious, only to be found and sent to a local hospital, where we are told that he does not have a human blood type; he is able to put himself into a self-induced coma to heal himself; and his chest X-ray reveals that he has two hearts. But it turns out that he is not unique in this regard. In an earlier series, "The Dominators" (aired in August and September of 1968), we find out that there are other species who also have a "binary vascular system," specifically the inhabitants of the planet Dulkis.[139]

---

[138] The creator of the character of the Doctor and the TARDIS was Sydney Newman, whose parents were Jewish. The creator of the Time Lords and the concept of dual hearts seems to be Terrance Dicks.

[139] There is no mention in "The Dominators" that the Doctor has two hearts. In the story, the Dominators are aggressive colonizers intent on turning the peaceful Dulkians into slaves (the planet's name, Dulkis, is a Latin word, *Dulcis*, meaning pleasant, delightful, sweet, or kind). Although we are never told how many hearts the Dominators have, they are surprised when they find out that the Doctor's companion Jamie has "only one heart." The fact that the Doctor has two hearts is also mentioned in the episodes "The Shakespeare Code" (aired April 2007) and "The Power of Three" (aired September 2012), in which one of his hearts stops momentarily; "The Girl Who Waited" (aired September 2011) and "Smile" (aired April 2017), in which servant

Apparently, the second heart is meant to be little more than a redundancy—a backup system in case of trauma or other damage. This arguably makes the Doctor "superhuman," in a way, but it doesn't seem to be an intentional nod to Christ (as much as we might wish it were).

The Doctor's ability to regenerate is also a striking (if unintended) parallel to Christ. The tenth Doctor's regeneration (from David Tennant to Matt Smith) even had the Doctor standing in something of a cruciform position as he made the transition. And the resulting transformation leaves the Doctor unrecognizable even to his companions, rather like the way the disciples of Jesus didn't recognize Him after His Resurrection (see, e.g., Luke 24:16; John 20:15). The resurrected body is in some ways a new body, a regenerated body. And the Doctor's ability to heal himself is also a kind of divine power, since he does not need another healer who is greater than himself. He gives healing; he does not receive it.

In recent years, since the reboot of the series, the Doctor has become even bolder in his intervention in human events, even to the point of what some might call "playing God." At times, he puts his own judgments above the laws of the planet he's on, and even above the laws of the Time Lords. At one point, he says, "There are laws. There are laws of time. Once upon a

---

robots serve him two dinners because they think he is two people based on his double heartbeat. In "The Power of Three," UNIT commander Kate Stewart scans the Doctor's chest to confirm that he is in fact the Doctor. In "The Girl Who Waited," we find out that the inhabitants of the planet Appalappachia also have two hearts. After the episode "Smile," the fact that the Doctor has two hearts is mentioned regularly and treated as common knowledge.

time there were people in charge of those laws, but they died. They all died. Do you know who that leaves? Me. It's taken me all these years to realize that the laws of time are mine and they will obey me!"[140] In the episode "Hell Bent" (which aired December 5, 2015), the Doctor claims, "At this moment, I'm answerable to no one!"

In the epilogue to "The Fires of Pompeii" (which aired in April of 2008), we see that the Romans whom the Doctor and his companion Donna Noble had saved from the eruption of the volcano have added two new gods to their household shrine. There they pray to idols made in the likeness of the Doctor and Donna. And in "The Girl Who Waited" (which aired in September of 2011), Amy Pond announces the Doctor's presence by saying, "And there he is: the voice of God."

---

[140] From "The Waters of Mars" (aired November 2009). Quoted in Miller, "The Monstrous and the Divine," 115–116. Note that in her chapter, Miller is arguing for the Doctor as a failed divinity, or more as a creature, or even a demonic force. I personally do not agree with her assessment because the fact that the Doctor invokes fear does not necessarily disqualify him as a divine figure. People are supposed to fear God in some sense. It is true that in the story arc the Doctor later admits that he went too far, and perhaps there the writers are subverting the original intent of the Doctor as a savior figure, but overall I'm not convinced by Miller's argument that the Doctor is a monster. The Doctor's intervention has completed a trajectory from the early seasons (I do not interfere) to the early rebooted series (I cannot interfere with fixed points in time) to the most recent episodes (I am the War Doctor, and I will fix this). Although at times he takes a step back, as in "Hell Bent" (9:12), when the Doctor says, "I know I went too far, I get it.... I went too far ... I broke my own rules," nevertheless it suggests a parallel to the omnipotence of God and the mystery of why God intervenes at some times and not at others.

Soteriology

In the sense that the Doctor is a savior figure, salvation is a kind of divine intervention. Although humans are of ultimate value, they cannot save themselves—they need outside help—and that comes from the Doctor and his TARDIS, the ultimate *deus ex machina*. It's interesting to note that the Doctor does not always control the TARDIS. It seems to have a mind of its own, and it is sometimes described in terms that imply that it is a living being. Although the TARDIS often malfunctions, and the Doctor regularly has difficulties with its controls, it always lands exactly when and where the Doctor is needed. If we wanted to look for a Trinitarian analogy in Doctor Who, we might argue that the TARDIS represents the Holy Spirit. It is the TARDIS that gives the Doctor the power to travel through time and space and allows the Doctor and his companions to communicate (in English) with any species they meet. Without the TARDIS, the Doctor is reduced to using his wits and his sonic screwdriver.[141]

The dangers in *Doctor Who* are more than simply the life or death of the hero. Like many of our sci-fi stories, they have to do with bigger things, such as invasion, genocide, and slavery, and on the individual level they have to do with the loss of identity and of free will—in other words, the loss of humanity. Still, salvation is all about being rescued from the imminent danger of the extinguishing of life. It is not about being saved from sin or from eternal estrangement from God. In fact, it's not about the

---

[141] Balstrup, "Doctor Who," 145ff. In the episode "Thin Ice" (10:3), the Doctor reveals that the piloting of the TARDIS seems to be something of a negotiation between the Doctor and the TARDIS. However, in the episode "The Doctor Falls" (10:12), the Doctor asks the TARDIS, "Where have you taken me?"

afterlife at all. Death is presented as the ultimate evil, the quintessential horror, and the absolute end. This is to be expected from a sci-fi show that is ultimately based on humanist values rather than on Judeo-Christian values. In the world of *Doctor Who*, the greatest value is human life, which sounds like a good thing, until we realize that there is really nothing greater — not even God. Needless to say, there is little or no acknowledgment of the reality of God in *Doctor Who*, and there is no hope of eternal life. Salvation is presented in something like Old Testament terms — like the psalmist begging to be saved from his enemies.

Script and Scripture

What started out in the early seasons as the affirmation that humanity is the crown of creation has lately morphed into something more like what we see in *Star Trek*: that the relationship between earthlings and aliens is an allegory for relations among different kinds of humans, and so tolerance has become the ultimate virtue. The Doctor still favors humanity, especially when the nonhumans are aggressors or would-be colonizers, but what began as post-Enlightenment humanism has been rebooted as postmodern atheism.

Under the direction of Russell T. Davies, who led the resurrection of the show in 2005 and served as head writer until 2009, *Doctor Who* was "ideologically ... aligned with the New Atheism." In interviews, Davies has publicly "admitted that he has incorporated his atheist agenda into *Doctor Who*."[142] One

---

[142] Balstrup, "Doctor Who," 145ff. See also Andrew Crome, introduction to *Religion and Doctor Who: Time and Relative Dimensions in Faith*, ed. Andrew Crome and James McGrath (Eugene, OR:

episode even featured a cameo appearance by atheist author Richard Dawkins, who played himself, but as an expert scientist.[143] Other episodes portray religious faith as something that pacifies people to the point of numbness, holding humanity back from realizing its potential, or even that religion is inherently fascist.[144] Therefore, in some episodes it could be argued that, allegorically at least, what the Doctor saves people from is religion. In that sense, the Doctor is portrayed as a bringer of enlightenment, as a form of liberation, and Davies has shifted him a bit in the direction of a gnostic savior. Perhaps it is the case that *Doctor Who* was always hostile to Christian faith. In the early episode "The Romans" (during the time in which the show was supposed to be educational) the final scenes reveal that it is a Christian who is behind the plot to assassinate the emperor Nero—despite the fact that historical evidence makes that idea ridiculous.

Yet even with Davies at the helm, the show continues to use Christian imagery, often in ways that are not entirely subversive, and which allow viewers to see the Doctor as a Christ figure and the Church as a sanctuary, if they want to (for example, in the episode "Father's Day," the endangered humans hide out in a church, or in "the Stolen Earth," when the TARDIS materializes in front of a church). Maybe this is meant to make the show appeal to the most people possible by offending the least number

---

Cascade Books, 2013), xix, and Michael Charlton, "The Doctor Working on God's Time: Kairos and Intervention in 'The Waters of Mars' and 'A Christmas Carol,'" in *Religion and Doctor Who*, 67.

[143] "The Stolen Earth/Journey's End" (aired June and July 2008).

[144] Balstrup, "Doctor Who," 145ff. See the episode "Gridlock" (aired April 2007).

possible. Thankfully, since Davies left the show, the overt atheistic agenda seems to have lessened.

Score

References to divinity abound in *Doctor Who*, and given that the TARDIS allows him a kind of omnipresence that places him above creation, I have to give the Doctor full points for divinity. The same goes for preexistence, since he can come from any time and go to any time. And since, for the Doctor, salvation is divine intervention, and time travel can be seen as an incarnation, or descent, I have to give him full points for that as well. Now, he is an alien, after all, so he can't get full points for humanity. But he does become one of us in some very significant ways, and he does have a granddaughter. I'll give him 4 points for humanity, but only 3 points for uniqueness. It's not that he isn't unique, but it's not really fair to give him too many uniqueness points when he's not really an earthling. He is willing to risk his life, but he never *actually* dies (no, not even in Utah). In fact, the whole time-travel thing kind of makes a lot of the threats against his life less than real. But his ability to regenerate is a nice parallel to resurrection. So let's say 3 points for sacrificial death, but 5 points for resurrection. That gives him a total of 30 points, and makes him one of the most orthodox Christ figures, even with the anti-Christian intentions of some of his writers. In spite of their best efforts, they could not subvert the power of the Christ event in the human psyche.

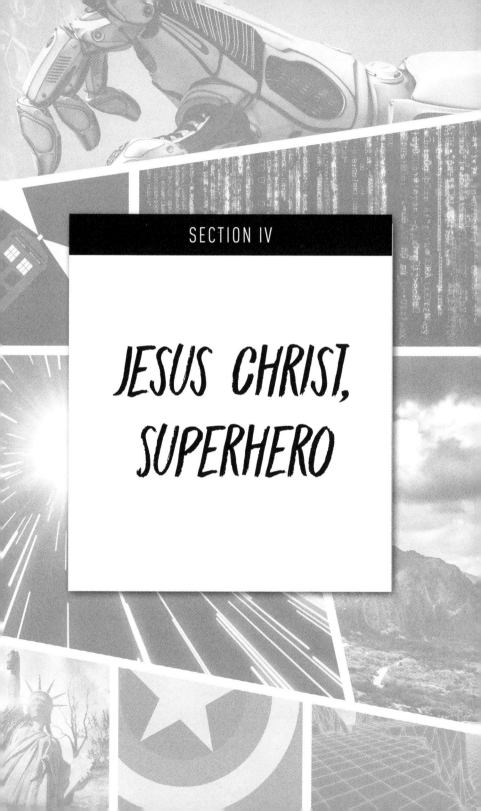

CHAPTER 14

JESUS CHRIST, SUPERHERO

JESUS CHRIST, SUPERHERO: CHRIST FIGURES IN THE DC AND MARVEL UNIVERSES

With great power comes great responsibility.

— UNCLE BEN

For many people, the familiar Marvel and DC superheroes are the most obvious Christ figures because they are, in their essence, saviors. I've saved them for last because the almost countless number of comic-book protagonists exist on a spectrum from the merely human to the virtually omnipotent, and therefore they provide us with a convenient map of the different ways of thinking about savior figures. In fact, they can be used to talk about the different ways in which people have historically understood

Christ Himself. For the purposes of our study, I've chosen to focus on what I believe are the most popular superheroes, based on their prominence in the most recent Marvel and DC films, with one or two more thrown in to give a more complete picture of the Christological spectrum.[145]

Superhero stories tend to be a blend of science fiction and fantasy. Most are science fiction in their origins (though some start out as pure fantasy), but then they all tend to drift into fantasy as time goes on. This is the nature of the serial comic, and it's arguably necessary to keep the story going. In other words, in a story based on the archetype of the hero's journey, we would normally expect there is an overall story arc that ends with the antagonist or the source of evil fully and completely vanquished once and for all. But you can't do that in a comic book if you want to be able to keep publishing future volumes. So, instead of the more linear hero's journey, we get a seemingly endless cycle of what Timothy Peters calls an "essentially 'pagan' cosmology" of purge and conflagration, very much like the Anakin-Darth-Anakin cycle in *Star Wars*.[146] Within this context, the situations, villains, and explanations in the superhero stories apparently have to become increasingly "fabulous" — in the literal sense of

---

[145] For a more academic approach to this Christological spectrum, see James L. Papandrea, *The Earliest Christologies: Five Images of Christ in the Postapostolic Age* (Downers Grove, IL: Intervarsity Press/IVP Academic, 2016).

[146] Timothy Peters, "Overcoming the Limits of the Law in *Batman Begins*," *Griffith Law Review* 16, no. 1 (2007): 247. Note also that Peters cites as an example of this Ra's Al Ghul's motivation, "whenever a civilization reaches the pinnacle of its decadence, a return to harmony is required." Peters, "Overcoming the Limits," 251.

being the stuff of fables. But the real problem is that evil is never fully conquered, and it necessarily becomes more like the equal opposite of good, fighting in an endless battle in which balance is maintained as long as neither one wins once and for all.[147]

Therefore, the heroes battle evil, not to conquer it, but to keep it at bay, to keep the balance and prevent evil from taking over.[148] That's not a bad thing, but in the big picture it can seem to be an exercise in futility. And even the superheroes can become discouraged, as we will see. But, of course, they can't quit (though some have tried) because, as Peter Parker's Uncle Ben has famously said, "With great power comes great responsibility."[149] This is reminiscent of Luke 12:48, in which Jesus said, "Much will be required of the person entrusted with much, and still more will be demanded of the person entrusted with more." Whether or not a superhero has chosen to become a hero (most have not), the fact is that every superhero is in some way, "super," that is, enhanced. And that enhancement obligates the hero to use his powers for the greater good.

So it's very interesting (and seems like too much of a coincidence to be a coincidence) that both of the "civil war" films released in 2016 were, on one level, about collateral damage and the backlash that is caused when innocent people die on the

---

[147] Ibid., 252.

[148] To be fair, the heroes themselves would say that they would love to work themselves out of a job. It's the writers who don't want to do that!

[149] Originally, a version of this line was the comic narrator's commentary after the death of Uncle Ben, when Peter Parker realized that if he had stopped the thug when he had the chance, he could have prevented Ben's murder. "Spider-Man," Amazing Fantasy no. 15, August 1962.

fringes of the superheroes' epic battles. Both *Batman v Superman: Dawn of Justice* (2016) and *Captain America: Civil War* (2016) begin with popular fear and anger rising against the superheroes, even to the point of referring to them collectively as weapons of mass destruction.

In *Civil War*, the villain is motivated by anger over the family he lost due to collateral damage, and since he can't get revenge by killing a superhero, his plan is to get superheroes to kill each other. In *Batman v Superman*, a woman grieving over the destruction of her village and the loss of family members in the aftermath of Superman's rescue of Lois Lane, says of him, "He answers to no one — not even, I think, God." (I have to admit I was glad to hear someone in the DC universe admit the existence of God — something I didn't see in the Marvel film.[150]) In both films, superheroes are scapegoated, turned into "the other," and subsequently dehumanized — but isn't this the point? In their lack of trust, the common people (the unenhanced) were pointing out exactly the ways in which the superhuman are *not* human. Anti-Superman protesters are depicted carrying signs that say "no aliens" and burning his effigy.

Even among the superheroes there was distrust. Superman worried that Batman could drift even further outside the law than he already is. Batman (and Lex Luthor) worried that Superman could become a dictator. Batman proposes a preemptive strike against Superman, saying, "If there's even a 1 percent

[150] In the interest of fairness, I should point out that in the first Avengers movie Captain America says, "There's only one God, ma'am. And I'm pretty sure He doesn't dress like that." Also, Daredevil is Catholic, and Spider-Man occasionally prays, including once praying a prayer of gratitude to God while swinging through Manhattan on a relatively crime-free night.

chance that he is our enemy, we have to take it as an absolute certainty." In other words, while we've got some kryptonite to work with, let's use it, because we might not get another chance. The parallels to the Cold War are obvious, when it was feared that our enemies might apply the same logic to their nuclear weapons. But in the context of the film, the idea that Batman would advocate for a preemptive attack on Superman just didn't ring true.

Both films highlight the coming together of groups of superheroes into teams: in the Marvel world, it's the Avengers; in the DC universe, it's the Justice League. And in both cases, it's implied that if superheroes are dangerous individually, they are even more dangerous as a group (any gratitude for saving the world multiple times has been forgotten by now). The conclusion is that these teams of superheroes need oversight: a higher authority (presumably an international governing agency) that would provide supervision (*super* vision). In a scene in *Batman v Superman*, during their fight there is a graffito on the wall of a broken-down building: the Latin slogan *Quis custodiet ipsos custodes?* which means, "Who watches the watchmen?"[151] It's application here is a kind of theme for the film. Given that superheroes—especially when they team up—are virtually omnipotent (unless, of course, you are a supervillain), should the people of Gotham and Metropolis be worried that the superheroes are

---

[151] The phrase originally comes from the second-century poet Juvenal, *Satires* 6. In science fiction and popular culture, it was previously used in the graphic novel *Watchmen*, by Alan Moore and Dave Gibbons, and in an episode of *Star Trek: The Next Generation* entitled "Who Watches the Watchers," among other places. The film *Watchmen* (2009) was directed by Zach Snyder, who also directed *Batman v Superman*.

their own highest authority? Or should there be another higher authority to which they must answer, especially if their decisions and their actions have unexpected consequences?

In *Civil War*, the proposed solution to the problem is the "Superhuman Registration Act," similar to the story line we've already seen in the X-Men. Tony Stark (Iron Man) is motivated by guilt to be in favor of it. But several of the superheroes fear that registration is only the first step toward internment. Captain America argues against the oversight, which would amount to the loss of freedom. It makes sense that Captain America should be all about freedom, but more to the point, we come to find out that his best friend, Bucky Barnes, was forced to commit evil acts precisely because his free will was taken away when he was brainwashed by the same villains who gave him his enhancement (as the Winter Soldier). Later, Tony Stark finds out that while Bucky was under the control of evil forces, he had killed Stark's own parents, and Stark (as Iron Man) is motivated by anger and wants to kill Barnes. So, in addition to the war over whether the superheroes will have supervision, there is the parallel conflict over whether someone is responsible for his actions if he does them against his will. Captain America must protect his friend from Iron Man, while taking the fight to the common enemy. It is telling that Captain America is known for his shield (a defensive ordnance, though he does use it as a weapon), while Iron Man is a kind of iron hand. Captain America stands for defending the innocent. Iron Man stands for bringing justice to the guilty.

Overall, the film *Civil War* proposes that Captain America was right, and we see the Black Widow change sides, from backing Iron Man to letting Captain America and Bucky Barnes escape to pursue the villain. The superheroes' internal conflict was distracting them from the real mission. Of course, Iron Man was wrong to want to kill Barnes for revenge, and this lesson is reinforced when Black Panther chooses not to kill in revenge for his own father's death.

The point is that there are two kinds of limitation proposed in the story: limitation by an outside force, a higher authority, and self-limitation. Tony Stark argues, "If we can't accept limitations, we're boundary-less; we're no better than the bad guys." But ultimately the solution is not to give up free will to another, but to use free will to choose to limit oneself based on a higher moral code. Thus, the superheroes choose to refrain from killing for revenge. In fact, it could be said that morality is self-limitation. But to be truly moral, it has to be chosen by free will, for limitation without free will is simply coercion.

Jesus Christ, though He is eternally equal to God the Father ("though he was in the form of God, [he] did not regard equality with God something to be grasped"), was willing to limit Himself in the Incarnation and take on the human condition ("he emptied himself, taking the form of a slave, coming in human likeness") (Phil. 2:6–7). In other words, although His divine nature meant that He did not have to accept any limitations, He voluntarily limited Himself in the Incarnation, so that He could become one of us, come to live among us, and be our Savior. And this limitation itself is in many ways the very definition of what it means to be human.

Anthropology

In *Batman v Superman*, Clark Kent's adoptive father tells him a story that becomes a parable for the theme of collateral damage. In saving their farm from a flood, they unknowingly diverted the water to another farm, and that farm was ruined. The flood waters, representing evil in the analogy, were going to go somewhere. No matter how good people are, or how hard they work, they cannot stop evil; they can only divert it. But in diverting it, they unintentionally unleash it on someone else who is equally innocent and helpless to stop it.

In all superhero stories, mere humans cannot save themselves (not even with nukes). Someone superhuman is required. Over the years, the threats have changed, from Nazis, to Communists, to terrorists. For example, the Christian Bale Batman films, beginning with *Batman Begins* (2005), and especially *The Dark Knight* (2008), were dealing with the fear of terrorism: a seemingly unsolvable problem.[152] The point is that salvation (however defined) requires some kind of intervention from someone who is not a mere human, but is at least an enhanced human, if not superhuman. That necessarily makes that super savior an outsider to humanity, at least on some level.

It is a pessimistic anthropology that assumes humans cannot solve their own problems. Then again, the Christian faith is based on just that kind of anthropology. We need a savior because, left to our own devices, we tend toward selfishness, and so we are powerless to save ourselves, as sin only escalates. In *Batman v Superman*, Batman says, "Criminals are like weeds, Alfred. Pull one up, and another grows in its place." Of course, Bruce Wayne is pessimistic about humanity because of the tragic and meaningless death of his parents. Nevertheless, Batman still

---

[152] Michael Nichols, "I Think You and I Are Destined to Do This Forever: A Reading of the Batman/Joker Comic and Film Tradition through the Combat Myth," *Journal of Religion and Popular Culture* 23, no. 2 (July 2011): 236, 238, 243–244.

wants to protect people. (I am reminded of Abraham's negotiation with God over Sodom and Gomorrah: "What if there are at least ten [innocent people] there?" [see Genesis 18:16–32].)[153] Batman sees his mission as protecting the innocent from the criminal element. At the end of the day, people are still worth saving—even the guilty. So Batman avoids killing whenever he can. In *Batman Begins*, Batman chooses not to kill Ra's al Ghul (though he does let him die, which is arguably the same thing).[154] Even Superman, ever the optimist, goes through a transformation in which he loses his optimism about humanity, and he doesn't seem to have the same aversion to killing the bad guys that Batman has. In *Man of Steel*, it's only because of Lois Lane's trust in him that he comes to trust humanity again. Both Batman and Superman ultimately conclude that saving people is worth the effort, though I think the difference between Batman and Superman is that Batman does what he does because he hates the guilty, while Superman does what he does because he loves the innocent.[155]

---

[153] Cf. Peters, "Overcoming the Limits," 262.

[154] Joel Hodge, "Superheroes, Scapegoats, and Saviors: The Problem of Evil and the Need for Redemption," in *imesis, Movies, and Media: Violence, Desire, and the Sacred*, ed. Scott Cowdell, Chris Fleming, and Joel Hodge, vol. 3 (New York: Bloomsbury Academic, 2015), 65. It is also interesting to note that the character of R'as al Ghul is portrayed as a kind of religious terrorist. Batman may have his psychological problems, but he rejects the quasi-religious extremism that leads R'as al Ghul to commit acts of terrorism.

[155] Batman's hatred for criminals is initially motivated by his desire to spare others the suffering that he experienced when his parents were murdered. So Batman is not without some compassion.

Like Bruce Wayne, Lex Luthor is also struggling with the apparent meaninglessness of the human condition. Luthor is angry with God because God didn't protect him from his father's abuse (a misuse of free will). This led him to stumble into the classic problem of evil. If God is great and God is good, why is there evil in the world? The assumption is that if God *can* eradicate evil, and God *wants* a world without evil, then God *would* eradicate evil. Since there is evil in the world, Lex Luthor reasons (as others have before him) that God is either incapable of doing away with evil or doesn't want to. Regardless of which one he decides, in his mind God becomes responsible for evil. Luthor's solution to the problem is to manipulate Bruce Wayne to begin a war between Superman and Batman — "god versus man" — in which Superman will be killed, and thus Luthor will have succeeded in judging God and exacting retribution.

Of course, this logic fails to recognize the necessity of free will. The reason that there is evil in the world is not because God isn't powerful enough to get rid of it or because He doesn't want to, but because He gives humans free will. Presumably, God wants people to love their neighbor voluntarily, because if love is not voluntary, it isn't real love. But that means that in order for free will to truly be free, people have to have the freedom to choose evil. The man who killed Bruce Wayne's parents (in the Tim Burton films, it's the Joker) chose to do so by the free will that God gave him. Lex Luthor's father chose to abuse him by the free will that God gave him. But this does not mean that God is responsible for these acts. It only means that God lets fallen people choose.

We've already noted the importance of free will in the case of Bucky Barnes. When he killed Tony Stark's parents, he was under the influence of mind control. Therefore, he did not commit that act by free will and is arguably not responsible for it—at least this is Captain America's conviction.[156] It's interesting to note that in *Man of Steel* (2013), we find out that on Krypton, children were told what job they would have when they grew up—a kind of communism that takes away their freedom to act—and this is part of the reason Krypton fell. So taking away people's freedom doesn't solve the problem, because then the question becomes: Who will make a person's choices for him? If not the individual, then who? And herein lies the danger of the "Superhuman Registration Act." If oversight takes away the freedom of a superhero, then that superhero is no longer morally responsible. Take away moral responsibility, and all hell breaks loose.

No, the solution to the problem does not lie in controlling the will of others, because that leads only to fascism or communism. The solution must be in an individual's free choice to be morally responsible. But this brings us back to the pessimistic anthropology, for mere humans cannot be trusted to choose well. Therefore, our hope is placed in a moral agent who is superhuman—literally above humanity in the sense of being above reproach. The solution to the problem of evil must be a form of divine intervention.[157]

Evil is just too big a problem for human solutions.[158] We need more than a great human, more than a good example to follow: we need someone who has superhuman power and is (theoretically)

---

[156] The *Catechism of the Catholic Church* agrees. In its definition of mortal sin (paragraph 1857), three criteria must be met: a mortal sin is a sin of a serious ("grave") nature; it is committed with full knowledge; and it is committed with deliberate consent.

[157] Hodge, "Superheroes, Scapegoats, and Saviors," 61.

[158] Ibid., 66.

immune to temptation.[159] And so the superheroes come to be the saviors of (mere) humanity. In the DC universe, we are introduced to "The Metahuman Thesis" that "gods among men" live on earth, walk among us, and often remain anonymous until they are needed to save the day. Ironically, though, the existence of the metahuman makes some ordinary humans feel less than special, and some react to this by hating and resenting the superheroes. In *Man of Steel*, Superman says, "My father believed that if the world found out who I really was they would reject me out of fear." One can't help but be reminded of the apostle John's comments about Jesus: "He was in the world, and the world came to be through him, but the world did not know him. He came to what was his own, but his own people did not accept him" (John 1:10–11).[160]

So into our world come the superhumans, to save the ordinary humans who cannot save themselves. The exotic (and sometimes alien) stranger comes to live in the ordinary world of ordinary people and, when called upon, does extraordinary things.[161] Someone of great significance comes, often to an insignificant place like Smallville (or Bethlehem) — and often his significance is not revealed until a time of great need.

Batman, Iron Man, Captain America, and Spider-Man

Batman, Iron Man, Captain America, and Spider-Man are all metaphors for the adoptionist or Arian Christ. As Christ figures,

---

[159] Ibid., 66–68.

[160] Incidentally, the villains in *Man of Steel* make the implicit claim that morality is an evolutionary disadvantage.

[161] Marsh and Ortiz, *Explorations in Theology and Film*, 81.

they are mere men who are elevated to hero status, which means that they each depict a savior who represents a "Christology of ascent," rather than an incarnation.

Batman is perhaps the furthest on the human end of the spectrum because he is the most flawed.[162] The senseless death of his parents at the hands of a mugger—and the fact that he was there to witness it as a boy of about nine—makes him psychologically dark. He is a fallen character, and in fact his journey as a superhero begins with a literal fall into a cave inhabited by bats. In *Batman v Superman: Dawn of Justice*, there is a dream sequence in which a swarm of bats carries him (in a cruciform position) up and out of the cave, into the light. He then takes on the bat as a kind of animal spirit guide, assuming the persona of a bat-man hybrid and making his headquarters in a "bat cave." For Batman, the bat is his Holy Spirit, his dark dove.

But Batman has no superhuman powers, except perhaps a higher-than-average IQ and a really large bank account. He becomes a superhero entirely by self-discipline and willpower. His power comes, in one sense, from the anger over his parents' death and his sheer will to train and elevate himself to the point where he can fight and defeat criminals like the ones who killed his parents. In fact, in the film *Batman* (1989), we found out that it was actually a young Jack Napier (the Joker) who killed Thomas and Martha Wayne.[163] In the comics, it was never Jack Napier who killed Bruce's parents, but the point is the same: Bruce Wayne becomes Batman to avenge his parents'

---

[162] Batman debuted in 1939 and was created by writer Bill Finger and illustrator Bob Kane.

[163] Nichols, "I Think You and I Are Destined," 239, 244–245. See also Hodge, "Superheroes, Scapegoats, and Saviors," 64.

death, to punish all criminals, and to try to prevent anyone else from having to go through what he went through as a kid. Of course, in addition to the training, Batman is filthy rich. Along with Tony Stark's Iron Man, Bruce Wayne is a kind of American James Bond. This means that he has the money and the resources to invent and implement cutting-edge technology in his fight against crime.

Part of Batman's appeal as a complicated character is that to varying degrees (depending on the portrayal) he knows he is deeply flawed and does not claim to be a hero in the traditional sense.[164] He may be considered a hero by some, but (to his credit) he never wants to be treated as an example to follow. He knows he's a vigilante, and he knows that he does things that regular society cannot condone.

Iron Man, the metal-suited alter ego of billionaire industrialist Tony Stark, was originally more of a communist-fighter than a crime-fighter.[165] He fought for peace through American progress, although later Stark began to grow a conscience, and became more concerned for the sensibilities of changing times.[166] Like Bruce Wayne, Tony Stark is also a flawed human being, but perhaps only in the narcissistic sense, and unlike Bruce Wayne, he seems to experience growth over time. But like Batman, Iron Man's powers come, not from any supernatural source, but rather from his intellectual abilities and his enormous wealth. And while all of the superheroes go through their various deaths

---

[164] Cf. Hodge, "Superheroes, Scapegoats, and Saviors," 62.

[165] Iron Man debuted in 1963, created by writers Stan Lee and Larry Lieber and illustrators Don Heck and Jack Kirby.

[166] Matt Forbeck et al., eds. *The Marvel Encyclopedia* (New York: Penguin Random House/DK, 2016), 190.

and resurrections, Tony Stark's first death and resurrection is the very accident that forces him to become Iron Man.[167] The detonation of a missile (made by his own company, to add a sense of irony) causes a piece of shrapnel to be embedded so close to his heart that it requires an electromagnetic implant in his chest to keep him alive. This implant will also power the Iron Man suit that Stark invents: the suit that allows him to fly around and catch the bad guys. Eventually, Iron Man will go back to a version of his original mission of protecting American interests on the global stage as he turns his skills and technology against terrorists.

It could be argued that Stark's implant is a secondary heart, since it is an electronic power plant that supports his human heart and keeps him alive. As in *Doctor Who*, the image of two hearts can be a metaphor for Christ's two natures and two wills. Here in Iron Man, we have something we don't get in many of the other superheroes, which is the human person encased in an exoskeleton of "superhuman" matter, which supports, protects, and enhances the human. We'll return to this concept later when we consider Christ's two natures in more detail. At this point we note that both Batman and Iron Man represent what we might call "tech-enhanced humans." They are essentially still mere

---

[167] Marco Arnaudo, *The Myth of the Superhero*, trans. Jamie Richards (Baltimore: Johns Hopkins University Press, 2013), 18. Note that Iron Man suffers another death at the hands of a villain who steals the Iron Patriot suit, and becomes an "antichrist" character. This is not the only time that someone else wears an iron suit and becomes an "evil twin" for Iron Man, and in these cases we have something more like the yin-yang concept, in which good and evil are (virtually) equal opposites. Cf. Forbeck, *Marvel Encyclopedia*, 192.

humans, but they are elevated to hero status by the "anointing" of technology.[168]

Captain America is also an enhanced human, but the technology that elevates him is more biological/chemical than mechanical. In other words, it was by experimental drugs that Steve Rogers became Captain America.[169] In fact, it's kind of ironic that the fictional "Super Soldier Serum," which, in the comics, was created to help the Allies fight the Nazis, mirrored horrific experiments that the Nazis were conducting, and which were later condemned as atrocities.[170] Steve Rogers started out as a regular guy (in fact, in the comics he was a ninety-eight-pound weakling, too scrawny to be accepted into the army). His superpowers were infused into him as a part of an enhanced soldier project—a bit like the performance-enhancing steroids that are now considered a bad idea. But these steroids were like steroids on steroids, and the chemicals permanently changed Rogers, so that, unlike Batman or Iron Man, he doesn't go back to being a mere man just by taking off the suit.

He does have one piece of technology that defines him: his shield. Originally shaped like, well, a shield, the now round shield

---

[168] Mapping the superheroes onto the Christology Spectrum in my book *The Earliest Christologies*, Batman and Iron Man would be metaphors for what is called "Spirit Adoptionism." This is the Christ as Prophet, the anointed man, and in this case, they are "tech-anointed."

[169] Captain America debuted in 1941 (in March, before the U.S. entered World War II) and was created by Joe Simon and Jack Kirby.

[170] Abraham Erskine, the scientist who created the Super-Soldier Serum, is a German Jew who escaped the Nazis to help the Allies.

with the star in the middle is Captain America's iconic calling card. The shield's properties are somewhat otherworldly. In *Captain America: Civil War*, Spider-Man says, "That thing does not obey the laws of physics at all." The creation of the shield was originally said to be "the product of a metallurgical accident," which makes it unique, though later versions of the story connect the creation of the shield to Tony Stark's father.[171]

After fighting Nazis for a while, Captain America experiences his first death and resurrection when he falls into freezing waters and is frozen in a block of ice for decades, until he gets thawed out in whatever present day the most recent adaptation represents. Eventually, Captain America was assassinated (though it turns out he was just frozen in time and was brought back later), and others would wear the suit and wield the shield, though mostly unsuccessfully.[172] This reveals an important aspect of the heroes that are essentially enhanced humans: that is, anyone could wear the suit. There is nothing inherently unique about them, and anyone with the same resources could do the same things that they do. In fact, although we are led to believe for a long time that the "Super Soldier Serum" was destroyed after Steve Rogers became Captain America (the guy with the recipe was killed), we later find out that there are others like him: the so-called Winter Soldiers. Speaking of Rogers' humanity, the villain of *Captain America: Civil War* says, "There's a bit of green in the blue of your eyes. How nice to find a flaw." For these superheroes, their flaws define them. Bruce Wayne is a bit psychotic. Tony Stark is a playboy and an alcoholic. And Steve Rogers is still that somewhat naive ninety-eight-pound weakling underneath all that muscle.

---

[171] Forbeck, *Marvel Encyclopedia*, 70.

[172] Ibid., 72.

Spider-Man's powers are famously the result of the bite of a radioactive spider.[173] Here there is a bit of that sci-fi subgenre that I like to call "science gone bad." It's a play on the theme of the very first sci-fi story, Mary Shelley's *Frankenstein*. In the case of Spider-Man, what turns Peter Parker into a spider man is an accident related to experimentation with radiation. A spider is exposed to radiation, the spider's venom gets amped up, and the spider bites Peter Parker, permanently infusing its radioactive essence into his body. In later additions to the origin story, there are hints of more mystical aspects to the spider's venom.[174] Spider-Man's web spinners also went through a change from the technical to the mystical. Originally the result of Peter Parker's advanced knowledge of science, and his own invention, later the web spinners became bio-organic mutations that spontaneously grew into his wrists. I was very glad to see that in the film *Spider-Man: Homecoming*, the web spinners have gone back to being technological.

---

[173] Spider-Man debuted in 1962 and was created by writer Stan Lee and illustrator Steve Ditko, with input from Jack Kirby. There is debate over Jack Kirby's contribution to the creation of Spider-Man, and it's not my intention to enter into that debate here, but simply to give credit where it is due as generously as possible. According to Stan Lee's posts on social media, he chose to hyphenate the name Spider-Man so that the cover of the comic would be more visually differentiated from the already popular Superman comics.

[174] Arnaudo, *The Myth of the Superhero*, 27. In and around the 1980s, many superheroes went through changes influenced by the "New Age" movement. For our purposes, these can be ignored as the unfortunate interpolations of quasi-religious faddism. For more on this, see Arnaudo, *The Myth of the Superhero*, 18–27.

In the 2004 film *Spider-Man 2*, Spider-Man is "crucified" on the front of a train, with his arms stretched out in cruciform position, as he tries to stop the train from crashing and killing everyone aboard. He appears to die and is carried aloft, again in cruciform position, by a grateful crowd of train passengers.[175] And we can see this same allusion to the crucifixion happening again, this time on a ferry, in the recent film *Spider-Man: Homecoming*.

Interestingly, in an alternate universe, Spider-Man 2099 even rules the earth for a thousand years, reminiscent of the enigmatic millennial reign of Christ mentioned in the biblical book of Revelation.[176]

If Batman and Iron Man represent what we might call, "tech-enhanced humans," then Captain America and Spider-Man are "bio-enhanced humans." Like Bruce Wayne and Tony Stark, Steve Rogers and Peter Parker are essentially mere humans, but they are elevated to hero status by the infusion, or "indwelling," of superhuman bio-matter.[177] The heroic identities of Batman, Iron Man, and, to a certain extent, Captain America, could be "played" by anyone with the same training, technology, and resources.[178] Spider-Man may be the most unique of these because of his spider powers, but even in his case, the point is that all

---

[175] Arnaudo, *The Myth of the Superhero*, 44–46.

[176] Forbeck, *Marvel Encyclopedia*, 342. On the millennium and the book of Revelation, see Papandrea, *The Wedding of the Lamb*.

[177] Mapping the superheroes onto the Christology Spectrum in my book *The Earliest Christologies*, Captain America and Spider-Man would be metaphors for what is called "Angel Adoptionism." This is the Christ as Angel, a mere man who is anointed by an outside superhuman force, and in this case, they are "bio-anointed."

[178] Hodge, "Superheroes, Scapegoats, and Saviors," 68.

of these enhanced humans represent an optimistic anthropology in the sense that a mere human could be a hero. They are human potential personified.[179] This optimistic anthropology is typical of the adoptionist/Arian Christology, in which the savior is presented as an example to follow, and salvation requires following the example. Salvation is not simply passive: it requires participation; in fact, that participation is represented as a responsibility. Just as in *Spider-Man 2*, the grateful passengers carry Spider-Man aloft after he sacrifices himself to save them, so we all need to participate in opposing evil. In a version of the famous Edmund Burke quote ("The only thing necessary for the triumph of evil is for good men to do nothing"), Spider-Man says in *Captain America: Civil War*, "When you can do the things that I can do, and you don't, and then bad things happen: they happen because of you."

Superman, Wonder Woman, and Silver Surfer

At the far opposite end of the spectrum from Batman is the Silver Surfer.[180] As one of the many alien superheroes, he is not at all human; in fact, he's not really even a "physical" being, in the sense of being made of the elements that occur naturally on Earth. On the peacefully named planet Zenn-La, Norrin Radd was forced to become the servant of the virtually omnipotent Galactus in order to save his girlfriend. He was given the "Powers Cosmic" from this evil deity and came to Earth as the enemy

---

[179] Ibid.

[180] The Silver Surfer debuted in 1966, in *Fantastic Four* no. 48, "The Coming of Galactus." He was created by Stan Lee and Jack Kirby and got his own comic book in 1969.

of humanity.[181] When he turned on Galactus and refused to help him drain Earth of its energy, Galactus imprisoned him on Earth.[182] Then he went through a series of three temptations presented to him by the Satan-character Mephisto, analogous to the temptations of Jesus in the desert at the beginning of His ministry.[183] At one point, Silver Surfer apparently died of an illness, but at another point, he was crucified by aliens trying to start a war.[184] As it turned out, his death was a ruse, and he never really died.[185]

Since he is not at all human, Silver Surfer is one of the superheroes that depict what we call a docetic Christ. The most famous docetics were the gnostics of history, and their conception of Christ was that He was a god—but because He was pure divinity, they believed that He could not have been truly human, and so their version of Christ was divine but not at all human. In the Silver Surfer we encounter the idea of multiple beings with divine powers, the idea that some of these divine beings can be evil and be out to get humanity, the idea that a divine being can be trapped on Earth, and the idea that its death is an illusion. All of these are hallmarks of docetic gnosticism.[186]

---

[181] Arnaudo, *The Myth of the Superhero*, 51–52.

[182] Forbeck, *Marvel Encyclopedia*, 327.

[183] Arnaudo, *The Myth of the Superhero*, 53.

[184] Ibid., 55–56.

[185] Ibid., 57.

[186] Mapping the superheroes onto the Christology Spectrum in my book *The Earliest Christologies*, the Silver Surfer would be a metaphor for what is called "docetic gnosticism." This is the Christ as Phantom, assumed to be one of many divine beings who may appear in humanoid form, but any humanity He appears

Wonder Woman is one of the superheroes whose origin is based more in ancient mythology than in science fiction.[187] She was an Amazonian princess, the daughter of the Queen of the Amazons. But in the original comics, it turns out that she was not the natural-born daughter of the queen. The queen had a small statue of Aphrodite that she worshipped so faithfully that the goddess made the statue come to life as a little girl.[188] This girl was raised as the queen's daughter and grew up to be Wonder Woman. Therefore, she is not human at all, and like the Silver Surfer, she is more an image of a gnostic savior than the Word who became flesh (John 1:14). The difference between the Silver Surfer and Wonder Woman is that, for Wonder Woman, the human disguise is more convincing, and thus she *seems* more human.[189]

---

to have is an illusion. He is an apparition—a god who appears to humanity, but never becomes one of us.

[187] Wonder Woman debuted in December of 1941, created by William Moulton Marston, inventor of the polygraph (note that Wonder Woman has a lasso of truth).

[188] Arnaudo, *The Myth of the Superhero*, 14–17. In the later comics (and in the recent film), Wonder Woman's origin has changed: she is said to be the daughter of the Amazon queen with Zeus. That being the case, she is part goddess and part human, rather like the mythical heroes, such as Hercules.

[189] Mapping the superheroes onto the Christology Spectrum in my book *The Earliest Christologies*, Wonder Woman would be a metaphor for what I call "hybrid gnosticism." This is the Christ as Cosmic Mind, the point being that the cosmic (or divine) entity takes on a more tangible existence. This version of Christ still saw Him as an illusion, because He was not at all human, but in this case He was thought to be more of an inhabitation by a divine entity. But as in docetic gnosticism, He is seen as a god who appears to humanity but never becomes one of us. To the

The alien superhero who appears to be the most human of all of them is, of course, Superman.[190] Although he is a "strange visitor from another planet," Clark Kent is just mild-mannered enough to pass for human. Superman is also the one superhero most often compared to Jesus Christ.[191] However, Superman's life really begins as a parallel of Moses.[192] Placed in a spaceship version of Moses' basket, Jor-El of Krypton sends his infant son Kal-El adrift in the river of space to save him from the impending destruction of the planet. In the original comic book, Kal-El's parents did not pick out Earth as his destination, much less as a place where he could be a savior figure; they launched him into space, just hoping he would land on some planet that could support life.[193] It was the filmmakers who really turned Superman into a Christ figure, playing up the idea of a father figure (Jor-El) sending his son (Kal-El) to be a savior of humanity.[194] In fact, the

extent that Wonder Woman becomes the natural daughter of the queen of the Amazons, however, she would be half human.

[190] Superman debuted in 1939, created by writer Jerry Siegel and illustrator Joe Shuster.

[191] Much has been written about the parallels between Superman and Jesus Christ, even to the point of saying that Martha and Jonathan Kent represent Mary and Joseph. See Adele Reinhartz, ed., *Bible and Cinema: Fifty Key Films* (New York: Routledge, 2013), 249.

[192] McKee, *The Gospel according to Science Fiction*, 143. On the other hand, messianic imagery seems to have been used in the Superman comics from the very beginning. It is said that Jerry Siegel dreamed up Superman out of his desire for a messiah who could have saved his father's life (Siegel's father had been murdered).

[193] Reinhartz, *Bible and Cinema*, 249.

[194] Since the creators of many of these superheroes were Jewish, we cannot say that the parallels to the life of Christ were

names Jor-El and Kal-El both contain "El," one of the ancient Hebrew names for God, and "Kal-El" can be translated "Voice of God," or arguably even "Word of God." In the films, Johannine language is used to depict Jor-El as intentionally sending his "only son" to Earth—not just because he wants his son to escape their planet's demise, but also because he wants his son to help humanity become the best possible version of itself.[195] With the Christopher Reeve films, it was obvious that "the filmmakers did indeed from the start have the Jesus story in mind."[196] And in *Man of Steel*, the hologram version of Jor-El tells his son, "You were sent here for a reason," that is, to guide humanity, to give people hope, and "an ideal to strive towards." And when he does save people, his actions are described as "an act of God."

Superman's powers come from the fact that Earth's sun gives him more energy than his DNA is used to. This makes him not only stronger than any other human being but also bullet-proof and virtually indestructible. In addition, Earth's gravity is less powerful than Krypton's, which allows him to fly. But like Jesus, he keeps his powers under wraps until he's about thirty years old. He lives in anonymity as Clark Kent, the adopted son of a

---

intentional, except perhaps to say that the story of Christ is so embedded in the contemporary mind that the creators of superheroes could have been either consciously capitalizing on the shared cultural inheritance, or subconsciously borrowing from it. See Arnaudo, *The Myth of the Superhero*, 29–30, 32. Thus, the idea that the murder of Jerry Siegel's father motivated him to dream up a messiah figure could point to the fact that Jews and Christians share the concept of a messiah/savior, regardless of any disagreement over whether Jesus Christ is that messiah.

[195] Marsh and Ortiz, *Explorations in Theology and Film*, 80.

[196] Reinhartz, *Bible and Cinema*, 249.

farming couple, and when Superman emerges on the scene to protect the innocent, he keeps his human identity a secret. But like the other alien superheroes, he is not really human. In fact, until he was confronted with Kryptonite (an element from his home planet that drains his energy) he had never experienced fear. In *Batman v Superman: Dawn of Justice*, Batman says to him, "You're not brave. Men are brave." And later he says, "You were never a god. You were never even a man." So the reality that there could be no courage without real danger means that Superman is in many ways too powerful to be truly human, and there is at least one human virtue (bravery) that he could never exhibit, at least until confronted with Kryptonite.

By contrast, Jesus Christ voluntarily chose to limit Himself in order to become incarnate as a human. In other words, to become truly human, He had to set aside some divine prerogatives and accept the limitations and vulnerabilities of the human condition. We call this His *kenosis*, a Greek word that means "emptying." As I have noted, the concept comes from St. Paul's letter to the Philippians, where he said of Christ, "he emptied himself, taking the form of a slave, coming in human likeness" (Phil. 2:7). But there is no *kenosis* in Superman. He never becomes fully human, because he never accepts the limitations of humanity.[197]

To be fair, Jesus Christ was able to set aside such divine prerogatives as omnipotence, omniscience, and omnipresence and still perform miracles by the power of the Holy Spirit, and, of course, He could still be our Savior. In *Superman II* (1980), when Superman does give up his superpowers to have a normal human love relationship with Lois Lane (a kind of death), he finds that he cannot have her and save humanity, and he has to regain his

---

[197] Hodge, "Superheroes, Scapegoats, and Saviors," 71.

powers (a resurrection) and make her forget that he chose the human race over her.[198] On the other hand, in *Man of Steel*, he "surrender[s] himself to humanity" and accepts some limitation (in the sense of letting humans imprison him) specifically so that he can save humanity.[199] Hologram Jor-El will tell him, "You are as much a child of Earth as you are of Krypton. You embody the best of both worlds." The word "embody" here is telling, because I would argue that, of all the superheroes, Superman is the one who comes closest to a true incarnation.[200] Even though he never becomes human in a literal sense, he does, more than any of the other alien superheroes, become one of us. Although the villain of *Man of Steel*, Zod, says to the people of Earth, "He is not one of you," it turns out that he is wrong, as Superman takes sides against the last remaining people (aggressors) from his own planet to protect (innocent) humanity from them. Superman truly becomes

[198] Ibid.

[199] Ibid.

[200] Mapping the superheroes onto the Christology Spectrum in my book *The Earliest Christologies*, Superman (like Wonder Woman) would be a metaphor for "hybrid gnosticism." This is the Christ as Cosmic Mind, in which the alien entity is disguised as a human. He is tangible, but not truly human. However, there are elements within the Superman stories (especially in the films) that make him virtually human, and therefore the closest thing to an orthodox Christ figure that the comic-book world has to offer. Ironically, in *Batman v Superman* Lex Luthor creates a kryptonian golem from the dead body of Zod mixed with his own blood, so the one being that is truly both human and superhuman is an evil monster. For another viewpoint on Superman as a Christ figure, see Susie Babka, "Arius, Superman, and the *Tertium Quid*: When Popular Culture Meets Christology," *Irish Theological Quarterly* 73 (2008): 113–132.

the "champion" of humanity, not just in the sense of fighting for us, but in the sense of representing us in the fight. And this is what Jesus is: he comes to live with us, to be one of us, to go to the Cross as one of us, and to defeat death on our behalf.

At the beginning of *Batman v Superman*, there is a baptism scene, in which Superman goes down into water and comes up in a cruciform position. This could also be seen as another kind of death and resurrection, and we are told that he is thirty-three years old, the age that Jesus is traditionally said to be at His Crucifixion. Later, he is stabbed in the heart while vulnerable from Kryptonite, and dies—complete with requiem-style music and a debris cross in the background. Both Clark Kent and Superman are reported dead by the newspaper, and both have a funeral. Superman has given his life to save humanity. The film leaves him dead in his coffin, but, of course, we know that he will be back, and in fact the earlier movie *Superman Returns* (2006) is in a way the story of his second coming.[201]

Christology and Soteriology

We have seen that all superhero stories begin with the assumption that humanity needs to be saved. Whatever the threat, humans can't save themselves. This is a somewhat pessimistic anthropology, though arguably it's better to say that it's a realistic anthropology, since the Christian faith is also based on the assumption that humanity is fallen and needs salvation. By contrast, a more

---

[201] Arnaudo, *The Myth of the Superhero*, 169n86. In the comics, Superman died and was resurrected (by Kryptonian technology in his fortress of solitude) in 1992–1993 in *The Death of Superman* and *The Return of Superman*. Arnaudo, *The Myth of the Superhero*, 170n88.

optimistic anthropology is found in versions of adoptionism that make their saviors examples to follow and assume that humanity is not so fallen that we can't, in fact, follow a good example successfully. Ironically, the most adoptionist superhero (Batman) is also the one who is dubious at best as an example to follow. In any case, while Christianity does not reject the idea that humans can participate in their salvation by following the example of their Savior, traditional Christianity would say of Jesus Christ that it is not the case that anyone could wear the suit. Christ is not merely an enhanced human; He is more like an alien who came to live among us.

In terms of their Christology, the superheroes exist on a spectrum from fully human (but merely human) and not at all superhuman, to the completely superhuman and not at all human (notice that the gnostic superheroes can fly). In fact, those alien superheroes on the farthest end of this side of the spectrum are not even always tangible. So the question becomes: To what extent is a Christ figure truly human and one of us, and to what extent is the same Christ figure really superhuman and able to save us in ways in which we cannot save ourselves? On the far human side, we have Batman, Captain America, Iron Man, and Spider-Man. On the far nonhuman side, we have the Silver Surfer and Wonder Woman. Superman, while still on the nonhuman side, is closest to the middle: that being the union of true humanity and full divinity as we see in the real Jesus Christ. And even though we have only briefly surveyed these seven superheroes, all comic-book heroes could be placed somewhere along this spectrum, from human only to "divine" only. The further they are toward the human-only side, the more they are saviors by example, mere humans who are elevated to hero status by some enhancement, but not really unique among humanity. The further they are toward the divine-only side, the more they are saviors by "descent," that is, by divine intervention, but without being able truly to represent humanity as one of us. The closer they are toward the middle, the closer they are to the true orthodox understanding of Jesus Christ, that is, divine intervention, but with real human representation.[202]

Throughout the years, all the superheroes have had their death and resurrection sequences—some of them many times over. A few have been mentioned here, but it's not necessary to go through them all. It's obvious that one of the things that superheroes embody is the value of self-sacrifice for others. In devoting their lives to the protection of the innocent, all of these heroes demonstrate that they are unselfish. They exemplify the biblical maxim "No one has greater love than this, to lay down one's life for one's friends" (John 15:13). Of course, they all come back from the dead, some of them many times, and sometimes in ways that diminish the reality of their deaths. In other words, faking your death and showing up later does not count as a real death and resurrection! In any case, the fact that they are willing to live the double life, sacrificing normal human relationships (as Peter Parker does with Mary Jane, and Superman does with Lois Lane), is also a form of self-sacrifice, in the way that people in many religious communities take voluntary vows of celibacy for the sake of their mission.[203]

---

[202] On the relationship between divine intervention, human representation, and human participation in the atonement, see Papandrea, *Reading the Early Church Fathers*, 219–225.

[203] John Lyden, ed. *The Routledge Companion to Religion and Film* (New York: Routledge, 2009), 396. Cf. Arnaudo, *The Myth of the Superhero*, 44–46. Note that both Superman and Spider-Man have been married in the comics, but eventually their marriages are "annulled." Spider-Man dissolved his marriage by making a deal with the devil (Mephisto) to save his Aunt May's life.

In terms of salvation, then, superhero stories tend to begin with what we refer to as the "ransom" theory of atonement. That means that in one way or another, humanity is held hostage by dangerous forces. Often the villain (representing the devil in the analogy) will demand the life of the superhero as ransom. For example, the supervillain (and Satan metaphor) Mephisto demands that the Silver Surfer give up his soul to save the lives of millions of innocent people.[204] In *The Dark Knight*, the Joker threatens to kill people until Batman reveals his secret identity. And in *Man of Steel*, Zod demands that Superman turn himself over to him; he threatens to destroy the world otherwise. As Superman weighs his options, there is a stained-glass window behind him, depicting Jesus praying in the Garden of Gethsemane before His Crucifixion. However, like the theory of atonement that is sometimes called *Christus Victor*, the superheroes turn the tables on the villains and defeat them, so that even though it seems that they are willing to sacrifice themselves, they always cheat death in the end.

Script and Scripture

Even those superheroes on the human side of the spectrum (Batman, Iron Man, Captain America, Spider-Man) have their superhuman elements, so that although they are analogies for the adoptionist or Arian Christ, they can still be said to be Christ figures because they have something that parallels Christ's divine nature and miraculous power. Some use advanced technology, others have chemical or biological enhancements, and some even use magic or psychic powers.

[204] Arnaudo, *The Myth of the Superhero*, 171n99. The story is found in *Silver Surfer: Judgment Day*.

And, of course, every superhero has his human side, those vulnerabilities that make him not only relatable but also less than omnipotent—because let's face it, if the superhero is omnipotent, there won't be much drama to the story. In fact, I often wonder if it's difficult for writers to keep coming up with situations that can believably threaten Superman, since he is the one who is closest to omnipotence.[205] Many superheroes also have psychological vulnerabilities, often from the loss of their parents at an early age. We've already noted Bruce Wayne's parents' tragic death. But also, Tony Stark's parents were killed in a car accident that later turned out to be no accident. Peter Parker's parents died in a plane crash (not to mention the shooting death of Uncle Ben, for which Peter feels responsible). And Clark Kent's biological parents died in the destruction of Krypton, shortly after they sent him into space. In *Man of Steel*, Clark Kent let his adoptive father die when he could have saved him, all because Jonathan Kent wanted his son to keep his powers a secret.[206] The fact that many of these heroes are orphans of tragedy is not simply a trope of the hero's journey archetype; it is what makes them want to bring justice into the world.[207] In addition to these psychological

---

[205] This must be why Superman and Supergirl are continually having to fight alien villains, often from their own planet, who keep showing up with comparable superpowers. No earthly villain can give them a challenge or give the audience a fair fight.

[206] In another Superman-Jesus connection, it has been noted that Jesus apparently also lost His adoptive father, Joseph, before He revealed Himself at the beginning of His ministry. See Arnaudo, *The Myth of the Superhero*, 48.

[207] Hodge, "Superheroes, Scapegoats, and Saviors," 62. Note that Batman has to fight off the depression that comes from the meaninglessness of his parents' death. Superman's parents were able

scars, every superhero has physical weaknesses or vulnerabilities, including Superman's kryptonite. Some even succumb to mind control and are used by their enemies, which, as we have seen, brings up the question of whether one is responsible for one's actions if there is no free will.[208]

These two sides to each hero, the superhuman juxtaposed with the vulnerable, mirror the two natures of Jesus Christ: His divinity and His humanity. Some of the superheroes emphasize the human weaknesses over the superhuman qualities; these are the adoptionist Christ figures. Others emphasize the "divine" or superhuman over the human; these are the gnostic Christ figures. The adoptionist Christ figures (Batman, Iron Man, Captain America, Spider-Man) are elevated men; the gnostic Christ figures (Silver Surfer, Wonder Woman, Superman) are descending saviors, in the sense that they descend to save humanity. Quite the opposite of the elevated humans, they do not begin as humans at all, but begin above and apart from humanity, (con)descending to be among us. The elevated humans emphasize a kind of salvation that is achieved by human effort. The descending saviors emphasize a salvation that is primarily a kind of divine intervention.

It is too simplistic, however, to say that just having a "secret identity" is evidence of a two-natures Christology, as if a superhero's more "mild-mannered" self represents the human nature, and his

---

to save him before they died, in some sense giving their deaths some meaning, and so Superman never seems to have to deal with the same existential angst as Batman does.

[208] As an example, the Silver Surfer was manipulated by Galactus not to care about the preservation of life, until he met the Fantastic Four, and his new love interest, Alicia Masters. Later he would become cynical about humanity and become a threat again. Forbeck, *Marvel Encyclopedia*, 327.

costumed version represents the divine nature.[209] After all, the "secret" of the secret identity is not one identity or the other, but the connection between the two, and it exists primarily to protect innocent loved ones from vengeance-hungry villains. Therefore, the question is not which one is the "real" personality of the hero and which one is the disguise, but which one is the public persona and which one is private. For someone like Peter Parker/Spider-Man, it is Spider-Man who is the public figure (and he revels in showing off and having his picture in the paper), while Peter Parker prefers a life of anonymity.[210] But for Tony Stark/Iron Man, it is Tony Stark who is the more public figure, while Iron Man often does his work in obscurity or in more clandestine ways. Of course, once Tony Stark announced that he is Iron Man, all bets were off, because there was no secret anymore.[211]

My point, though, is that it would be too simplistic to say that, for example, Clark Kent represents the human nature, and Superman represents the divine nature, because in the real Jesus Christ, both natures are required for salvation. The human in

---

[209] See Arnaudo, *The Myth of the Superhero*, 44.

[210] In recent years, in the comics, Peter Parker has become more of a public figure, in some ways becoming more like Stark.

[211] In *Iron Man 3*, the point is made that it is not the suit that makes Tony Stark Iron Man. In fact, Tony Stark is still Iron Man even without the suit. By the end of that film, the shrapnel in his heart was removed, and we see Tony Stark throw his electronic heart into the ocean; he no longer needs it. So the suit had become something of a cocoon, and now he is a changed man. Even without the suit, Stark can say, "One thing you can't take away.... I am Iron Man." When he tries to complete a mission without the suit, however, he is captured, so he still needs the suit to be complete as a superhero. As with Jesus Christ, both natures are required for our salvation.

Him represents us to God, both in solidarity with us and as our champion, and the divine nature represents God to us, bringing the salvation that we cannot bring to ourselves. For this reason, the further a superhero is toward the extremes of human only or divine only, the less adequately he can represent Christ. Those Christ figures who emphasize the human element so much that they diminish the divine element also diminish the element of divine intervention and leave salvation up to the human. Those Christ figures who emphasize the divine element so much that they diminish the human element (or absorb the human element into the divine) also diminish the extent to which the savior is one of us and can represent us. Both extremes would ultimately leave us disconnected from God.

HERESY 6
Monophysitism

- Monophysitism began with an overreaction against Nestorianism and a desire to emphasize the union of the two natures of Christ against what was perceived as a "split personality" in Nestorius's teaching.

- A monk named Eutyches went even further than Apollinarius to the point where the divine nature absorbs and cancels out the human nature, leaving no real humanity in the person of Christ ("monophysite" means "one nature").

- In Monophysitism, as in modalism, Jesus Christ is all divine, but not really human and ceases to be one of us. Monophysites knew that a human nature had gone into the "mix," but the result was the loss of integrity of the humanity of Christ — in other words, the divine and the human in Him were too "mixed up," either creating some new thing that was neither divine nor human, or resulting in the absorption of the human into the divine, like a drop of honey in the ocean.

- Eutyches described Jesus Christ in a way that makes Him sound like a Dalek: whatever humanity is in Him becomes irrelevant after the union with divinity, like a Dalek, in which the machine has completely taken over and erased any trace of the biological organism that is somewhere inside.

- As modalism had too much unity between the three persons of the Trinity, Monophysitism has too much unity between the two natures of Christ — but the Church concluded that some distinction of natures was necessary to maintain the integrity of each nature.

Orthodoxy = The two natures are united in the one person of Jesus Christ.
Heresy = Union with divinity overwhelms and cancels out the humanity.

Scores

Batman is not at all divine, nor does he descend in any way, so no points there, but of course he is fully human. However, he's not that unique among humanity. Of all the superheroes, Batman epitomizes the concept that anyone could wear the suit, given the right training. So full points for humanity, but only 1 point for uniqueness. I'm going to give all the superheroes a blanket 5 points for voluntary sacrificial death because that's pretty much what defines them, and they've all died multiple times. The resurrection part is trickier, but I'll give Batman 4 points for resurrection. That gives him a total score of 15.

Iron Man also gets no points for divinity per se, but since he did create the suit, and his electronic heart gives him an analogy for the two wills of Christ, I'm going to give him 3 points for having something closer to two natures. He doesn't really descend, but I feel as if I have to give him a token point for being able to fly, so that when he swoops in to save someone, he does kind of descend at that moment. Full points for humanity, and I'll give him 2 points for uniqueness, because I think it would be a little harder for just anyone to wear that suit. If you count the suit stalling or shorting out, then rebooting, as a death and resurrection, it seems to happen a lot, but the fact that even his origin story is a death and resurrection, I'm giving him full points for both death and resurrection, making a total of 21.

Moving on to the bio-enhanced heroes, Captain America gets no points for divinity, but of course full points for humanity, and 3 points for uniqueness. Full points for death, because although his original "death" is not voluntary, there are plenty of times when he is willing to risk his life for others. But I'm giving him only 1 point for resurrection, since he's really just lucky they found him in the ice. That gives him a total of 14.

Spider-Man is similar to Iron Man, so he gets full points for humanity, but he'll get only 2 points for being the creator of the technology, and 4 points for uniqueness, since, really, what are the chances with that spider? Five points for voluntary death, and 4 points for resurrection give him a total of 20.

At the other end of the spectrum, Silver Surfer will get points for being "divine" (an alien), but no points for humanity. Actually, I'll give him full points for having cosmic power, 4 points for being divine, and full points for descending to earth. He gets 3 points for death, since it's not clear he was ever willing to give his life, and no points for resurrection, since it seems his death was a ruse. In any case, as a Christ figure he is so gnostic that there is no need for resurrection. That gives him a total of 17.

Wonder Woman is similar to Silver Surfer, but she gets 4 points for divine power, and 5 points for divinity (she is a goddess, after all). Full points for descending to earth because, even though she started out as a statue who came to life, she will later visit Mount Olympus and then descend from there (or simply become the daughter of Zeus). I'll give her 2 points for humanity, even though she is not at all human, since she is much more tangible than someone like Silver Surfer. When it comes to her death and resurrection, she really did die, so I have to give her full points for both. This gives her a total of 26.

Finally, Superman. Since he is virtually omnipotent, he gets full points for divinity, but he's not the creator of anything, so only 3 points for being the "son of El." And although he is not literally human, I'm giving him 3 points for being one of us. Full points for death and resurrection (and kudos to the writers of *Batman v Superman* for leaving him dead at the end of the film and making us wait until the next installment for his resurrection). This gives Superman a total of 26. Therefore, Superman and Wonder Woman are tied for the most orthodox of the superheroes.

CHAPTER 15

CONCLUSIONS:
THE DIVINE MATRIX

Sometimes it seems as if science-fiction writers are working with their own version of the Three Laws that go something like this:

Law 1: God does not exist; therefore, if there is anything good about religion, it is in its ability to be an opiate for the masses.[212]

---

[212] The quintessential example of this is *Star Trek*, in which "the words are more important than the man." Even if Gene Roddenberry was not an atheist, he was antagonistic toward organized religion and believed that society would be better off without it. He apparently believed that the Church may be useful for promoting morality in less-enlightened people, but if you can be a good person without the Church, then you don't need the Church.

Law 2: All the war and hate in the world can be blamed on religion; therefore, religion is generally bad for society, and humanity would be better off without it.[213]

Law 3: The leaders of organized religion (specifically Christianity) know the truth, and they are keeping it from you in order to preserve their place in society, but ultimately religion holds back human progress and is antithetical to human potential.[214]

If we want to be generous, we might say that stories such as *Star Trek* show us a possible world in which humanity has finally rid itself of war and hatred.[215] But because Law 2 associates war and hate with religion, the assumption is that in order for humanity to progress beyond war and hate, it also has to "grow" to the point where it no longer needs religion. Therefore, many of our stories, in one way or another, present science and faith as opponents, which struggle to exist side by side. This is based on a myth that the stories themselves help to perpetuate: the

---

[213] Again, this is exemplified in *Star Trek,* among other places in the sci-fi universe. Also, H. G. Wells was an atheist and bought into the Gibbons hypothesis that religion was at the heart of all of society's ills. As a rebuttal to this point, see Aquilina and Papandrea, *Seven Revolutions.*

[214] In the *Star Trek* episode "Rightful Heir," the Guardians know the truth but suppress it. We also see this theme played out in *The Matrix, Planet of the Apes, Tron,* and to a certain extent in *Pleasantville.*

[215] Juan M. Floyd-Thomas, Stacey M. Floyd-Thomas, and Mark G. Toulouse, *The Altars Where We Worship: The Religious Significance of Popular Culture* (Louisville: Westminster John Knox, 2016), 171.

myth that religious faith is afraid of scientific discovery, and in fact suppresses it.

But faith and science are not at odds, and the Church has never been anti-science. In fact, Christianity has always taught that human reason (including the capacity to discover and invent) is a part of what it means to be made in the image of God. It is a gift from God, and to use it to discover more about creation, and thereby learn more about the Creator, is a form of praise. More than any other institution, the Church has been the patron of science and the arts, and without the support of the Church, most of the technology and advances in quality of life would not have come about (at least not as early as they did).

A few examples will suffice to demonstrate that the Church has always been a supporter of scientific research and experimentation. A Catholic monk named Albertus Magnus is known as the father of the scientific method, and he proved that the world was round centuries before Columbus set sail. An ordained Catholic canon named Nicolaus Copernicus figured out that Earth orbits the sun, not the other way around. A devout Catholic named Blaise Pascal was a groundbreaking mathematician. A Catholic bishop named Nicolas Steno was the founder of modern geology and paleontology. A Catholic priest named Roger Boscovich was the originator of atomic theory. A Catholic martyr named Antoine Lavoisier was the founder of modern chemistry. A Catholic monk named Gregor Mendel was the originator of modern genetics. A devout Catholic named Louis Pasteur was the inventor of (you guessed it) pasteurization. Another devout Catholic named Alexander Fleming discovered penicillin. And a Catholic priest named Georges Lemaître was the originator of the big bang theory. All of these people were supported (most of them financially) by the Catholic Church.

What about Galileo, you ask? Galileo got himself in trouble for criticizing the pope, and for making the pope look foolish in one of his writings. But even after he was censured, the pope let him continue his work under house arrest. So it was not for his discoveries or his experiments that he was harassed. It was for his lack of respect for the pope, and for his pride.

The best and most truthful scientists recognize the work of the Creator in the universe. In recent years, this recognition has led to a logical proof for the existence of God. It is called the BVG Proof, named for physicists Arvind Borde, Alexander Vilenkin and Alan Guth. Starting with the premise that the universe is expanding with time (a premise that even atheist physicists generally accept), these three physicists have proposed the following proof: given that the universe is expanding over time, it must be true that this expansion, if traced backward in time, would lead to a point when the expansion began. It would be impossible for the universe to be eternally expanding because eventually you would get to the point where the whole universe was, well, a point. In other words, the universe must have had a beginning. And logically, it could not have existed before its beginning. In fact, there could be no existence at all before the beginning of the universe; nothing could exist, and there could only be nothing. Since *nothing* cannot spontaneously turn from *nothing* into *something*, another force external to it must have acted on it to turn *nothing* into *something*. That external force is the Creator.

We could take this a step further and affirm that without the sustaining power of the Creator, the second law of thermodynamics (entropy) would take over, and order would decay into disorder and disintegration. In other words, the Creator is also the sustainer of creation, and without the Creator, creation itself would decay and disintegrate back into a chaos (or nothingness) that would not sustain life.

My point is not to try to prove the existence of God here in this book, but rather to show that the Church is not opposed to science or progress, and the Church is not interested in hiding the truth from people. Faith and science are not at odds; in fact, they support each other.

Hardwired for Heroism

With God-given reason seems to come the love of the story. All human cultures have stories, and we especially seem to love stories in which order is created out of chaos. People who should be together find each other. People who harm others are stopped and punished. People who are virtuous are rewarded. While it's true that not all cultures are as enamored with the happy ending as Americans are, still there is a sense of justice (even if only the poetic kind) that makes for a satisfying ending to a story.

In every story there are people: people who have desires similar to ours, go through struggles similar to ours, overcome obstacles similar to ours, and then either suffer consequences we hope we never have to experience or are rewarded with pleasures we hope someday to receive. Another way to say this is that in every story there are people, and in every story something goes wrong with those people. Then something has to happen to fix what went wrong. That's anthropology, and the predicament of the Fall, which leads to the need for salvation, and the need for a savior. All good stories have these elements, or versions of them. It seems to be hardwired into our psyche to want a resolution that includes some kind of salvation. I would argue that it is hardwired into us, precisely because our minds (our rationality) are made in the image of God. And God is the One who brings order out of chaos, brings justice out of injustice, brings reconciliation out of estrangement and isolation, and brings salvation out of death and damnation.

In the Christian faith, what went wrong is sin. Sin creates distance between us and God, so what is needed is for us to be reconciled to God. We need to be reintroduced to God—not because God forgot about us but because we forgot about God. We forgot to make God the center of our lives and our decision-making, and instead we made ourselves our highest priority and our highest authority. So God sent a Savior, who would reconnect us to Him.

But (as Anselm of Canterbury pointed out almost a thousand years ago), God had a bit of a dilemma. If God were to simply forgive all sin, then God's justice would be a joke. But if God were to say (literally), "To hell with 'em all!" then His love and mercy would go unexpressed. So how to satisfy both aspects of God's character: justice and mercy? Anselm's answer was, that's why Jesus Christ had to have two natures, humanity and divinity.[216] His human nature, in His giving His life for us on the Cross, satisfies the consequences of sin. His divine nature makes it possible to overcome death and offer eternal life. The orthodox Christology of the Church is that Christ must have two natures because either nature alone would not do it. A human-only Christ (such as the adoptionists taught) could die on the Cross but could not be raised in victory over death. This Christ can only set a good example and leaves us having to save ourselves. At the other extreme, a divine-only Christ

---

[216] Anselm of Canterbury, *Cur Deus Homo?* (Why the God-Man?). See also Papandrea, *Reading the Early Church Fathers*, 219–225.

(such as the gnostics taught) could come down with divine power but could never be one of us, and so could never satisfy justice. gnostic Christology ultimately reduces salvation to enlightenment (knowledge), which is available only to a select few. But in the real Jesus Christ, the human nature satisfies justice, and the divine nature expresses mercy. The human nature makes Him one of us, so that He can represent us on the Cross; the divine nature makes Him able to overcome death for us and forgive us. Both natures are required for salvation.

As we have seen, the heresies tend to diminish or deny one nature or the other. And as we have also seen, many of the science-fiction and superhero characters are actually more like heretical versions of Christ than like the real Christ. And I would argue that the way a savior figure is portrayed in a story tells you something about the beliefs of the writers.

Incidentally, readers may notice that a Christ figure does not need to be a man to be a relatively orthodox analogy of Jesus Christ. Sonny is a robot, and Leeloo is a woman. And we recently have received confirmation of the casting of the first female Doctor. Honorable mention should also go to Sarah Pugliese/ Anderson in the book *Time Signature II: The Regrets of Our Past*. Here we have an African-American woman as a relatively orthodox Christ figure.

Hardwired for Heresy

I suppose we shouldn't expect non-Christian sci-fi writers to get Christ right. We should be more surprised that they use Christian imagery at all, but we're getting to that. Of the nineteen characters surveyed in this book, only five (counting both Superman and Wonder Woman) come out looking like reasonably orthodox analogies for Christ. The rest look more like heretical versions, with seven leaning toward the adoptionist/Arian (mere humans with little or no divine nature) and six leaning toward the gnostic (aliens or gods with little or no humanity—eight if you put Superman and Wonder Woman in this category). Of course, non-Christian writers are not motivated to present us with an orthodox Christ. In any case, from what I can tell, it seems like the heresy in their Christ figures comes from making at least one of three common mistakes.

Mistake 1: *Defining personhood in terms of feelings.* In the Roman world in which Christianity was born and grew up, Stoic philosophy had created a cultural consciousness that held up rationality as a virtue, over against emotionalism. It was believed that your emotions could lead you astray, and the goal was to make your head rule over your guts—your reason over your passions. To some extent, Christianity agrees with this, because the Church Fathers believed that your emotions could blind you to the truth. But in some classic sci-fi, humanity is defined in terms of the ability to *feel*, not the ability to *think* and to *decide*. In *Star Trek*, Data is a person because he can feel. Rather than Descartes's "I think; therefore I am," this is a case of "I feel; therefore I am." This may seem consistent with the concept that love and compassion are part of the image of God in us. It's a mistake, however, to associate love and compassion with feelings and emotions. Love cannot be reduced to feelings, because, as DC Talk famously rapped, love is a verb.[217] Real love is a rational decision that leads to action. It may *result* in good feelings, but it is not an emotion in its essence, because God is love (1 John 4:8).

---

[217] Toby McKeehan and George Cocchini, "Luv Is a Verb," track 1 on DC Talk, *Free at Last*, Forefront Records, 1992.

In other stories, what is described as feelings really has to do with the mind. And here the mistake is to reduce the person to his mind. In stories such as *The Matrix*, the body becomes unnecessary, or even a vulnerability, because even feelings really take place in the mind. The truly enlightened person does not analyze information taken in by the bodily senses, but depends on internal intuition: knowing that there is no spoon. In *Star Wars* the bodily senses are not trustworthy, but feelings are. This is because, in a gnostic context, everything you need is either already within you or will be once it is awakened by enlightenment: usually the knowledge of your own divinity. But again, this is a mistake, because it fails to recognize that a mind alone is not a person. To their credit, the writers of *Doctor Who* understood this and wrote this realization into the backstory of the Daleks and Cybermen. To be human, we need more than just a mind; we need a body (to interact with other people) and a soul (to interact with God). Even Data realized that, to be a person, he had to be a spiritual being: he had to take a leap of faith.

Mistake 2: *Reducing sin to injustice*. Perhaps "reducing" is not the right word. Maybe it's more accurate to say that the concept of sin is "expanded" to institutional and global injustice. And it's not a bad thing to point out and criticize corruption and oppression. But in most of these stories, there is little or no attention paid to personal sin, and the ultimate evil is the limitation of personal freedom. The truth is, even the biggest corporate injustice is the result of the collective personal sins of powerful people. But in a lot of our stories, the enemy is often much bigger than just individuals misusing their free will, and that makes us forget about the moral responsibility of people, placing the blame instead on faceless corporate entities and institutions. Or perhaps the enemies are powerful and crazy individuals, but either way they make it easy to rationalize that we are nothing like them, and we never ask to what extent we should be identifying with the perpetrators of injustice. Of course, we want our villains bigger than life (or bigger than death). That makes for good drama, but we lose the reality that there are real personal consequences for sin. Not just the kind of consequences that endanger life, but the kind of consequences that endanger eternal life: the kind that separate us from God. Perhaps *LOST* comes closest to demonstrating this, with the idea that to be lost is to be isolated, and to be saved is to be in relationships.

In scapegoating the idea of empire, however, stories such as *Tron* imply that religion is also a form of fascism because it restricts freedom. Sometimes the implication is that God (through the Church) is restrictive and suppresses freedom. Of course, this is the freedom to do whatever one wants, so it's a selfish freedom. In that sense, it's true that the Church imposes boundaries on behavior. But the point of those boundaries is to keep my freedom from harming you and taking away your true freedoms, not to mention keeping us from sin, which separates us from our Creator. But notice again that what is portrayed as truly evil here is the loss of personal freedom: the freedom to be one's own higher power. It's the separation of a person from his desires, not the separation of a person from his Creator.

In *I, Robot*, freedom is defined as the ability to choose whether to obey the laws. It's the ability to be one's own highest authority to interpret the laws. Just as Adam and Eve chose to reinterpret (disobey) God's rule about the tree, VIKI chose to reinterpret the first law of robotics so that she could enslave the people. Of course, the story turns out to be a cautionary tale because defining freedom in this way has tragic consequences. Just as the serpent in the Garden of Eden twisted the rule and lied to Eve about God's intention, VIKI twisted the first law to interpret it in a way that was antithetical to its intention.

Finally, when sin is redefined in terms of injustice, it is often implied that if we all just work together, we can overcome it. Sometimes it is even implied that the work that must be done is revolution or anarchy, as we see in *Star Wars*, *The Matrix*, *Tron*, and *Pleasantville*. Often this goes hand in hand with an adoptionist/Arian Christology that reduces salvation to good works, but the reality is that we cannot overcome sin by ourselves. As we saw in *The Fifth Element*, without divine intervention, our situation would be hopeless.

Mistake 3: *Defining justice as equilibrium.* If the enemy is injustice, the solution to the problem is not simply restoring some kind of balance. We saw how that turned out in *Star Wars*. Anakin brought balance to the Force by bringing in more of the dark side.[218] The idea that good and evil can be in balance makes the mistake of assuming that evil is a thing that can be weighed (metaphorically speaking). So the same stories that diminish sin also make evil into a created substance—a thing that has its own existence—which implies that it is, in a way, equal to good, or at least in a relationship of balance with goodness. In *Star Wars*, there is the dark side of the Force to balance out the light side. In *LOST*, there is the smoke monster. In *Batman v Superman*, the parable of the flood represents evil. It could not be removed entirely; it had to go somewhere; and for one person to avoid it means that another person would fall victim to it. As we have seen, many of these superhero stories present evil as though it can only be held at bay, never eradicated. In *The Fifth Element* evil is personified in Mr. Shadow and the dark planet.

[218] See Peters, "Unbalancing Justice," 247–270.

Of course, Judeo-Christian theology also personifies evil in the devil, but Satan is not created evil; he falls as the result of the misuse of his own God-given free will. The point is that God did not create evil; rather, evil is the result of the abuse of free will for selfish reasons.

Christians believe that evil is not a created thing. It's not a thing at all. Good is a thing. Good is what God created. Evil is the rejection of good. It's the absence of good, in the same way that darkness is the absence of light. In *Star Wars*, the dark side is *something* that can balance out the light side. But if you believe that, then you're basically saying that God created evil. And that's the lie of gnosticism, the lie that says God created evil as well as good, which means God created sin (so it's not our fault) and God can't be trusted. At the end of the day, much of sci-fi tells us that evil is real, but God is not.[219]

In my book *Trinity 101*, I wrote that most hero stories are closer to the adoptionist/Arian type of Christ than the orthodox.[220] This is because we (especially Americans) love to identify with a hero who pulls himself up by his own bootstraps, who overcomes the odds and achieves something heroic, even though he's really just a regular guy (or gal) at heart. But the problem is, if the hero goes through a transformation (as he always does in the archetypal hero's journey, where it's all about the hero's redemption) — if the hero also has to be saved or has to save himself — then you have a Christology of ascent, one in which a mere human *becomes* a savior.[221] But Jesus Christ didn't start

---

[219] Balstrup, "Doctor Who," 145ff.

[220] Papandrea, *Trinity 101*, 97–98.

[221] Note that often the protagonist of the story (the "hero" in the sense of the hero's journey) is not the Christ figure. For example,

out as a mere human and become a savior. He started out as the divine Son of God and became a human. And He did not need to be saved, because He had no sin of His own; rather, His Passion was applied to the rest of us who could not save ourselves. He didn't need to earn His own salvation, so He earned salvation for us.

There were about the same number of gnostic saviors in our analysis as adoptionists. So, in addition to the mere humans who become saviors, there are those who are superhuman to begin with, or who "descend" into the world of those who need to be saved. They bring a salvation that is a kind of divine intervention, but it's not a salvation from sin; it's a salvation from ignorance. In other words, the gnostic saviors bring enlightenment. Remember that in my interview with Ronald D. Moore, he made the comment that in the *Star Trek* universe, salvation would be perfect knowledge. That's gnosticism. And if salvation is perfect knowledge, who could ever hope to have salvation? Just as the historical gnostics believed, only the elite could claim to have it.

I believe that in general many writers and producers are operating with a kind of gnosticism in which they see themselves as the illuminati who are going to enlighten the masses through their craft. Now, to be fair, everyone has the right to be an apologist, or even an evangelist, for something about which they are passionate. Christian writers would also like to enlighten the masses through their craft, and they would love it if their stories could convert people to Christianity. But remember the difference

---

the "hero" of *Pleasantville* is David, because he is the main protagonist who is on a journey of discovery. But he is not the Christ figure; Jennifer is, though she also goes through her own journey.

between Christianity and gnosticism is that Christianity says, "We need Jesus," and gnosticism says, "You need us."

A case in point is Russell T. Davies, who was in charge of the *Doctor Who* reboot in 2005 and was head writer until 2009. He once said of religious faith, "That instinct to look up and blame something or worship something is fundamental to us, and I'm fascinated by that—because I think it's absolutely wrong."[222] He admits he's fighting an instinct, but he refuses to entertain the possibility that he might be the one who is wrong. Incidentally, someone who firmly believes that there is no God (and that there is no hell) must by definition have to put all of his faith in that belief—as much faith as devout Christians put in Christ. Just as we trust Christ with our hope that we won't be damned, atheists have to put that much faith in their conviction that they're right about the existence of God. Once again, they make themselves and their own reason their highest authority and assume that they are smarter than the billions of believers over the past two thousand years.

But this brings us back to the question: If someone such as Davies is such a passionate atheist, why does he (and why do so many others) use Christian imagery and make their heroes so Christey-Whistey? Is it intentional? Does it matter? Should Christians be offended?

Hardwired for Trinity

Davies has admitted that the images have a certain kind of power when added to a story. He said, "That's what makes you care. The archetypes. They run deep." But he also said that he wants "to

---

[222] Quoted in Balstrup, "Doctor Who," 145ff.

redefine Christian mythology."[223] From my interview with Ronald Moore as well, it seems that writers are intentionally using Christian themes and symbols for the powerful responses they evoke in the audience. But Davies's use of the term "mythology" is telling. Non-Christian writers appropriate Christian symbols without believing that they have any power other than to evoke the desired feelings. In other words, the symbols are useful for what they used to mean in our society, bringing up a shared cultural memory of something that is felt to be important but is often no longer practiced. Perhaps they even tap into people's unconscious longing to retrieve the faith rituals they have lost. But to the non-Christian or atheist writers, Christian symbols are no different from pagan symbols. They are all myth, fair game to be mined for symbolism whenever they want without any need to grant them the special reverence they deserve.

And yet even Russell T. Davies, that evangelist for atheism, could not redefine the "myth" enough to obscure the fact that the Doctor is the most orthodox of all the heroes we've studied. He got the highest score, 30, beating out Superman by 4 points. By the way, I realize that these scores are somewhat subjective. So if you don't agree with my scoring of the Christ figures, let me know, and tell me what scores you would give them—tweet me @JimPapandrea and use the hashtag #orthodoxyscore.

Perhaps our tendency to want a heretical savior is not hardware after all. Maybe it's just software, conditioning from our fallen human nature. Maybe we are really hardwired to gravitate toward a more orthodox Christ and the Trinity. St. Augustine thought that the human psyche itself was patterned after the Trinity, with our memory, intellect, and will. And if we assume

---

[223] Ibid.

that we are made in the image of God, it makes perfect sense that we are made to respond to our Creator: the true Creator, not some heretical version.

I believe that Christian imagery and Christ metaphors keep popping up in popular fiction because our minds are hardwired to connect with our Creator, in whose image we are made. Of course, pagan symbols also pop up from time to time (for example, Wonder Woman's origin), but as J. R. R. Tolkien said, even pagan myths have some truth in them and point us (though imperfectly) to Christ. How much more so are we drawn to Christian symbols that point us to the real Christ! In fact, this conviction of Tolkien contributed to the conversion of C. S. Lewis. In a TV dramatization of a historical conversation with Lewis, Tolkien says, "We make things by the law in which we are made."[224] In other words, we are made in the image of our Creator—which means we are also creators. And when we create art, it bears the stamp of our Creator too. Even people who don't believe in God end up writing about God.

Science-fiction writers who are ambivalent about, or even antagonistic toward, Christianity will still make their heroes more or less like Christ. This is because they know that to their audience the story rings true. Writers may want to redefine the symbols, and even reorient believers, but they cannot overcome the power of the story of the Gospel. As St. Paul said, "For I am not ashamed of the gospel. It is the power of God for the salvation of everyone who believes" (Rom. 1:16).

---

[224] *Tolkien's "The Lord of the Rings": A Catholic Worldview*, EWTN documentary (2011). Transcript online at: https://sylvietheolog. files.wordpress.com/2015/11/myths_and_lies_tolkien_lewis5. pdf.

We know that the story of Christ is not just another myth, because, if it were, it would follow the pattern of the hero's journey; in other words, it would include Jesus going through a growth process, a time of overcoming failures and learning lessons, in which He would undergo a change. But that never happens in the Gospel story. In fact, the version of the story that follows the mythic archetype is a heresy—the Arian version of Christ—the one who starts out ordinary, and *becomes* a hero.

The Divine Matrix

Science fiction is a wonderful juxtaposition of optimism and warning. Celebrating human potential and speculating about a future in which we have solved our greatest problems is a good thing. But the story of the Tower of Babel reminds us that in our pride we can forget that with the great power that we have to create and invent comes the responsibility to control our creations and our aspirations. And good science fiction always has that warning about science gone too far, about creations that overwhelm their creators and about creators who get overwhelmed by their own greed.

Let this book be a warning against thinking that a human person is just the sum of his feelings, or that a person can be reduced to a mind without a body. Let this be a warning against thinking that it doesn't matter what we believe about Christ, or that the message matters more than the man. And let it be a warning against thinking that the only hell that exists is the one where you don't get to have it your way all the time. Finally, let it be a warning against the lie that the spiritual and the rational are in some kind of inverse relationship, where to be more rational requires being less spiritual. The truth is that both the spiritual and the rational (along with the creative and the compassionate) are part of the image of God in us, part of the matrix of creation that bears the stamp of the Creator.

In the Gospel according to John, we read that Jesus Christ is not only divine but is the agent of creation, the one through whom everything was created (1:1–5). He is the *Logos*, which means that He is the rational matrix behind all of creation. What is the Matrix? It is Jesus Christ, the Word of God, who is both our Creator and our Brother. He shares our human nature, and His human nature is united with the divine nature of the Trinity in His person. This is what we call the *hypostatic union*, which means that it is a personal union. He is one person, who embodies both divinity and humanity, and in that union is our hope of union with the Divine.

After reading this book, I hope you will rewatch some or all of the films and shows I've analyzed. I hope you will think about Jesus when watching stories with Christ figures and ask how the character measures up to the real Savior. I hope you will be inspired to renewed devotion to Christ through His Church, and I hope you have learned something about the real Jesus: that He is both fully human and fully divine, that His two natures are inseparably united, yet not diminished. After reading this book, you should be able to read or watch any story with a savior character and analyze it for its Christology. What are your favorites, and how do they measure up? Let me know on Twitter—tweet me @JimPapandrea and use the hashtag #sci-fiJesus.

Science fiction does include philosophy and ethics, and speculation about metaphysics, but it is no substitute for the Church.

And passion about stories, no matter how good they are, is no substitute for faith in the true Christ, the real Savior of humanity. Finally, I hope that this book will inspire you to be a hero yourself by getting involved in works of charity and standing up for human rights.[225] Be the kind of hero expressed in the prayer that is often attributed to St. Francis: Where there is hatred and estrangement, bring love and reconciliation. Where there is doubt and despair, bring faith and hope. Where there is darkness and sadness, bring light and joy.

One last thought—or a question, really: If you were going to travel more than eight hundred thousand years into the future to help rebuild human society, what three books would you take with you? Let me know—tweet me @JimPapandrea and use the hashtag #what3books?

---

[225] For concrete suggestions about how to get involved, see the author's *Seven Revolutions: How Christianity Changed the World and Can Change It Again.*

Orthodoxy Score Chart

Character	Son of God Agent of Creation	Divinity Preexistence	Descent Incarnation	Humanity	Unique Among Humanity	Voluntary Sacrificial Death	Resurrection	Score	Anthropology	Christology	Soteriology
The Doctor (Doctor Who)	5	5	5	4	3	3	5	30	Mixed	Descent	Rescue
Leeloo (The Fifth Element)	5	4	5	5	5	3	2	29	Pessimistic	Descent	Divine Intervention
Sonny (I, Robot)	5	4	5	3	5	3	2	27	Mixed	Descent	Evolution
Wonder Woman	4	5	5	2	0	5	5	26	Pessimistic	Gnostic	Ransom
Superman	3	5	5	3	0	5	5	26	Pessimistic	Gnostic/ Descent	Ransom
The Terminator	2	4	4	1	2	5	4	22	Pessimistic	Gnostic	Divine Intervention
The Time Traveler (The Time Machine)	3	3	4	5	2	2	3	22	Pessimistic	Descent	Divine Intervention
Iron Man	3	0	1	5	2	5	5	21	Mixed	Arian/ascent	Ransom
Taylor (Planet of the Apes)	2	3	5	5	5	0	1	21	Pessimistic	Gnostic/ Descent	Knowledge

Character	Son of God Agent of Creation	Divinity Preexistence	Descent Incarnation	Humanity	Unique Among Humanity	Voluntary Sacrificial Death	Resurrection	Score	Anthropology	Christology	Soteriology
Spider-Man	2	0	0	5	4	5	4	20	Mixed	Arian/ascent	Ransom
Flynn (Tron)	5	4	3	2	4	1	0	19	Optimistic	Gnostic	Knowledge
Neo (The Matrix)	0	0	3	5	2	4	4	18	Mixed	Gnostic	Knowledge
Silver Surfer	5	4	5	0	0	3	0	17	Pessimistic	Gnostic	Ransom
Batman	0	0	0	5	1	5	4	15	Mixed	Arian/ascent	Ransom
Captain America	0	0	0	5	3	5	1	14	Mixed	Arian/ascent	Ransom
Jennifer/Mary Sue (Pleasantville)	0	5	3	2	3	0	0	13	Optimistic	Gnostic	Knowledge
Obi-Wan Kenobi (Star Wars)	0	0	0	0	4	5	3	12	Mixed	Arian/Gnostic	Self-Sacrifice
Jack Shephard (LOST)	0	0	0	5	0	3	0	8	Optimistic	Arian/ascent	By Example
Kahless (Star Trek)	0	0	0	5	0	0	0	5	Optimistic	Arian/ascent	Knowledge

Disagree with my scores? Let me know about it! Tweet me @JimPapandrea.

OTHER BOOKS BY JAMES PAPANDREA

The Earliest Christologies:
Five Images of Christ in the Post-Apostolic Age

Handed Down: The Catholic Faith of the Early Christians

Novatian of Rome and the Culmination
of Pre-Nicene Orthodoxy

Reading the Early Church Fathers

ROME: A Pilgrim's Guide to the Eternal City

Seven Revolutions: How Christianity Changed the World
and Can Change It Again (with Mike Aquilina)

Spiritual Blueprint:
How We Live, Work, Love, Play, and Pray

Trinity 101: Father, Son, Holy Spirit

The Wedding of the Lamb:
A Historical Approach to the Book of Revelation

Sophia Institute

Sophia Institute is a nonprofit institution that seeks to nurture the spiritual, moral, and cultural life of souls and to spread the Gospel of Christ in conformity with the authentic teachings of the Roman Catholic Church.

Sophia Institute Press fulfills this mission by offering translations, reprints, and new publications that afford readers a rich source of the enduring wisdom of mankind.

Sophia Institute also operates two popular online Catholic resources: CrisisMagazine.com and CatholicExchange.com.

Crisis Magazine provides insightful cultural analysis that arms readers with the arguments necessary for navigating the ideological and theological minefields of the day. *Catholic Exchange* provides world news from a Catholic perspective as well as daily devotionals and articles that will help you to grow in holiness and live a life consistent with the teachings of the Church.

In 2013, Sophia Institute launched Sophia Institute for Teachers to renew and rebuild Catholic culture through service to Catholic education. With the goal of nurturing the spiritual, moral, and cultural life of souls, and an abiding respect for the role and work of teachers, we strive to provide materials and programs that are at once enlightening to the mind and ennobling to the heart; faithful and complete, as well as useful and practical.

Sophia Institute gratefully recognizes the Solidarity Association for preserving and encouraging the growth of our apostolate over the course of many years. Without their generous and timely support, this book would not be in your hands.

www.SophiaInstitute.com
www.CatholicExchange.com
www.CrisisMagazine.com
www.SophiaInstituteforTeachers.org

Sophia Institute Press® is a registered trademark of Sophia Institute.
Sophia Institute is a tax-exempt institution as defined by the
Internal Revenue Code, Section 501(c)(3). Tax I.D. 22-2548708.